BRITISH FINANCIAL CRISES SINCE 1825

British Financial Crises since 1825

Edited by

NICHOLAS DIMSDALE
AND ANTHONY HOTSON

OXFORD
UNIVERSITY PRESS

OXFORD
UNIVERSITY PRESS

Great Clarendon Street, Oxford, OX2 6DP,
United Kingdom

Oxford University Press is a department of the University of Oxford.
It furthers the University's objective of excellence in research, scholarship,
and education by publishing worldwide. Oxford is a registered trade mark of
Oxford University Press in the UK and in certain other countries

First Edition published in 2014

Published in the United States of America by Oxford University Press
198 Madison Avenue, New York, NY 10016, United States of America

British Library Cataloguing in Publication Data
Data available

Library of Congress Control Number: 2014936187

ISBN 978–0–19–968866–1

Foreword

The invention of money by human cultures was an important step in the creation of the complex and sophisticated societies in which we live today. Liberated from the constraints of simultaneous exchange and coincident proximity in the bartering of goods, resources could be traded for mutual benefit across time and space. Money was such a valuable invention that it became a universal attribute of advanced societies and in doing so, the fact that it was ever invented at all has been more or less forgotten; we can scarcely now imagine a world without it.

The invention of money was approximately coincident with the invention of agriculture and these two inventions must have played a part in paving the way for the development of larger-scale human social organizations; for towns, for armies, for kings, and for emperors. In due course, money in turn gave rise to its own institutions within these societies; banks, currencies, interest, and salaries. Taken together the idea of an economy was born, the set of trading and commercial interactions, mediated by money that occupied and sustained human life. Reflecting on the functioning of such systems the study of economics very naturally turned for sources of metaphor and analogy to the workings of the human body. The role assigned to money within these analogies is always that of blood, the life-giving substance that, in coursing through the substance and organs of a body, is believed to animate it. The analogy is, like all analogies however, imperfect and whilst it may sometimes inform it may equally at other times obscure understanding.

Given their central importance to the idea of civilization, economies and the role of money and its institutions within, they do plead for scholarly attention. They exhibit behaviours and give rise to phenomena. They have, however, generally resisted the attempts of economic scientists to unmask their guiding principles more successfully than Mother Nature's resistance to the scrutiny of physical scientists. The physical sciences have had great success with general, overarching descriptive theories; electromagnetism, relativity, quantum theory, genetics. By contrast, in our attempts to codify the principles guiding the functioning of economics it sometimes seems that we are no further forward than where we started!

One of the phenomena that is observed in the behaviour of economies is that of the financial crisis. These are often labelled as panics and sometimes precede what are known as depressions in economic activity. Such events are of profound import in human history, sometimes even precipitating wars or revolutions. It is no wonder that many consider study of such phenomena to be of the utmost importance. This is a book of such studies in relation to the history of Britain. Let us hope that it will bring some small measure of enlightenment to those who feel that an understanding of the economic past can help to inform better economic policy development and governance in the future.

David Harding

Contents

List of Figures

List of Tables

List of Contributors

Gareth Campbell is a lecturer in Finance at Queen's University, Belfast. His research, which has focused on asset pricing bubbles and financial history, has been published in journals such as the *Economic History Review*, *Explorations in Economic History*, *Business History Review*, and *Financial History Review*. He teaches Mathematics for Finance and Corporate Finance, and he is Programme Director for the BSc Finance at Queen's.

Forrest Capie is Professor Emeritus of Economic History at the CASS Business School, City University, London. He has taught at the London School of Economics, the University of Warwick, and the University of Leeds. He has been a British Academy Overseas Fellow at the National Bureau, New York, and a Visiting Professor at the University of Aix-Marseille, and at the London School of Economics, and a Visiting Scholar at the IMF. He has written widely on money, banking, and trade and commercial policy. He was Head of Department of Banking and Finance at City University from 1989 to 1992; Editor of the *Economic History Review* from 1993 to 1999. He recently completed the commissioned history of the Bank of England (2010, Cambridge University Press). His latest book (with G. E. Wood) is *Money over Two Centuries* (Oxford University Press, 2012).

Youssef Cassis is Professor of Economic History at the European University Institute. His work mainly focuses on banking and financial history, as well as business history more generally. His numerous publications on the subject include *City Bankers, 1890–1914* (Cambridge University Press, 1994), *Big Business: The European Experience in the Twentieth Century* (Oxford University Press, 1997), *Capitals of Capital: A History of International Financial Centres, 1780–2005* (Cambridge University Press, 2006), and *Crises and Opportunities: The Shaping of Modern Finance* (Oxford University Press, 2011). He was the co-founder, in 1994, of *Financial History Review*.

Nicholas Dimsdale is Emeritus Fellow in Economics at Queen's College Oxford and an Associate Fellow of Nuffield College, having retired as Fellow and University Lecturer in Economics. His interests are in monetary economics, macroeconomic history, and financial history. His papers have been published in leading journals and he has edited several books. For many years he was an editor of *Oxford Economic Papers* and is a member of its editorial board. He has been an active member of the Winton Institute for Monetary History and has collaborated closely with Dr Anthony Hotson, including the editing of this volume.

Marc Flandreau is a graduate of the Ecole Normale Supérieure in Paris. Professor Flandreau joined the Institute de Hautes Etudes in Geneva in 2008 and holds a joint appointment in the International History and in the International Economics Departments. His areas of expertise include the history of the international monetary and financial system, banking history, the history of reputation and white-collar criminality, and the history of financial information. He previously held teaching and research positions at the Centre National pour la Recherche Scientifique in Paris (where he was an award winner) and he was Chair of International Finance at Sciences Po between 2003 and 2008. He is finishing a book, *Anthropology and the Stock Exchange*, which revisits the relations between science, power, and white-collar criminality in Victorian Britain.

Nicholas Horsewood is a senior lecturer at the University of Birmingham, where he is Director of MSc Programmes and Director for Internationalisation. He has been the local organiser of the Royal Economic Society's Training Schools for the last 12 years. His research interests are eclectic and he has published over 30 articles in learned journals, co-authoring the economic history articles with Nicholas Dimsdale. He has worked as a consultant for the World Bank and has been involved in numerous EU-funded projects into the role of home ownership on the wider economy in EU countries.

Anthony Hotson is a Research Associate at the Centre for Financial History, Cambridge, and a member of Wolfson College, Oxford. He worked at the Bank of England in the 1980s and subsequently as a market practitioner. More recently, he has been a Research Fellow at the Winton Institute for Monetary History in Oxford where he collaborated with Nicholas Dimsdale, including the editing of this volume. Dr Hotson teaches financial history and is co-editor of a book to be published this year on the Thatcher Government and the 1981 Budget. He is a non-executive director of Cenkos Securities plc.

Avner Offer is Chichele Professor Emeritus of Economic History at the University of Oxford, and a Fellow of All Souls College. He initially studied land tenure and the economics of war, and published *Property and Politics 1870–1914* (Cambridge University Press, 1981), and *The First World War: An Agrarian Interpretation* (Oxford University Press, 1989) as well as many articles. Subsequently he focused on consumption and the quality of life and has published *The Challenge of Affluence: Self-control and Well-Being in the United States and Britain since 1950* (Oxford University Press, 2006). Currently he is studying the transition from social democracy to market liberalism, and is completing a book on the origins and consequences of the Nobel Prize in economics.

Richard Roberts is Professor of Contemporary Financial History at King's College London. He is a specialist in the development of financial institutions, banks, and markets and author of many scholarly publications in this area including, *Schroders: Merchants and Bankers* (Macmillan, 1992), *Take Your Partners: Orion, the Consortium Banks and the Transformation of the Euromarkets* (Macmillan 2001), *Saving the City: The Great Financial Crisis of 1914* (Oxford University Press, 2013), *The Media and Financial* Crises (co-edited with Steve Schifferes) (Routledge, 2014), and (with David Kynaston) *The Lion Wakes: A Modern History of* HSBC (Profile, 2015). His publications on international financial centres include (with David Kynaston) *City State: A Contemporary History of the City of London and How Money Triumphed* (Profile, 2001), *Wall Street* (The Economist, 2002), and *The City* (The Economist, 2008). He writes reports with City consultants Lombard Street Research that provide long-term perspectives on topical financial issues, and recently: *Did Anyone Learn Anything from Equitable Life? Lessons and Learning from Financial Crises* (ICBH, King's College London, 2012).

John Turner is a Professor of Finance and Financial History at Queen's University Belfast. He is the founder and director of the Queen's University Centre for Economic History. His research focuses on the long-run evolution and development of banking, banking crises, bubbles, corporate law, and financial markets. He also writes a blog (<http://www.financelongrun.co.uk>) which centres on the past, present, and future of finance. He has held several distinguished visiting positions during his career—he has been a Houblon-Norman Fellow at the Bank of England and an Alfred D. Chandler Fellow at Harvard Business School. He has recently published *Banking in Crisis: The Rise and Fall of British Banking Stability, 1800 to the Present* (Cambridge University Press, 2014).

Stefano Ugolini is Assistant Professor of Economics at the University of Toulouse 1 (Institute of Political Studies and LEREPS). After graduating in humanities from Scuola Normale Superiore di Pisa, he obtained a PhD in international finance from Sciences Po, Paris. Focused on monetary and financial history, his research has appeared in international journals such as the *Economic History Review* and the *European Review of Economic History*. Dr Ugolini has also provided his historical expertise to a number of central banks, including the Federal Reserve, the Bank of France, the Bank of Norway, and the Central Bank of Luxembourg.

1

Introduction

Nicholas Dimsdale and Anthony Hotson

This book examines British financial crises since the Napoleonic wars. Recent crises have led to a revival of interest in the history of money and banking, and a desire to understand past financial crises. Earlier generations of economists and historians were familiar with these crises, but interest lapsed during the generally benign financial conditions which followed the Second World War. Other areas of academic inquiry came to the fore, notably Keynesian demand management for regulating the economic cycle, monetarism for countering inflation, and, more recently, the stabilizing role of inflation targets. However, the study of banking markets and financial crises has returned to centre stage following the credit crunch of 2007–8 and the subsequent Eurozone crisis.

The foundation for this volume was a seminar series held at the Winton Institute for Monetary History in Oxford during Hilary Term 2010. The seminar was organized by Nick Mayhew and Luke Samy, and speakers were invited to give papers on a wide range of topics relating to British financial crises since the early nineteenth century. Amy Trevethan provided editorial assistance. Adam Swallow and Aimee Wright at Oxford University Press gave support and advice on the preparation of this volume. As editors, we are most grateful to all these contributors to the project.

Originally it was envisaged that each crisis would be discussed individually, but in the event the seminar took a rather different course. While some contributors spoke about individual crises, others covered common aspects of a number of crises. The papers are rooted in the tradition of describing crises in detail as well as keeping abreast of new developments in the analysis of financial markets. Forrest Capie's chapter provides an account of British financial crises since 1825 and serves to draw the collection together, providing a unified view of the course of British financial experience. The chapter by Nicholas Dimsdale and Anthony Hotson likewise reviews developments since 1825 with particular reference to the interaction of financial crises and the economic cycle. The next group of chapters review the course of individual crises: Gareth Campbell examines the railway mania and the 1847 crisis; Marc Flandreau and Stefano Ugolini assess the Overend Gurney crisis of 1866 and contrast it with the Baring crisis of 1890; and Richard Roberts examines the international financial crisis of 1914. Nicholas Dimsdale and Nicholas Horsewood consider the 1931 crisis and the effect of the Great Depression on the UK. Banks come under scrutiny in the chapters by John Turner and Avner Offer, and developments in regulation are assessed by Youssef Cassis. These chapters are reviewed briefly below.

In his chapter, Forrest Capie asks what distinguishes financial crisis from a lesser financial disturbance. He argues that the threatened breakdown of the payments mechanism constitutes a financial crisis, whereas individual bank failures are to be expected without necessarily leading to systemic problems. He suggests that the long period of financial stability, following the 1866 crisis, depended in large measure on the Bank of England's emerging role as lender of last resort. With the benefit of Walter Bagehot's advocacy, the Bank learned how to lend freely in a crisis at a high rate and to relieve pressures in the money market. Capie notes that the Bank provided market assistance anonymously, via the discount market, rather than dealing directly with individual banks. He argues that the threatened insolvency of Barings in 1890 did not impinge on the payments system and therefore it was not a financial crisis in his sense. Capie questions what he sees as a change in the Bank's policy away from anonymous market support in favour of individual bank rescues, starting with the secondary banking crisis in the early 1970s. This may have encouraged greater risk-taking and played a role in developments leading to the 2007–8 crisis.

Nicholas Dimsdale and Anthony Hotson take up themes introduced in Capie's chapter, in particular the financial crises of the mid-Victorian period. They place more emphasis on the disruption of credit flows resulting from financial crises and the consequential impact on the wider economy. They argue that improved stability after 1870 was assisted by the rise of acceptance houses which led to an improvement in the quality of bills and the resilience of the money market. The authors examine the dismantling of the system, starting with Competition and Credit Control in 1971 and extended by the Thatcher Government from 1979. They suggest that these reforms, including the deregulation of home finance, contributed to the severity of the financial crisis in 2007–8.

Dimsdale and Hotson explore the causes and consequences of financial crises by examining the relationship between the business cyclical and money market crises. The connection was relatively close in the period before 1866 and was present in the crisis of 2007–8. The authors argue that, without the countervailing effect of a resilient money market, financial risk tends to be pro-cyclical, rising during economic upturns. Financial crises often occur close to the top of the cycle and a freezing of the money market can lead to a credit crunch. This, in turn, can exacerbate a cyclical downturn. The interaction between the money market and the wider economy is therefore bi-causal. Abuses which occurred in the bill markets before 1870 are described and it is suggested that similar types of behaviour occurred in the recent financial crisis, although on a larger scale. The authors conclude that the severity of the 2007–8 crisis, and the length of the subsequent recession, were unique in British financial history and that 'This Time Things Really Were Different'.

Gareth Campbell focuses on government policy during the railway mania and the subsequent financial crisis of 1847. He argues that the government's policy was ineffective in containing the upsurge in share prices during the railway boom of the 1840s and, when the bubble burst, calls on shareholders' partly paid stock forced share prices down. Government policy was equally unsuccessful in preventing wide fluctuations in wheat prices through its tariff policy on wheat imports. The collapse of the price of wheat in 1847, following its upsurge in 1845–6, had serious implications for the money market, leading to widespread failures. The Bank could do little to alleviate the crisis due to the low level of its reserves and the restrictions built into the Bank Charter Act of 1844. In the event, the suspension of the 1844 Act was sufficient to quell the panic and it was not necessary to exceed the fiduciary issue.

Campbell's chapter contrasts the effective measures to relieve the crisis compared with the ineffectiveness of the rule-based approach embodied in the 1844 Act. He argues that crisis management is likely to be more effective in resolving a testing situation than regulatory measures drawn up before the event. An implication of this argument is that designing policy to anticipate crises may be doomed to failure.

Marc Flandreau and Stefano Ugolini argue that the collapse of Overend Gurney and the ensuing crisis of 1866 was a turning point in British financial history. According to the authors, the achievement of relative stability was due to the Bank's willingness to offer generous assistance to the market in a crisis, combined with an elaborate system for discouraging moral hazard. They suggest that the Bank's assistance was not anonymous because it monitored the names on its discounted bills. It recorded not just the house that discounted a bill, but the acceptor and drawer. They argue that this allowed the Bank to maintain the quality of bills in the market by threatening misbehaving money market participants with exclusion from the discount window.

Flandreau and Ugolini consider the factors that led to the decline of Overend Gurney. During the 1860s, Overend invested in speculative bills and longer-term investments which declined sharply in value at the time of a setback in the stock market in 1865. The firm sought extraordinary assistance from the Bank, but their request was refused on the grounds that the bills offered did not comply with standard eligibility rules. The Bank's refusal forced Overend to suspend payments and there was a general panic in the market. The Bank responded by lending freely and raising Bank rate to very high levels. The new policy was not lost on market participants who learned that to receive assistance from the Bank it was necessary to behave prudently. The improved standing of London's money market helped to establish sterling as an international currency.

Richard Roberts' chapter examines the breakdown of international payments at the outbreak of the First World War. He notes that this exposed London's money market, the leading international market in short-term capital, to severe problems. The acceptance houses were exposed to the risk of default by debtors and their failure could have undermined the discount market and the banking system. Roberts examines the nature of the crisis and steps taken by the authorities, the Bank and Treasury, to deal with the situation. The reactions of the authorities showed some inventiveness and flexibility, including a payment moratorium, purchases of impaired bills and advances to acceptors. The government decided to issue Treasury notes in small denominations and these were readily accepted by the public. The general panic was rapidly stilled, but the supply of commercial bills contracted paving the way for an expanded issue of Treasury bills. Measures were also taken to protect the viability of the Stock Exchange which became the conduit for long-term government borrowing during the war. In this way the crisis was used to redirect the short- and long-term capital markets to meet the needs of an economy mobilizing for war. A crucial decision was taken to remain on the gold standard on the advice of J. M. Keynes who assisted the Treasury at the start of the crisis.

The chapter by Nicholas Dimsdale and Nicholas Horsewood examines the impact of the financial crisis of 1931 and the effect of the Great Depression on the British economy. The chapter starts with a discussion of the events leading up to the decision to abandon the gold standard, starting with an examination of the reasons for sterling's vulnerability in 1931. These arose from underlying problems of the balance of payments, which had been further weakened by the decline in world trade. In the face of financial turmoil in Austria and Germany, adherence to the gold standard depended on the support of the Federal Reserve and the Banque de France. The Bank of England faced increasing difficulty meeting the conditions set by its creditors, who pressed for reductions in the British government's budget deficit as a condition for the renewal of credits. Following the fall of the Labour government and its replacement by a coalition, some progress was made in curbing the budget deficit, but there was increasing uncertainty about the government's electoral prospects and a looming exchange rate crisis. The authors draw on a model of currency crises developed by Morris and Shin (1998) to provide insights into the course of events. The chapter emphasizes the importance, for the restored gold standard, of cooperation among central banks, rather than reliance upon the traditional Bank rate mechanism.

In the second part of the chapter, the effects of the Great Depression on the British economy are assessed using an econometric model. The simulations confirm that the depreciation of sterling after its departure from the gold standard had powerful effects. They also suggest that the decline of world trade had a major effect, reducing British exports, output and employment. Consumption might have been expected to fall, but actually increased in the recession. This may be explained by the fall in import prices, which boosted real incomes, allowing consumer spending to rise despite the depressing effects of the fall in exports and investment. Finally, there is a brief assessment of the factors contributing to recovery. The simulations indicate that a modest rise in exports from the depressed levels of 1931–2 made a valuable contribution to recovery. By contrast, the reduction in interest rates, while boosting investment in housing, did not have a major macroeconomic effect. Aggregate public spending did, however, make a valuable contribution to the rising level of economic activity.

John Turner's chapter seeks to explain the relative stability of the British banking system in terms of its capital structure. Prior to 1826, the only joint-stock banks with limited shareholder liability were the Bank of England and four other state-chartered banks in Ireland and Scotland. All other banks had to be partnerships with unlimited liability. From 1826 joint-stock banking was allowed, but shareholder liability was jointly and severally unlimited. Limited liability banks were allowed from 1857–8, but these banks issued partly paid shares with an obligation on shareholders to subscribe for uncalled capital, if required by directors. One way or another, contingent capital offered additional protection to bank note holders and depositors (other than those of state-chartered banks).

Contingent capital meant that shareholders and managers would suffer losses in the event of failure and this discouraged risk shifting at the expense of note-holders and depositors. Turner argues that the British banking system remained relatively stable and free from systemic failure during the contingent capital era from 1826 to 1958. Although individual banks collapsed, the failure rate of banks (in terms of number or capital) did not reach a critical level—10 per cent—beyond which the payments system might have been threatened. Turner argues that agency problems and systemic risk rose after the abolition of contingent share capital in 1958.

In his chapter, Avner Offer argues that Britain's era of banking stability from 1870 to 1970 was the exception rather than the rule. He suggests that functional specialization of financial institutions played a key role during this period. High Street banks with responsibility for operating the payments mechanism were not significantly exposed to the risks of longer-term lending. Whereas today it is standard practice for banks to take short-term deposits and lend long term, the clearing banks of the pre-1970 period did not attempt the magic of maturity transformation. Their balance sheets were more liquid and their assets of better credit quality than today. Traditionally, clearing banks shunned home finance and commercial property lending because of their long maturity and the poor protection offered by real property when used as security for loans. This did not deter banks from taking security over property for short-term loans, but this was icing on the cake. In any event, domestic property prices slumped by more than a third over the Edwardian period and the sale of foreclosed properties proved to be difficult. Offer notes that the property cycle did not impinge on the clearing banks because they were not seriously exposed as lenders.

Offer sees the deregulatory package, known as Competition and Credit Control as a major turning point. Launched in 1971, the new arrangements were aimed at creating a more competitive market for credit and were followed by further deregulation introduced by the Thatcher government from 1979. Building societies were liberated from restrictions which governed their activities and banks entered the mortgage market, while some building societies converted from mutual status and became publicly listed banks. The liberalized credit system increased funds for house purchase and supported a house price boom. In the financial crisis of 2007–8, banks with lending secured on residential and commercial property became vulnerable, particularly if financed by short-term borrowing.

Offer moves on to consider proposals which have been put forward to strengthen the banking system. He supports a reversion to functional specialization in the financial sector, and notes that the Vickers proposals for ring-fencing are a step in this direction. However, he suggests that they are far from being sufficient and they fail to separate banks with responsibility for the payment system from property-related lending. Nor does the government's policy on banking reform seek to put the credit genie back in her bottle. On this point, Offer suggests that the restoration of stability may require a return to the credit rationing of the Radcliffe era.

Youssef Cassis presents a wide-ranging review of financial crises and the regulatory responses which followed them. His scope is international and he adopts a long-run historical perspective. A major financial shock may well prompt a regulatory response seeking to curb excesses that led to the crisis. In general such responses are short lived, although the response in the US to the Great Depression led to long-lasting changes in regulation. A clear contrast can be drawn between the Baring crisis of 1890, which led to little change in the organization of financial markets in London, and the New York panic of 1907 which prompted a major review of the US financial system and the setting up of the Federal Reserve System in 1913. The system was tested again in the Great Depression and found to be seriously defective. This led to further wide-ranging reforms introduced in the New Deal.

Movement towards an international form of regulation started in 1974 with the formation of the predecessor of the Basel Committee. It was followed by the Basel I agreement in 1988, which focused on the measurement of bank capital and risk measurement. At a time when some form of international regulation was being discussed, there was also a swing in ideology towards the deregulation of financial systems. The neoliberal view became predominant in Anglo-Saxon countries during the Thatcher government and Reagan administration. The outcome was a reduction in state intervention, which was not challenged until the crisis of 2007–8. This trend towards liberalization did not prevent the Basel Committee from introducing the Basel II regulations in 2004 after long negotiations, but their effectiveness has been questioned and they may have aggravated pro-cyclical fluctuations.

All the authors in this volume agree that there was a golden era of banking stability in Britain from around 1870 to 1970, although Turner suggests that the starting date should be set somewhat earlier. The authors agree on the need to distinguish between financial disturbances and major crises, but there are differences of view on what constitutes a systemic threat. Capie and Offer stress the importance of the payments system and the need to protect it. Dimsdale and Hotson accept that a resilient payments system is important, but argue that crises that interrupt credit flows also need to be avoided. They argue that the main cost of a financial crisis may be a cyclical downturn in the economy, rather than just disruption in the financial sector.

The Bank of England's role as lender of last resort is generally accepted, but other contributors to stability are suggested as well. Turner focuses on banks' capital structures, notably contingent capital. Offer stresses the importance of functional specialization and the systemic risks of universal banking. There are also differences of emphasis on how the Bank's market assistance maintained stability in the golden century while guarding against moral hazard. Capie points to the anonymity of lending against good collateral—what rather than who. Dimsdale and Hotson look to the new-style acceptance houses and the primacy of the bill on London. Flandreau and Ugolini emphasize the Bank's strict monitoring of money market participants and their leverage.

It also becomes clear that there is a need to distinguish between the origins of crises and the means used to resolve them. Campbell considers the opportunities missed and measures eventually taken to resolve the banking and commercial crises of the 1840s. He concludes that political realities meant that it was often easier to take decisive action in the midst of a crisis than to devise rules to prevent one. Roberts discusses the emergency measures taken in 1914 and comes to a broadly favourable view about the approach taken and its implementation. Here again, it is difficult to see how the financial problems of 1914 could have been mitigated significantly in advance. Cassis's consideration of regulatory responses to crises, including more recent ones, gives further support to the notion that cure is often easier than prevention. This implies that the periodic crises may be the norm and that Britain's century of stability (1870–1970) may have been exceptional.

It is too early to establish the full ramifications of the systemic crisis of 2007–8. It precipitated a severe recession and it is arguable that this time really is different. The feeling of 'never again' has become widespread and reforms to the financial system have been discussed at length. As before, radical changes are being resisted by defenders of the status quo and there is a risk we will end up with partial regulatory reform.

2

British Financial Crises in the Nineteenth and Twentieth Centuries

Forrest Capie

2.1 INTRODUCTION

Financial crises were frequent in England in the nineteenth century, then disappeared for a hundred years, and then they reappeared in the latter part of the twentieth century. The Bank of England and the banking system gradually learned how to deal with and then prevent financial crises and a long period of stability followed. But lessons on all sides get forgotten and crises reappear.

What constitutes a financial crisis? Some working definition is useful and one to work with is that a crisis is the result of a disturbance that threatens the payments system. The payments system is key (see Norman et al., 2011, for a lucid description of the history and central role of the payment system). In the words of a great authority: 'A financial crisis is fuelled by fears that the means of payment will be unobtainable at any price and, in a fractional reserve banking system leads to a scramble for high-powered money. It is precipitated by actions of the public that suddenly squeeze the reserves of the banking system . . . The essence of a financial crisis is that it is short-lived, ending with a slackening of the public's demand for additional currency' (Schwartz, 1986).

It is not the failure of an institution or of a municipality or anything else like that. There will always be such failures and so long as they do not threaten to impinge on the payments system they can be ignored for these purposes. Movements in asset prices might be indicators of what might follow and therefore useful to watch, but no more than that. A collapse in asset prices is not a financial crisis on its own. Only when it impinges on the banking sector does it threaten to provoke one.

2.2 WHAT HAPPENS IN A CRISIS?

The pattern of events in crises is well known. Many authors have set it out and Kindleberger and Aliber (2011) have produced a good summary of what typically happened in a financial crisis. Something happens to begin with that shocks the system, however mildly, what Irving Fisher called displacement; that exogenous event then opens up profitable opportunities. That could be something such as the discovery of a new technique or the discovery of a new resource. New investors are then attracted into the activity. After that, interest turns to other assets. The next stage is borrowing to buy. The boom is well underway by this stage and feeds on itself. A state of euphoria is reached. Bit by bit credit then becomes overextended and there will invariably be fraud and other kinds of skulduggery along the way. At some point some of the keener participants or insiders will decide it is time to take their profits and get out and the writing is then on the wall. The monetary authorities often take fright and tighten conditions at this stage. Collapse follows. Historically, banks (commercial and central) have played a central part in the process since it was largely bank credit that financed the boom; and then banks failed in the collapse.

The money multiplier is a useful means for thinking about how the main elements in the system operate. The multiplier captures how the public hold cash in relation to deposits, and how the banks hold cash reserves in relation to deposit liabilities. If broad money growth is threatened by the public's response to fears of a liquidity shortage (a flight to cash and out of deposits) and the multiplier shrinks, the monetary authorities can take the necessary offsetting action by increasing, to whatever extent is required, the monetary base.

One further comment should be made. Fractional reserve banking is a prerequisite for financial crises. But even so it is difficult to see how a banking crisis (which is really at the heart of this) gets underway before there has developed a banking multiplier of some significance. If banks are simply cloakrooms, as they were close to being in their earliest days, then it is hard to see how they fail or at least bring wider problems. So it is only after financial intermediation has progressed a reasonable distance that we get a multiplier of sufficient size to result in banking problems.

In England it is not until the beginning of the nineteenth century that that point is reached. In the eighteenth century there was certainly movement towards it but by the end of that century the multiplier is no more than about 1.3 times. Typically, developing countries with nascent banking systems have multipliers between 1.2 and 1.5 times. There was undoubtedly a great growth of banking in England in the eighteenth century but regulation constrained that growth (see Capie, 2004). By the mid nineteenth century the multiplier is close to 4 times, where it remained for more than a century (Capie and Webber, 1985).

2.3 NINETEENTH CENTURY FINANCIAL CRISES IN ENGLAND

From the 1820s onwards there was a long series of financial crises that ran through much of the nineteenth century: 1825, 1836–7, 1847, 1857, and 1866. There were some other episodes after that to which I will return, episodes that do not qualify as financial crises but are often thought of as such: (1873), 1878, 1891, (1907), 1914, and 1931.[1] But from 1866 onwards there were essentially a hundred years of financial stability without any financial crises. Then they reappeared albeit in milder form in: 1973/4, 1982–3, and 1991–2; and then in a major form in 2008.

I will describe these genuine nineteenth-century crises briefly, simply to bring out the important similarities between them, and comment more briefly still on those in the twentieth century.

In the few years before the 1825 crisis there was what would come to be recognized as a distinguishing feature of most crises: easy money and abundant credit. On this occasion it was 'improvident finance on the part of the country banks' that was the source (King, 1936). They were guilty of over-issuing banknotes. But the Bank of England joined in, reducing its discount rate to 4 per cent and extending the life of bills from 65 days to 95 days. Abundant credit and speculative activity broke out across a range of commodities. There were also several development schemes for the newly established South American republics. In the three years from 1822 to 1825 there were twenty loans for a total of £40 million (when British national income—gross domestic product—was about £300 million). In early 1825 the Bank, scenting trouble ahead, sought to correct things by refusing to discount bills. Alarm began to spread and when Sir Peter Pole and Co. failed at the end of the year panic ensued. According to one report the country was, 'within twenty-four hours of barter'. Remarkably, in recent times the same thing was in effect being said—the banking system was within twenty-four hours of complete collapse. In 1825 the Bank was slow to act but did so eventually, quelling the panic. As a director of the Bank (and a former Governor) Jeremiah Harman put it at the time:

> We lent it by every possible means and in modes we had never adopted before; we took in stock on security, we purchased Exchequer bills, we made advances on Exchequer bills, we not only discounted outright, but we made advances on the deposit of bills of exchange to an immense amount, in short, by every possible means consistent with the safety of the Bank, and we were not, on some occasions over-nice. Seeing the dreadful state in which the public were, we rendered every assistance in our power. (Bagehot, 1873: 52)

[1] The years given in brackets were crises in other parts of the world which did not appear in England.

Bagehot added: 'After a day or two of this treatment, the entire panic subsided, and the "City" was quite calm' (1873: 52).

In the 1830s there were some similarities, at least in terms of easy money. In 1830 the Bank had sanctioned the opening of discount accounts for bill brokers in what was agreed to be an improvement to the functioning of the money market. Then in 1834 the Bank had especially large deposits from the East India Company and went out of its way to find employment for the funds. But in addition there was a reckless use of the new facilities for discounting. Yet again, according to King, the Bank should take responsibility for the crisis because it not only permitted but fostered the easy money which encouraged the growth of paper of doubtful quality. The unprecedented ease in the money market was the Bank's responsibility. As ever there was an increasingly adventurous spirit abroad in the commercial world and a host of new joint stock flotations. As an anonymous pamphlet of the time said, these were, 'losing sight of caution and common rules'. There followed excessive discounting of poor quality paper. In the mid 1830s many of these related to the Anglo-American trade. The same pattern followed with the Bank first refusing to discount the paper of the Anglo-American houses, then deciding it could not let them fail and so coming to their assistance to allow for an orderly liquidation. In 1836/7 and 1839 European bank promotion added problems and the crisis ebbed and flowed.

In the mid 1840s it was the railways that were the new thing and they were growing rapidly. But they were not growing as rapidly as the prospectuses for new projects. In the middle of this the Bank launched an aggressive lending policy apparently encouraged by the passing of the 1844 Act. After the Act the Bank believed it had an obligation to discount competitively and immediately cut its discount rate to 2.5 per cent and offered temporary advances with a wider definition of acceptable collateral 'until further notice'. In 1845 the *Bankers' Magazine* warned, 'if this line of conduct continues a monetary crisis will be inevitable'. But the easy money did continue and the railway mania really took off. There were many new projects, though many were entirely fictitious. The share prices of some companies rose by as much as tenfold in as many months. Even after the boom in railway shares collapsed, the feverish activity spread to other ventures. In the middle of this the Bank kept its rate at 2.5 per cent and its security portfolio grew apace and the Bank could not see any problem. Not everyone in the Bank was guilty. George W. Norman stood apart. He wrote:

> During the course of the year (1847) I did not fail to impress upon the Court my views of the propriety of acting earlier, and more efficiently by raising the rate of discount. I did this by formal motion in March of this year, by which and my subsequent conduct, I acquired no little obloquy and unpopularity on the part of certain members of the court, some of whom had overtraded and regarded an

> easy state of the money market as vitally important to them. The fact that I was out of business, and could thus look without alarm as to my private interest upon the storm raging around, did not tend to make my counsels more acceptable. (O'Brien and Creedy, 2010: 417–18)

It was only when fears of poor harvests spread fear further afield and the Bank realized late the threat to its reserve, that it raised the discount rate and imposed increasingly onerous terms until it was impossible to discount bills or to raise money on first-class securities. A paralysis of trade followed. Attribution of blame changes little over the years too. The defenders of the 1844 legislation put all the blame for the crisis on the 'commercial world for the reckless overtrading, its foolish speculations and its irrational exuberance' (King, 1936: 149).

In the 1850s the feverish speculation that developed had its origins in the gold discoveries of the decade. In 1853 the Bank's discount rate went up to 3.5 per cent but the speculation continued unabated. It was also fuelled by developments in California and in what was said to be gross over-investment in land, railways, and mining such that by 1854 all the ingredients of a financial crisis were present. But instead of a crisis breaking at that point it was fed for another three years by the gold inflows from Australia. As the market rates fell the Bank imprudently followed the rates down. Then as usual the Bank decided enough was enough and tightened. When bad news filtered through from the American West, and particularly the failure of Ohio Life and Trust Co. at the end of August with liabilities of $7 million, it was followed by wholesale bank failures. Panic spread to Glasgow and Liverpool—the most exposed cities. Again, the Bank's reserves fell, the Bank rate was raised, and panic followed. In fact the Bank had vacillated over a couple of years before finally breaking the boom.

In March 1858 the Bank decided to change access to the discount window. It was a decision that would be tested a few years later in 1866 (see Calomiris, 2011; but also Flandreau and Ugolini, 2010). In 1866 there were some differences. The crisis became focused on a major firm, Overend Gurney. Overend Gurney's origins were Quaker and they were highly respected in the financial sector from at least as early as the late seventeenth century. Few, it was said, were as wise in the ways of the City or more judicious than Samuel Gurney.

The decade of the 1860s was the high point of the mid-Victorian boom. In early 1866 the Chancellor of the Exchequer, Gladstone, was decidedly upbeat about the economy. In May the Bank's reserves were in good shape. But on 10 May Overend Gurney & Co failed. Overend's had become a giant financial institution dominating the discount market. But it got involved in bad asset management and became grossly over-committed to risky enterprises. Many of the booming firms of the 1860s failed and after Overend's failure panic set in immediately. It was the worst panic since 1825: 'this ruin of its (the Bank's) most famous neighbour and sometime rival, "the Corner House", the greatest private firm in England' (Clapham, 1966: 261).

Overend's 'losses were made in a manner so reckless and so foolish that one would think a child who had lent money in the City of London would have lent it better' (Bagehot, 1873: 19). Samuel Gurney's old sound business called for 'great care with every bill, great knowledge of the "standing of parties", and considered use of that knowledge. The younger men now in charge held bills of doubtful subordinate. Portfolios were filled with all sorts of flimsy paper, including the so-called "finance securities"'—toxic assets again (Clapham, 1966: 261). These latter were 'issued in advance by company promoters, perhaps before the public had even subscribed, to contracting firms, and by them discounted'. And Overend's had gone far beyond dealings in bills, good or bad. They were mixed up in all sorts of financing, were 'partners in almost every kind of speculative and lock-up business' (Clapham, 1966: 262).

On 11 May 1866 there was an unprecedented fall in Bank of England reserves. Bank rate went to 10 per cent and stayed there for three months, and more banks failed. Bagehot criticized the Bank for lending 'hesitatingly, reluctantly, and with misgiving. In fact to make large advances in this faltering way is to incur the evil of making them without obtaining the advantage' (Bagehot, 1873: 64–5). But they nearly got it right.

2.4 RESOLUTION AND PREVENTION

How was it that these crises occurred at regular intervals and then stopped? My argument is that there were three parts to the solution. First, the banks learned how to behave and found their own way to prudence. Secondly, the Bank of England learned how to perform the role of lender of last resort. And third, government provided what it believed to be the appropriate regulatory environment.

2.4.1 The Commercial Banks

At the beginning of the nineteenth century banks were generally small and without branches. Any shock to the system that cast doubts over the security of deposits could result in a run, and the nature of a bank's balance sheet meant even well-behaved banks could fail. So they had to find their own way to the most suitable capital/asset ratio, cash/deposit ratio, and liquid/asset ratio that was consistent with acceptable profitability. The ratios, as might be expected, all started out fairly high and gradually came down as banks found what could work consistent with an acceptable level of profitability.

Caution was learned and by mid-century was essentially the byword. A major contribution to this was made by, not surprisingly, a Scot—people known the world over for their caution. But within Scotland there are those who are noted for their extreme caution. They are from Aberdeen. They are said to give nothing away. George Rae was from Aberdeen. He learned his trade as a banker there and in the 1830s decided he needed to test himself in England. He joined a Liverpool bank, the North and South Wales Bank, and did well before he was embarrassed in the crisis of the 1840s. Amid the various difficulties the bank experienced, in October 1847 a London newspaper carried a story that the bank had failed, a story that was false. But not surprisingly panic followed and the bank was forced to suspend payment. Other difficulties followed that set Rae pondering further on the nature of banking.

Rae then went on to write a handbook for bankers which was still being used in the twentieth century, *The Country Banker* (1885), and indeed editions of which were produced in 1930 and again in 1976. It had gone through several nineteenth-century editions. Rae covered every aspect of banking but central to his instruction was caution. He wrote: 'There is . . . a possibility of being over cautious; but in banking that is one of the cardinal virtues, compared with the opposite evil and mischief of being over credulous' (Rae, 1885: 3). Bagehot agreed: 'Adventure is the life of commerce, but caution, I had almost said timidity, is the life of banking' (Bagehot, 1873: 232).

Nevertheless, even the best behaved banks could still be embarrassed when a shock hit the system and the second part to the solution was the lender of last resort. The banks learned caution and they were supported by the lender of last resort.

2.4.2 The Bank of England

At the end of the eighteenth century and the beginning of the nineteenth there were many contributors to a developing literature in the changing financial and monetary environment. And many of these addressed the question of the role of a lender of last resort. Francis Baring was probably the first to use the phrase and describe what was meant. But Henry Thornton gave a fuller, even comprehensive, treatment. He described how the Bank should behave in normal times letting the money supply 'vibrate only within certain limits' (Thornton, 1802: 259), but that in times of liquidity squeeze the Bank should relieve the pressure. However, 'It is by no means intended to imply, that it would become the Bank of England to relieve every distress which the rashness of the country banks may bring upon them: the Bank by doing this might encourage their improvidence'. Others such as Thomas Joplin contributed too, exhorting the Bank how to behave in the middle of the crisis of 1825.

The Bank, he said, should increase its note issue to offset the loss of circulation. Bagehot, writing in the 1840s, brought greater clarity following the crisis of 1847:

> It is a great defect of a purely metallic circulation that the quantity of it cannot be readily suited to any sudden demand; . . . as paper money can be supplied in unlimited quantities, however sudden the demand may be, it does not appear to us that there is any objection in principle of sudden issues of paper money to meet the sudden and large extensions of demand. (Bagehot, 1848: 267)

But the Bank of England learned its role as lender of last resort slowly. It resisted for a long time the advocacy of theorists. The lender is the ultimate source of cash and is therefore usually the central bank. The lender should provide liquidity to the market as a whole, and not bail out individual firms (banks). It can provide liquidity without limit, but should do so at an increasing price. It is the knowledge in the markets that the supply cannot run out that serves to assure the market and allay the panic. In its ideal form it should do this anonymously. There should be no commercial rivalry that might deflect the Bank from its task, or involve a conflict of interest. If it is known in advance that this is how the bank will behave (pre-commitment) then the picture is complete.

Any commercial bank may, from time to time, extend loans to customers who are illiquid or even insolvent. They may do so even when the present expected return from the new loan itself is zero or negative if the wider effects on their own reputation for commitment, or the knock-on effects of the failure of the first customer on others warrant it. By the same token, a nascent central bank—an institution still some way short of maturity as a central bank—may 'rescue' some client or correspondent bank, just as the commercial bank may support its business customer. But we would not want to describe such ad hoc exercises as involving a conscious assumption of a systematic lender of last resort function. Nor would we want to see a mature central bank endeavouring to rescue individual banks. There is simply too much moral hazard involved. No central bank would want to pre-commit itself to giving special support to *any* individual bank that was running into liquidity problems. A bank liquidity problem that is not caused by some technical problem is likely itself to be a reflection of some deeper suspicions about solvency. Consequently, an unqualified pre-commitment to provide assistance to an individual firm would involve too much moral hazard.

Besides, it is worth pausing to consider what could reasonably be meant by 'bail out'. Central banks in general do not have the capital resources to salvage single-handedly an institution of any significant size—significant in the sense that it could have damaging consequences for the rest of the system. If the central bank discounted at face value the inferior assets of an individual institution in difficulty, then if these assets were subsequently marked to market, their values would appear much lower on the bank's balance sheet. Thus the central bank would be seen to be damaging its own balance sheet since it has parted with cash and exchanged that for lower-value assets. If this in turn required government assistance in raising more capital, the central bank would in effect have taken a fiscal decision. Thus, in the case of an individual institution, all the central bank can really do is oversee or organize a rescue operation, perhaps putting pressure on others to subscribe new capital.

How can the ideal operation of lender of last resort be achieved? The lender of last resort supplies funds to the market in times of need; it does not supply individual institutions. In its proper form it should not engage in bailing out firms of any kind, be they banks or non-banks. Therefore, if the operation could be carried out where the identity of those seeking funds was not known to the Bank that would be ideal. Institutions holding good-quality assets will have no difficulty in getting hold of the funds they need. Institutions with poor-quality assets are likely to suffer. In times of panic the interest rate would rise.

By something of a happy accident this was in effect the system that developed in England. At the beginning of the nineteenth century the Bank's monopoly offended the rest of the banks. Such was the antipathy that the new joint stock banks preferred to keep a distance. Discount brokers emerged who conveniently transacted business between the commercial banks and the Bank of England. These discount brokers gradually acquired the capital base to finance their own portfolios and by the third quarter of the nineteenth century had developed their modern form of the discount house.

When the commercial banks were under pressure in a liquidity squeeze their first line of defence was to call in their loans to the discount houses; this in turn sent the discount houses off to the Bank of England. If the commercial banks had to cash in bills they would do this at the discount houses and the latter would in turn take them to the Bank. In this way the central bank never needed to know from whence the great bulk of the demand was coming. The precise source of the demand is largely an irrelevance. Good bills get discounted.

Some confusion in the discussion over the nature of the lender of last resort function may have arisen from too cavalier a treatment of this model. Central banking was more advanced in Britain than in other countries, and the British model of central banking was often adopted elsewhere. But the actual mechanism did not always exist elsewhere. Thus a key feature of the British system, its inbuilt protective device for anonymity, was ignored. This meant that in most other countries the institutions themselves went to the central bank, losing their anonymity by so doing. Difficulties were exacerbated when the government's bank and the commercial banks were in competition for commercial business. This seems to have been ignored in most of the literature, and it may be this that accounts for the way in which bailing out has been treated.

Prior to the latter part of the nineteenth century, central banks were generally expected to carry out a commercial banking function. In some cases, when they were first established, they offered the only source of commercial banking services and they were often the most important and largest commercial bank in their country. Consequently, the early relationship between central banks and commercial banks was often one of business rivalry and competition. This adversarial relationship was resolved around the beginning of the twentieth century in most cases by a largely uncodified concordat whereby, in return for the central bank's withdrawal from commercial banking, the commercial banks voluntarily accepted the central bank's leadership (see Capie, Goodhart, Fischer, and Schnadt, 1994). A central bank assumes the function of lender of last resort when it accepts responsibility for the banking system as a whole that overrides any residual concern with its own profitability. It is the appreciation of how they should behave in a crisis, rather than any individual act of rescue, that signals acceptance of the role.

It is worth pausing here to consider the 'too-big-to-fail doctrine' as it might have applied to Overend Gurney. Overend had become banker to the London and country banks and on the day it failed *The Times* said it 'could rightly claim to be the greatest instrument of credit in the Kingdom' (*The Times*, 11 September 1866). Its balance sheet was roughly ten times the size of the Midland Bank and the Westminster Bank—two of the biggest banks in the country, and while they operated with capital/asset ratios of about 9 to 11 per cent, Overend's was 2 per cent. (Discount houses do have lower ratios, but Overend was conducting banking business.) Overend's appeal to the Bank for help was refused: 'The Governor took the view that the Bank could not assist one concern unless it was prepared to assist the many others which were known to be in a similar plight' (King, 1936: 242). In any case, there was considerable animosity between the two institutions. Nevertheless, the refusal to help Overend can clearly be seen as a further step on the road by which the Bank came to see its function as coming to the aid of the market as a whole rather than bailing out imprudent and insolvent institutions. The panic of 1866 was huge. But in spite of Overend's size and apparent centrality to the system, the panic passed and the system went on to become strong and stable. The Bank's refusal, then, can be regarded as a signal that was an important step on the road towards a sound policy towards financial crises in the Schwartz sense of the term.

The Bank of England learned how to do all this over a long period, beginning with the crisis of 1825 and continuing until the crisis of 1866, and then putting it into practice if ever the need appeared to be arising (Ogden, 1991; Capie, 2002). There followed over a hundred years of financial stability; banks failed as they should indeed be allowed to, but there were no financial crises. And that was across a long period of alternating fortunes of growth and recession, of war and different exchange-rate regimes, deflation and inflation, and so on.

2.4.3 Regulatory Environment

The third element in the story is the role of government and regulation. The striking thing about all this to a modern eye is that it was all done in a period of laissez-faire, and banking followed that course. The preceding period that ran through the eighteenth century was that of mercantilism—the supremacy of the state. And in that century banking in England was severely circumscribed. But the reaction to the inefficiency and corruption in government that mercantilism produced, was to seek small government, free trade, and sound money. And so in that new climate of laissez-faire, after each financial crisis the authorities deregulated.

The first stage in this process came with relaxation of the usury laws, at least for the Bank of England. The laws had been in force for centuries. In 1825 when the crisis blew up, the Bank did lend but it could not lend at a rate above 5 per cent which in the context of the times was hardly high enough. After the crisis the usury laws were relaxed and at the next crisis the Bank raised its rate above 5 per cent.

At the same time the restrictions on banks being limited to partnerships of no more than six was also abandoned and joint stock banks were allowed to form. Initially, they could only operate away from London—outside a radius of 65 miles. But a few years later in the 1830s they were also allowed to operate within London.

The gold standard had been more strictly defined in the 1844 Act but it proved too restrictive and when the 1847 crisis developed it was clear that the Bank could not hold to the law and do what was required for financial stability. The Chancellor then wrote to the Governor and relieved him temporarily of the need to stick to the requirements of the Act and so the limitless lending (at a high rate) could take place.

There was a growing discussion on the merits and demerits of limited liability in the second quarter of the nineteenth century, and after the 1857 crisis the laws were relaxed and limited liability was available for those who chose to avail themselves. Not all did, but it was an option.

After that banking was extremely lightly regulated and everything was then in place that would allow the Bank to act as a lender of last resort. Generally speaking it did so, though on occasions it might have blurred the issue.

2.5 SOME NON-CRISES

There are, as mentioned earlier, some other episodes which have sometimes been portrayed as financial crises but are better described otherwise. They were the events of (1873), 1878, 1890, (1907), 1914, and 1931. In 1878 the large and heavily branched bank, the City of Glasgow Bank, failed. The bank was of unlimited liability and its failure caused considerable distress. But the bank was fraudulently run. It was not the system that was at fault or at risk. The failure did, of course, have an effect on other firms and even on some other banks. But there was no financial crisis; there was no threat to the payments system. There was no need for action by the Bank or the Chancellor. There was no need for action of any kind.

In 1890 Barings bank failed. Barings was an old and distinguished British name. But it was a merchant (investment) bank and not directly involved in the payments system. Of course its demise might still have impinged on the payments system had it been taken as a sign of more general difficulties and fears then spread elsewhere. But it quickly became clear that Barings' problems derived from difficulties in Argentina. The rest of the system was sound. The Chancellor enquired of the Governor if a letter was required relieving the Bank of the necessity of holding to the 1844 Act and the answer was no. The Bank did take action and organized a 'lifeboat' rescue, an action that is better described as crisis management.

In 1914 there was a major problem in the financial system on the outbreak of war. There were, though, none of the common features of the build-up to a crisis. There was no boom and no downturn. There were simply the seriously disruptive problems produced by the failure of remittance from continental Europe. The solution, however, was similar in many respects to that for normal crises. An injection of liquidity was required and was provided. But there were also some guarantees given to the accepting houses and the discount houses on their bills. The liquidity injection happened to coincide with the abandonment of the gold standard for reasons of war and thereafter there were failures in not retracting the liquidity. While 1914 is a good guide as to how to deal with imminent systemic collapse, it is not a good illustration of a typical financial crisis.

There was no great depression in Britain between the wars. Neither was the 1920s a depressed decade. There was a recession between 1929 and 1932 with a fall in output of 5.6 per cent. The financial system remained robust throughout the whole period and British growth in the 1930s was faster than it had ever been. There were serious financial problems in most of the rest of the world and great depression too. But financial stability remained in Britain. What happened in 1931 was an exchange-rate crisis. The return to gold in 1925 had taken place at an over-valued rate, one that could not be held to, and was abandoned in mid 1931. But there were few financial ramifications. The payments system was essentially undisturbed. Bank profitability was hardly dented.[2]

So, following the crisis of 1866, while there were many bank failures and there were episodes when other kinds of problems blew up, there were no financial crises. The system was stable for over a hundred years.

2.6 THE END OF THE INTERMISSION IN MERCANTILISM

By the Second World War financial stability was taken for granted and it continued for another 25 years. But then, as is frequently the case, after a period of increased and deliberately encouraged competition in banking between 1971 and 1973, and of expansionary monetary policy, there was a huge growth of the fringe (or shadow) banking sector. This sector lay outside the banks which were subject to credit controls (in many ways was a consequence of the controls being in place) and its business model was to borrow in the short-term money markets—the inter-bank market—and lend on property. A great property boom developed. When the monetary authorities then tightened policy in the face of spiralling inflation, the market turned down, the euphoria turned to gloom, property companies failed and then too the fringe banks which had lent on property were in danger. There were also the usual accompanying dodgy practices that are expected.

There were then fears that the difficulties might spread to other parts of the banking system and the Bank launched a rescue operation that came to be called the lifeboat. This should properly be called crisis management of the kind that was organized for Barings in 1891. The question that arises is: why not rely on that former stabilizer, the lender of last resort, if indeed it were needed? Any bank in difficulty that held good assets could have got the necessary liquidity by the traditional means. If they did not hold the appropriate assets then that might be considered poor management and they could be left to fail. If they were thought sufficiently good risks then a clearing bank might well have thought it worthwhile extending them credit.

Instead of which the Bank became involved in a long process (lasting over many years in some cases) of propping up or winding down a large number of institutions at considerable cost in terms of the resources devoted to the exercise, and in some cases in substantial financial losses. And that does

[2] But for some modification to that view see Accominotti (2012) who argues that the Bank chose internal stability over external, and the position of London as an international financial centre.

seem to have been the Bank's approach thereafter, quietly to bail out or otherwise arrange the affairs of banks in trouble no matter how small and insignificant they were. In the mini-crises of the early 1980s related to the Latin American debt crisis, in the small bank crisis of the early 1990s, and from year to year across the last third of the century that was the practice (Jackson, 1996). How much moral hazard was being stoked up is hard to say but it must have become clear that financial institutions in difficulty would be rescued. It is sometimes argued that the idea was that equity holders should lose their stakes and management teams should be dismissed while the system was preserved. These are good principles but if they were indeed followed why the need for secrecy and hence obscuring the lesson for all? It was several years later in the case of most of these events that outsiders discovered what was going on.

2.7 LESSONS CAN BE LEARNED FROM HISTORY

There are many similarities between the financial turmoil of 2007/8 and financial crises of the past. But there are always differences. No two crises are ever identical. But if the first crisis of the twenty-first century was characterized as deriving from a period of easy money stimulating an asset price boom (in this case housing) and then turning down as monetary policy tightened, there would be the essentials of many, or even most, previous crises. The tightening led to the credit crunch which in turn affected the real economy.

There are few, if any, simple lessons that can be drawn from historical experience; there is no manual to which one can refer. History is better used when the patterns or the rhythms of the past are understood and absorbed. (As Mark Twain is reputed to have said, 'History does not repeat itself; it rhymes'). Nevertheless, lessons do appear to have been learned in the course of the nineteenth century for how else do we explain the long period of stability in England that followed the long period of recurrent crises, particularly so when the crises continued to appear in other countries around the world. The banks had to learn what shape their balance sheet should have. They did and stuck to it. They did suffer abuse for the next hundred years for being too conservative. Perhaps the main lesson from the English experience (though I believe it extends elsewhere) is that periods of monetary expansion produce booms that then collapse. But it is still monetary expansion that is required to then restore confidence and stimulate the economy. A second lesson was that it needed to be clear in advance that liquidity would be available. The Bank had to accept this as a primary function and it did, and its role as lender of last resort was understood by the market. (There is a danger that a lesson might be over-learned; a fear of lack of liquidity should not be sufficient to call forth ever-increasing injections of liquidity). Perhaps a third general lesson is that when something goes wrong it is not necessarily a good thing to identify the problem (past) and disallow it in the future. Regulation is not necessarily the solution; it is just as likely to be the problem.

There are some other smaller points. These might seem too obvious to mention, and I hesitate to do so, and yet they do keep reappearing. If some activity is growing extremely rapidly it should probably be looked at closely. If high returns are being offered on some investment then it too should be examined closely.

3

Financial Crises and Economic Activity in the UK since 1825

Nicholas Dimsdale and Anthony Hotson

3.1 INTRODUCTION

The literature on financial history and business cycles is conventionally discussed separately. The aim here is to bring them together.[1] A financial shock, or a series of incidents, can lead to a systemic crisis in the money market, and this may—or may not—have a serious impact on the rest of the economy. Conversely, the economic cycle may affect the resilience of the money market and its ability to cope with financial shocks. We want to find out whether disturbances in London's money market affected the wider economy, and vice versa. To put it another way, we want to know whether conditions in Lombard Street affected the High Street, and vice versa. This question is particularly relevant in view of the debate on the causes and consequences of the financial crisis of 2007–8.

In section 3.2 of this chapter, we examine the timing of financial crises relative to the business cycle, and possible interactions between the two. In section 3.3, we examine developments in London's money market in more detail, and assess the causes and consequences of financial crises in London since 1825. Our conclusions are set out in section 3.4.

3.2 CRISES AND CYCLES

3.2.1 Bi-causality and Pro-cyclical Risk

The peaks and troughs of UK business cycles are set out in Table 3.1 below. The data have been compiled by Broadberry, Campbell, Klein, Overton, and

[1] We are grateful to Alan de Bromhead for research assistance.

Table 3.1. British economic fluctuations and financial crises, 1819–2013, major cyclical peaks and troughs, and the timing of financial crises

	Sub-period	UK business cycle		Disturbances affecting London's financial markets	
		Trough	Peak	Systemic failure	Incidents and shocks
1	1819–1841	1819	1825	1825	Run on country banks
		1832	1836	–	–
		1837	1839	1837–9	US crisis (1837), UK balance of payments crisis (1839)
2	1842–1866	1842	1846	–	–
		1847	1849	1847	Bill market crisis (1847)
		1850	1857	1857	US panic (1857); Borough Bank of Liverpool (1857)
		1858	1866	1866	American Civil War (1861–5); Overend Gurney (1866)
3	1867–1892	1867	1872	–	German and US crises (1873)
		1879	1883	–	City of Glasgow Bank (1878)
		1885	1890	–	Barings (1890)
4	1893–1914	1893	1899	–	–
		1903	1907	–	US crisis (1907)
		1908	1913	–	–
		–	–	1914	Outbreak of war and threat to accepting houses (1914)
5	1921–1943	1921	1925	–	–
		1926	1929	–	Stock market crash (1929)
		1931	1937	–	Standstill agreement and gold parity crisis (1931)
6	1952–1974	1952	1973	–	Secondary banking crisis (1973–5)
7	1975–1979	1975	1979	–	–
8	1981–2007	1981	1990	–	Latin American debt crisis (from 1982)
		1991	2007	2008	Lehman Brothers (2008)

Sources: Broadberry et al. (2011) for 1819 to 1829; Hills et al. (2010) for 1830 to 1947, updated from Office of National Statistics (2013).

van Leeuwen (2011) and Hills, Thomas, and Dimsdale (2010), and updated using more recently published official statistics.[2] Aldcroft and Fearon (1972), Matthews, Feinstein, and Odling Smee (1982) and Dimsdale (1990) give similar, but not identical classifications of peaks and troughs.

Dates of peaks and troughs since 1819 are shown in the table alongside dates of financial sector disturbances, and instances when London's money market faced a systemic crisis. We identify five systemic crises in the mid nineteenth century, a sixth at the outbreak of the First World War in 1914, and a seventh in 2008. Financial shocks and disturbances have occurred much more frequently, but since the 1870s they have rarely led to systemic market failure. We examine why this has happened, and whether the crisis of 2007–8 leaves open the possibility of a reversion to periodic systemic crises, akin to those experienced between 1825 and 1866.

The general pattern is one in which financial crises occur close to business cycle peaks, and are followed by a downturn in the wider economy. The 1914 crisis arose from the outbreak of world war, but it also followed a prolonged cyclical upturn. The credit crunch of 2007–8 followed a prolonged upturn and was, itself, followed by a cyclical downturn.

This pattern is consistent with the notion that risk in money and banking markets is pro-cyclical (Financial Services Authority, March 2009: 22). Financial disturbances are more likely to lead to systemic market failure when the wider economy is enjoying a sustained upturn, collateral values are at cyclical highs, and market practitioners are willing to accept more risk. The data are also consistent with the idea that causality runs both ways: an upturn in the High Street may leave Lombard Street more exposed to a financial crisis, and a financial crisis in Lombard Street may contribute to a downturn in the High Street. The aim of this chapter is to assess whether the interaction between the two has been bi-causal, and whether risk in the money market has been pro-cyclical.

3.2.2 Financial Shocks and Systemic Market Failures

From the 1870s until 1913, there were no systemic crises in the London money market akin to those experienced in the previous fifty years. Although the cyclical plateau of 1872–3 did coincide with financial crises in Germany and the US, there was no systemic crisis in the UK. The collapse of the City of Glasgow Bank in 1878 disrupted the money market, but the economy was growing slowly and systemic failure was avoided. The threat to Barings in 1890 coincided with a cyclical peak and could have led to a systemic crisis, but this

[2] Office of National Statistics, Quarterly National Accounts Time Series Dataset Q1 2013, 16 July 2013 update, accessed 26 July 2013.

was averted by the Bank of England's prompt action. As a result, Baring's problems had little impact on the domestic economy, but deteriorating conditions in the international economy did lead to a downturn in the early 1890s.

The outbreak of war in 1914 did result in a crisis in the London money market, but the problem was managed by the joint action of the Bank and the Treasury (Morgan, 1952). During the interwar period there were three cyclical upturns, but no crisis in the domestic financial system. There was, however, a major external crisis in 1931, which could have affected the London money market. The Bank's standstill agreement for foreign bills successfully prevented a systemic failure in the domestic market, and the departure from gold parity stemmed the external crisis. 1931 was, of course, a cyclical trough.

Turning to the post-war period, we find that there were no systemic crises until 2007–8, although balance of payments and exchange rate crises were relatively frequent. There were two near misses: the secondary banking crisis of 1973–5, and the Latin American debt crisis from 1982. The UK's departure from the European exchange rate mechanism (ERM) in 1992 brought rapid relief from severe financial pressures arising from an overvalued exchange rate.

3.2.3 Business Cycle and Financial Crises

During the mid nineteenth century, the business cycle followed a classic pattern of economic upturn interrupted by a financial crisis, leading to a contraction of credit and a hike in the Bank of England's base rate for lending (Bank rate), followed by economic downturn. The five systemic crises of the mid nineteenth century and the overseas financial crisis of 1873 all coincided with a raised Bank rate (Table 3.1). The Bank rate was also raised at the time of the cyclical peak in 1836, although there was no financial crisis (Figure 3.1).

The financial crises of 1847, 1857, and 1866 each had a major impact on the money market, but only short-term effects on the real economy. Real output (output) recovered within one to two years with an easing of financial pressures (Figure 3.3). In contrast, the crisis of 1825 coincided with sharp swings in output and was followed by a period of slow growth. The 1839 crisis was followed by a recession which lasted until 1842 (Figure 3.2).

In some cases, cyclical peaks in economic activity were associated with a sharp rise-and-fall in price inflation, for example, the cyclical peaks of 1825, 1836, and 1866 (Figure 3.4). Interconnections between commodity and credit markets meant that an upturn in commodity prices could encourage an easing of credit, and a downturn could lead to defaults and restraint in the supply of credit. These interactions are considered in more detail in Section 3.3.

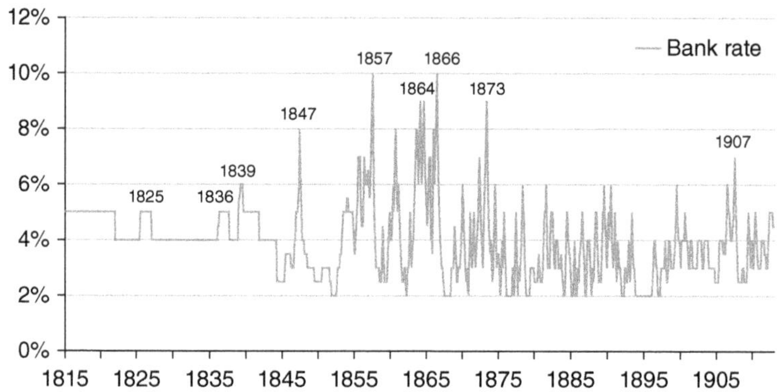

Figure 3.1. Bank rate, 1815–1913
Bank of England

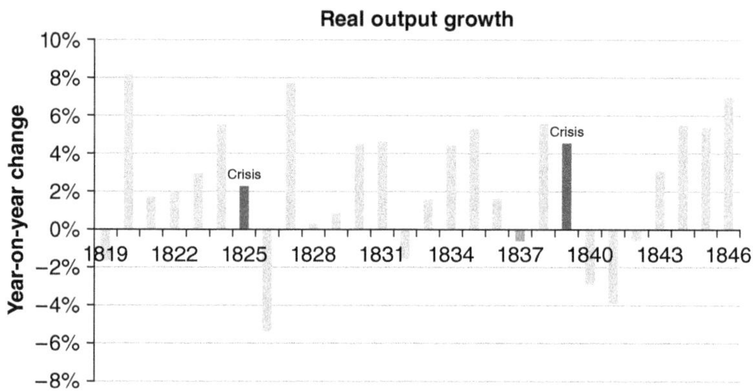

Figure 3.2. UK business cycles and financial crises, 1819–42
Broadberry et al. (2011); Hills et al. (2010)

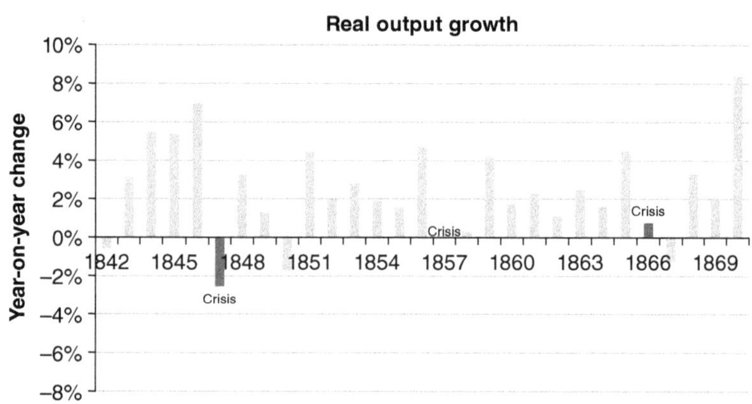

Figure 3.3. UK business cycles and financial crises, 1842–67
Broadberry et al. (2011); Hills et al. (2010)

In the late 1830s, bad harvests and the need to import more grain led to a drain on bullion. The Bank of England raised Bank rate in 1839 and restrictions on credit appear to have had a contractionary effect during the early 1840s (Matthews, 1954: Ch. 12). Gold discoveries and an influx of bullion in the late 1840s allowed Bank rate to be cut and an easing of credit. This appears to have had an expansionary effect in the early 1850s and led to an inflation peak in 1853. The interplay of these factors is discussed in more detail in the next section. From the mid 1870s, there was a marked reduction in the variability of prices over the trade cycle, and a steady fall in prices in the period 1874 to 1879. There were price rises close to cyclical peaks in 1882 and 1889, but these were soon reversed. A prominent rise in prices occurred in 1900, following the outset of the Boer War, when the price level rose by 5 per cent, but this was reversed in the following year (Figures 3.4 and 3.5).

In the late nineteenth century, a number of financial disturbances were followed by downturns in the economy, but the causal linkages are not clear. The collapse of the City of Glasgow Bank in 1878 did not coincide with a cyclical peak and it did not lead to systemic problems in the money market. It was, however, followed by a brief contraction in the wider economy (Figure 3.6). The New York panic of 1907 did not lead to systemic failure in London, but there was a downturn in the UK economy in 1908 (Figure 3.7). This reflected a deterioration in international trade, rather than credit problems in London.

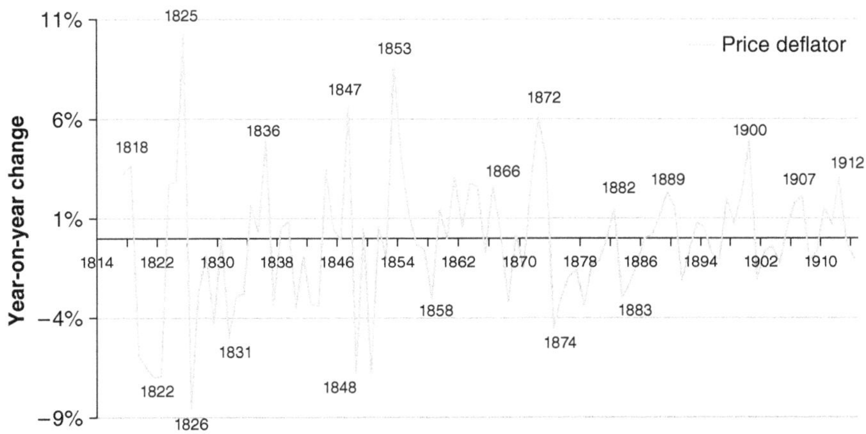

Figure 3.4. UK inflation

Broadberry et al. (2011); Hills et al. (2010)

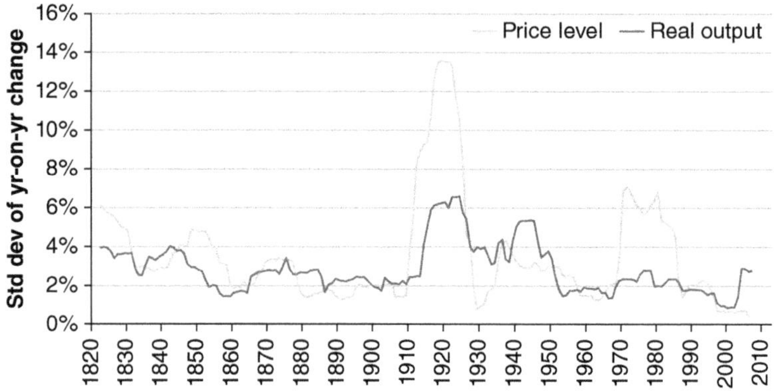

Figure 3.5. UK price and real output variability

Broadberry et al. (2011); Hills et al. (2010); ONS (2013)

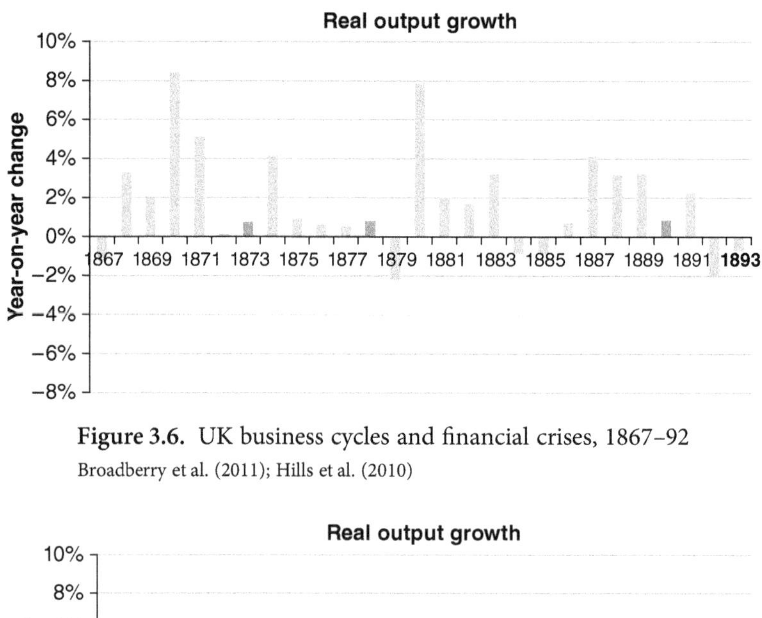

Figure 3.6. UK business cycles and financial crises, 1867–92

Broadberry et al. (2011); Hills et al. (2010)

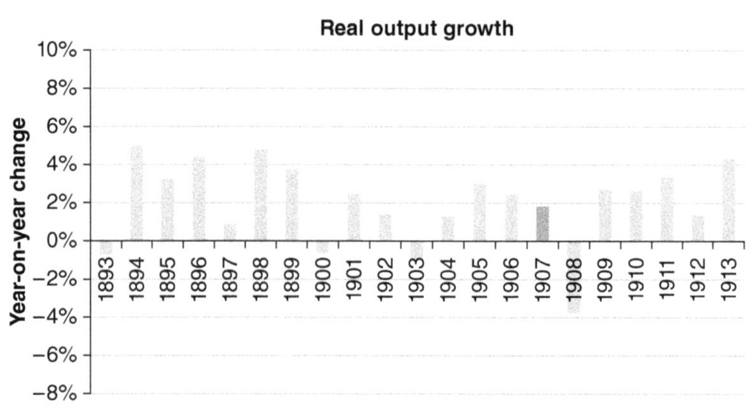

Figure 3.7. UK business cycles and financial crises, 1893–1913

Broadberry et al. (2011); Hills et al. (2010)

3.2.4 Longer-term Growth and Variability

The trend rate of growth of output was about 2 per cent before 1914 and its variability was moderate. In the interwar period, the mean growth rate was lower and its variability was higher than before the First World War. In the Golden Age of 1952–73, real growth rose sharply and its variability was reduced. Following the oil price hike of 1973, there was a decline in growth and a rise in variability. After Britain left the European ERM in 1992, there was a rise in the trend growth rate which lasted until 2007. This period became known as the Great Moderation, although in the US it started a decade earlier (Table 3.2 and Figure 3.9). Price inflation, and its variability, dropped dramatically and real growth rates matched those of the Golden Age (Figure 3.8).

The apparent state of grace of the Great Moderation was brought to an abrupt end in 2008 with a systemic failure in a number of major interbank markets including London, which led to a contraction of credit and a severe recession. The sustained upturn during the Great Moderation and the scale of the

Table 3.2. Annual growth rate of gross domestic product (%), means and standard deviations

Periods	Observations	Mean	Standard deviation
1822–1866	45	2.25	2.85
1867–1913	47	1.92	2.32
1920–1938	19	1.25	4.52
1952–1973	22	2.91	1.73
1974–1992	19	1.73	2.19
1993–2007	15	2.94	0.62

Source: Hills et al. (2010).

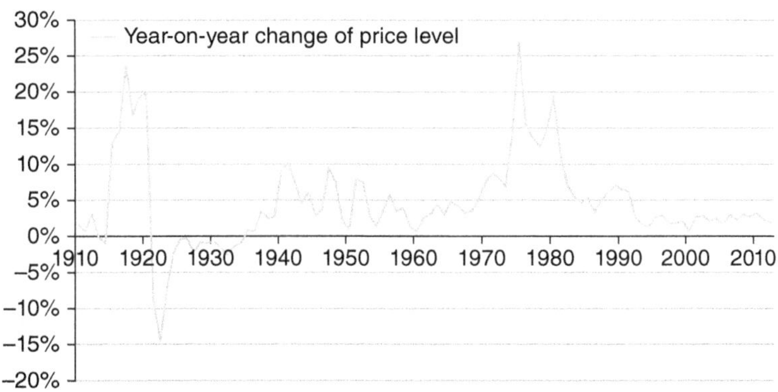

Figure 3.8. UK price inflation

Broadberry et al. (2011); Hills et al. (2010)

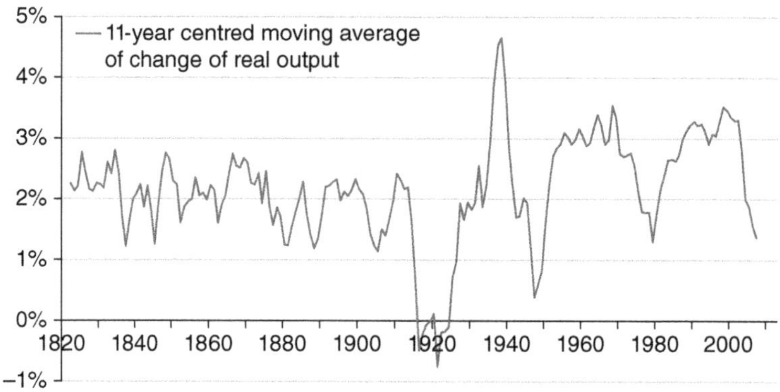

Figure 3.9. Trend UK real output growth
Broadberry et al. (2011); Hills et al. (2010); ONS (2013)

downturn following the financial crisis were both exceptional—This Time Really Was Different.

A more detailed account of the UK's economic cycles is given in the appendix to this chapter. In the next section we examine the linkages between the financial sector and the wider economy by examining London's money market in more detail. We want to gauge the extent to which business cycles and financial crises have had a bi-causal relationship, and whether money market and banking risk has been pro-cyclical.

3.3 MARKET COMMENTARY

3.3.1 Crisis of 1825 and its Aftermath

Our starting point is the crisis of 1825, which was not only severe, but also had major consequences for the structure of the financial system (King, 1936). The crisis was the outcome of a boom which was stimulated excessively by inept monetary and fiscal measures for which the Bank and the Treasury were responsible. Britain prepared to return to the gold standard after the Napoleonic Wars and there was a period of deflation with weak economic activity. The economy reached a cyclical trough in 1819 and revived thereafter largely in response to a rise in exports, in particular cotton textiles. The subsequent boom was supported by home and foreign investment, helped by a financial stimulus brought about by the authorities. The financial stimulus had two elements. First, the Treasury was keen to reduce the cost of servicing the high level of debt accumulated in the Napoleonic Wars. To this end, it reduced the coupon paid on government debt, leading to a fall in long-term yields. This encouraged investors to acquire riskier investments, offering a higher return than public debt. Secondly, the Bank of England expanded credit. It had accumulated substantial bullion reserves to replace small denomination notes circulating with the public. These notes had been issued by country banks during the period of the paper pound, 1797–1821, when the convertibility of notes into specie (gold and silver coins) was suspended. It was planned that these notes would cease to circulate in 1822, but in the event the withdrawal of small notes was postponed for ten years (Feavearyear, 1963). This decision meant that the Bank's bullion reserves were higher than usual, and it responded by reducing Bank rate from 5 per cent to 4 per cent, while discounting freely. The combined effect of these measures was to reduce the cost of borrowing and to encourage an appetite for risk (Neal, 1998; Gayer, Rostow, and Schwartz, 1953: Ch. IV).

Risk-taking took the form of financing speculative projects at home and abroad. Public utilities were favoured and bonds of recently formed South American states. There was a keen interest in investing in mining, and an upsurge in mining stock prices (Gayer, Rostow, and Schwartz, 1953: 184). The bubble burst in 1825 when high levels of external investment and a surge in corn imports, due to a disappointing harvest, led to pressure on the Bank's bullion reserves.

The public lost faith in country banknotes and there was a run on these banks. Public demand for specie put pressure on the Bank's reserves. Loss of confidence in country banknotes led to a breakdown of the payments mechanism—a genuine financial crisis in the terminology of Schwartz (Schwartz, 1986). The Bank responded initially by rationing its discounting (purchases) of bills and other financial instruments from the market. This aggravated the panic and fears were subdued only when a policy of unconstrained discounting was adopted. Whether the crisis was due to an over-issue of small notes by the country banks, as claimed by contemporaries is uncertain, but the loss of public confidence precipitated the crisis (Neal, 1998). The collapse of the speculative boom and the pressures arising from higher wheat imports were major factors causing the crisis. The sharp contraction of credit led to a recession, followed by a period of stagnation. High wheat prices squeezed real wages and consumer spending. This period was notable for political unrest leading up to the Reform Bill of 1832 (Matthews, 1972).

A major consequence of the financial panic was a reconsideration of the Bank's monopoly of joint-stock banking. This had resulted in banking outside London being conducted by note-issuing banks which were small and vulnerable partnerships. The Act of 1826 allowed the formation of joint-stock banks which were predominantly recipients of deposits, rather than issuers of notes. The development of joint-stock banking did not take off until it was made clear that joint-stock banks could operate in London, provided they did not issue notes. This point was clarified in the Bank Charter Act of 1833. In exchange for losing its monopoly of joint-stock banking, the Bank was compensated by being permitted to open branches in the provinces. In practice, this change did not lead to increased competition for existing bill brokers because the new branches would discount bills of only the highest quality, but it did provide an effective means of transmitting funds to London. In this way it assisted the business of brokers in London (King, 1936).

Prior to the 1825 crisis, London's private bankers had held trade bills and exchequer bills as liquidity reserves. In times of stringency, they relied upon the Bank to let them rediscount (sell) these assets, or provide loans secured against them. In the turmoil of the 1825 crisis, they found that they were unable to secure this form of assistance. They decided that in future they would hold liquidity reserves in the form of deposits at the Bank and funds lent to the money market. The next stage came in the early 1830s when bill brokers were permitted to open accounts at the Bank. This created a structure of the financial system in which the Bank dealt with the money market, but not with commercial banks, whether inside or outside London. Finally, the 1825 crisis made the Bank recognize that it had some responsibility for supporting the financial system in times of severe stringency (King, 1936; Gayer, Rostow, and Schwartz, 1953: Ch. IV; Collins, 1990).

3.3.2 Crisis of 1837–9

When recovery did come in the early 1830s, it was due to the buoyancy of exports followed by a home investment boom in which railway building played a major part. British exporters benefited from the vigour of US economic growth in the 1830s, but there was a setback in 1837. The US dollar depreciated and US importers faced problems meeting their obligations to British exporters. Default by US importers put pressure on Anglo-American finance houses that had accepted American bills. A leading finance house failed and the Bank refused to discount paper issued by the houses. This resulted in a financial panic which was only stilled when the Bank relented and provided assistance to the market. However, the shock was sufficient to check the boom, and the economy went into recession in 1837 (Matthews, 1954: Chs. V, XII; Gayer, Rostow, and Schwartz, 1953: Ch. V). Activity was maintained in 1837 and 1838, in part, due to the continuing strength of expenditure on existing railway projects, but it fell away in 1840 and 1841. Harvest failure contributed to the recession in the early 1840s. The shortage of wheat at home necessitated increased imports which strained the balance of payments. Monetary conditions were tightened as the Bank's bullion reserves weakened. There were doubts about Britain's ability to remain on the gold standard (Matthews, 1954: Ch. XII, Section 5; Deane, 1968). High corn prices contributed to social stresses associated with the Hungry Forties (Matthews, 1954: 215; Dimsdale, 1990: 160).

It is reasonable to ask whether the new financial system created by the legislation of 1826 and 1833 was to blame for the crisis. The main change was the growth of joint-stock banking, both in London and the provinces. The new banks behaved differently from the note-issuing private partnerships which preceded them. They competed for deposits and did not hold bills to maturity, but rather rediscounted them in the London money market. This meant that London's bill brokers did more business than under the old system. This was important because it accommodated the increasing need for credit in a growing economy (King, 1936: 39–50). The previously established pattern of surplus funds being channelled from agricultural districts to industrial districts continued, but on a larger scale (Pressnell, 1956). Banks in the industrial borrowing areas accepted bills drawn by local traders. Once the bills carried a bank's endorsement, they could be rediscounted in the London market and provided a source of liquid assets for banks in agricultural districts. The new banks sought to attract funds by paying interest on their deposits.

Savings were mobilized effectively, but there were some problems with the operation of this system. Banks in the borrowing districts could engage in excessive discounting. They found it more profitable to rediscount bills rather than to hold them to maturity. This had been the practice under the old system based on note-issuing private banks, which had developed in the late eighteenth century. When a bank rediscounted (on-sold) a bill which it had endorsed, it remained liable in the event of default by the drawee of the bill. Banks could ignore these contingent liabilities and rediscount excessively relative to their capital. There were growing complaints about excessive rediscounting and one of the most prominent joint-stock banks had rediscounts which were a high multiple of its subscribed capital. If there were defaults among the bills which it had endorsed, there was a risk that its capital would be seriously depleted or possibly wiped out (King, 1936: 91–101; Matthews, 1954: Ch. XI).

Bill brokers were generally willing to rediscount bills provided they bore the endorsement of a bank. In the event of default by the drawer of the bill, the bill broker would have recourse to the bank which had endorsed it. Defaulting on bills need not disturb the money market unless it undermined the solvency of an endorsing bank. This could happen if banks indulged in excessive endorsing of bills drawn by questionable traders. A related problem was the use of short-term accommodation paper to finance long-term business activities. Accommodation paper had to be rolled over and refinanced, whereas bills used for trade finance could be repaid upon delivery of goods. In Lancashire, bills were commonly used to finance investment in plant and machinery and faced refinancing risk (Matthews, 1954: 198). These sources of weakness contributed to a lack of stability in the financial system.

3.3.3 Crisis of 1847

The next major crisis occurred in 1847. It is discussed in more detail in Campbell's chapter and only a brief account is provided here. By the mid 1840s the economy was recovering strongly from the previous recession which had started in 1840. The money market expanded during this period and bill brokers started to be replaced by discount houses, trading with their own capital. They borrowed short-term money from joint-stock banks, including money at call, and used this funding to hold bills on their own account. Banks obtained a profitable outlet for their reserves which enabled them to pay more competitive rates on their deposits. In this way the capacity of the market was increased, but its stability might be jeopardized as discount houses had to be ready to repay call loans on demand.

There was a revival of interest in railway building and a major change in the monetary regime. The Currency School triumphed over the Banking School in the controversy over the way in which monetary policy should be conducted (Feavearyear, 1963: Chs. X, XI). This controversy will not be discussed here, but the views of the Currency School had important consequences for the conduct of the Bank in the 1840s. Under the Bank Charter Act of 1844, which reflected the views of the Currency School, the Bank's balance sheet was divided into the Issue Department and the Banking Department. The separation of the two departments was intended to ensure that currency in the form of Bank notes would be readily convertible into specie, so preventing a currency crisis like the one that occurred in 1825. The notes of Issue Department had to be backed by holdings of bullion and specie, plus a stipulated limit on the fiduciary issue of notes. This was intended to maintain confidence that note convertibility would not be compromised (Feavearyear, 1963: 272–4). However, strict observance of the limit on the fiduciary issue might restrict the ability of the Bank to provide assistance to the money market at a time of crisis. According to the doctrine of the Currency School, financial stability would be safeguarded by the rules prescribed for Issue Department, leaving the Banking Department free to operate as a profit-making commercial bank. Indeed, it was stated by a leading Currency theorist that it was the duty of the Banking Department to act as a competitive commercial institution (King, 1936: Ch. 4).

The Bank responded to the 1844 Act by introducing a new discount policy. This involved abandoning the previous practice of holding Bank rate above market rate. Instead, Bank rate was set closer to market rates enabling it to compete more aggressively (King, 1936: 115, 163). Bank rate was reduced to 2.5 per cent, which encouraged a speculative boom in the mid 1840s, bidding up the price of railway shares. The share boom peaked in mid 1845 and, by then, there were gathering clouds associated with the Irish potato famine.

There were expectations of an upsurge in wheat prices, which reached 112 shillings per quarter, the highest level since 1817. Interest rates remained low despite higher imports of cereals and the erosion of the Bank's bullion reserves.

In the event, the harvest in 1847 was better than expected, easing the shortage of wheat and causing a sharp fall in prices. There were heavy losses among corn merchants who had entered into forward contracts to buy wheat at previous high levels. These problems caused difficulties for money market traders who had discounted corn merchants' bills (Ward-Perkins, 1962; Gayer, Rostow, and Schwartz, 1953: Ch. VI). These pressures gave rise to a general panic, prompted by fears about the quality of bills and other paper circulating in the London market. The problems with commercial bills, which had first appeared in the financial crisis of 1837–9, were repeated in 1847 but on a larger scale. Abuses arose from excessive rediscounting by banks which accepted contingent liabilities far exceeding their capital. There was continuing abuse from various forms of lending long and borrowing short through the use of finance bills, otherwise known as accommodation paper. These practices ranged from the imprudent to the fraudulent (Ward-Perkins, 1962: 83–4; King, 1936: 123–8, 134–43).

The activities of the money market did not, of themselves, trigger the 1847 crisis. Contributory factors included an inappropriate policy for Bank rate, speculation in the wheat market and possibly the large cash demands arising from the obligations of shareholders on partly paid railway shares. However, the questionable quality of short-term paper in the market was a factor aggravating a loss of confidence. The Bank's duty to provide assistance to the market at a time of crisis depleted its reserves conflicting with the 1844 Act. This was resolved only by a temporary suspension of the Act. After the 1847 crisis, Bank rate was held above market rate, but remained close to it (King, 1936, Ch. V: 161–9). Active competition with other lenders was discontinued and Bank rate was raised to 5 per cent in early 1847 and then by steps to 8 per cent in October 1847 as the Bank sought to protect its declining reserves.

The judgement of Ward-Perkins (1962: 90) on financial innovation in the crisis of 1847 bears repeating, as it is relevant to other financial crises:

> The Bill of Exchange, an ingenious and beautiful credit instrument, and the new form of finance and banking were in their way as momentous as Watt's steam engine, yet both were peculiarly liable to clumsy and criminal mishandling. It would take two more crises before the London Money Market learnt its lesson in this respect or the Bank had gained the necessary experience and authority to control the situation.

3.3.4 Crisis of 1857

The economic recovery which started after the 1847 crisis gathered momentum during the early 1850s. The driving force behind the developing boom was the influx of newly mined gold from California and Australia. Interest rates declined as the Bank's gold reserves rose; Bank rate was reduced to 2 per cent and the market rate to 1.5 per cent in 1852. The influx of gold to other countries increased economic activity and strengthened the demand for British exports. There was vigorous growth in exports in 1852–3, while the reduction of interest rates led to a boom in the floating of new companies and domestic investment. Activity was also stimulated by rising government spending on the Crimean War in 1854–6. In 1856–7 exports again grew strongly, but at this time gold was flowing out of the reserves and interest rates were rising (King, 1936, Ch. VI: 170–4). Growth was checked by the financial crisis in 1857, which resulted from deteriorating financial conditions and a panic in New York. Output stagnated in 1857–8, but there was renewed growth in 1859 (Hughes, 1960: Ch. 2). While the 1857 crisis had a major impact on financial markets, the real economy escaped more lightly. It can be argued, as Temin (1974) does, that the major setback to the economy came from the outbreak of the American Civil War in 1860, rather than the financial crisis of 1857.

The boom of the 1850s was accompanied by a rapid growth in bill finance. An increasing number of joint-stock banks sought to attract deposits and to acquire portfolios of trade bills. The bills were not held for long, but rapidly rediscounted in the London money market. The new discount houses had the capacity to hold bills on their own account and were not just agents, like the former bill brokers. Discount houses attracted money at call, which enabled them to increase their holdings of bills. Competition for call money narrowed the margin between call rates and bill yields. Large risks were taken to exploit small interest differentials.

There were continuing abuses of bill finance of the same kind which had been practised in the 1840s. These included banks discounting excessively in relation to their capital, and discount houses rediscounting bills of doubtful quality provided they bore the endorsement of a joint-stock bank. At this stage, the Bank was willing to discount bills if offered by a respectable institution even though the provenance of the bills might be unknown. The growth of call loans made the discount houses more vulnerable to withdrawals at short notice (King, 1936: Ch. VI; Hughes, 1960: Ch. 10: 256–74 and Appendix 5).

As in 1847, the financial system became more exposed as the boom proceeded. The shock which precipitated the crisis in London came from New York, following the failure of the Ohio Life & Trust Company in August 1857.

British banks and trading houses with close trading links with the United States became vulnerable. The starting point of the British crisis was the failure of the Borough Bank of Liverpool, which was not only exposed on account of its links with the US, but was also vulnerable on account of its risky discounting policy. There were further failures, including the Western Bank of Scotland (King, 1936: 193–9).

The response to this shock was for banks to strengthen their cash reserves by recalling their call money from the money market. This put pressure on the discount houses, who found they were unable to finance their bill portfolios and turned to the Bank for assistance. The Bank provided assistance, but found itself acquiring bills of doubtful quality, which it would not normally have discounted. As demand for liquidity increased, there was an internal drain putting pressure on the Bank's bullion reserve despite a steep rise in Bank rate to 10 per cent. Such was the pressure on the Bank that the Bank Charter Act of 1844 was suspended, enabling it to increase the note issue beyond the limit of the fiduciary issue. Even then, the stilling of the panic in the money market was not immediate. The crisis was followed by a steep fall in interest rates as the fears of the market were pacified, while the economy stagnated in 1858.

There was, however, unfinished business as far as the Bank was concerned. The Directors decided that the conditions for providing assistance to the discount market needed to be tightened. This took the form of an announcement that assistance would not normally be available except on the Bank's own terms (King, 1936: 199–205). The prospect of a reduction in the Bank's assistance caused serious concern and led to a persistent dispute between the Bank and the market. At one point the dispute became so bitter that a leading firm, Overend Gurney, threatened the Bank's liquidity by suddenly withdrawing funds deposited with it. There was a disturbed relationship between Bank rate and market rates as the money market sought to reduce its dependence on the Bank (King, 1936: 205–16).

3.3.5 Crisis of 1866

There was a sustained recovery of output from 1859 to 1865, but the pace of growth was constrained by the American Civil War. Shortage of raw cotton arising from the interruption of imports from the US caused a cotton famine in Lancashire. As a result exports of cotton goods were checked and total exports stagnated in the early 1860s. There was, however, a strong boom in fixed investment, which rose by 50 per cent in which railways and construction played a major part (Cottrell, 1988).

During the early 1860s there was an upsurge in new company flotations, including banks and discount houses (Collins, 1988). The record of two discount companies launched in the 1850s was regarded as sufficiently promising to encourage further company promotions in the 1860s (King, 1936: Ch. VII). A further market development was the growth of finance companies, which undertook major construction projects and financed these activities by issuing short-term paper. This form of finance had been pioneered by Credit Mobilier in France, and it spread to Britain in the 1860s (King, 1936: 231). Refinancing risk meant that these arrangements were likely to cause problems if markets were disturbed and investors lost confidence.

Monetary conditions in the early 1860s were disturbed by fluctuations in interest rates, which did not follow a normal pro-cyclical pattern, but had a major spike in 1864 in the middle of the recovery, when Bank rate was raised to 9 per cent. Some of this volatility was a consequence of the American Civil War. It was necessary to replace US cotton with supplies from India as a substitute. This led to a drain of bullion to India which reduced the reserves of the Bank and put upward pressures on interest rates. A financial crisis was narrowly averted in 1864, but further problems emerged two years later in 1866.

These developments had a major bearing on the discount market as its leading firm, Overend Gurney, became involved in a range of long-term activities, which were riskier than its normal business of holding sound commercial bills. Its discounting was conducted in a risky manner and several of its debtors defaulted, leaving it holding long-term assets. These assets had to be financed by short-term accommodation paper, but this became increasingly difficult to renew in disturbed market conditions. As its problems became more widely known, Overends found it could not get assistance from the discount market, or the Bank of England. Since the firm was unable to offer good collateral to the Bank, it was forced to suspend payments (King 1936, Ch. VII: 242–5). The Bank did not feel compelled to assist Overends on the grounds that its dominant position in the money market made it too big to fail, but the Bank took active steps to relieve the panic which followed news of its failure. The Bank's conduct in lending freely on good collateral at a high interest rate relieved the crisis. This accorded with the recommendations of Bagehot in Lombard Street (1873). Its liberal lending checked the internal drain, but necessitated the suspension of the 1844 Act. The raising of Bank rate to 10 per cent checked a threatened sterling crisis and the rate was held at this level from May to August.

Considering the period 1825 to 1866 as a whole, there was an improvement in the Bank's responses to pressures in the money market. Thornton (1802) and Bagehot (1873) made important contributions to the principles of money market management and helped avoid domestic money market crises after 1866.

3.3.6 London's Money Market from the 1870s to 1971

The 1866 crisis was the last systemic crisis of the mid nineteenth century. King argues that the stability of the London money market after 1866 resulted from the development of the international bill on London and the rise of the acceptance houses (King, 1936: Ch. VIII). According to this view, the 1866 crisis served to discredit the London discount market and its indigenous discount houses. This enabled bankers from continental Europe, such as Schroder, to obtain a foothold in London (Roberts, 1992: 47). The Franco-Prussian War and suspension of the gold standard by France made London the dominant financial centre. When the new-style acceptance houses accepted (i.e. guaranteed by endorsing) a foreign bill, they sought to verify the standing of the parties. This contrasted with the less careful use of acceptances in the finance of overseas trade before 1870. Perhaps the most striking example of this had occurred in 1837 when the Anglo-American trading houses failed to honour their acceptance obligations following the default of American importers. Similar problems had arisen in the 1857 crisis. The improved credit processes of the acceptance houses after 1870 ensured that the London money market was better able to withstand shocks. Holders of accepted bills could rely on them being discounted in the market and accepted by the Bank as security for loans. The provision of good collateral by the market enabled the Bank to act as lender of last resort by discounting freely in a time of financial stress (Balogh, 1947; Truptil, 1936). King argues that this development was a gradual process, which was assisted by the displacement of inland bills by international bills during the latter part of the nineteenth century.

In their chapter in this book, Flandreau and Ugolini argue that the transformation came more quickly as the discount market rapidly learned the lessons of the 1866 crisis. The discount market made sure that in future it would be able to provide bills of high quality for rediscount at the Bank. The resilience of the bill market served to limit the severity of financial disturbances after 1866. Whether the change was gradual, as suggested by King, or more rapid, as argued by Flandreau and Ugolini, it produced the same result. The London money market became a centre for international finance and was not troubled by the periodic disturbances of the pre-1866 era. The operation of the bill on London is explained in the classic work by Gillett Brothers (1964). In modern parlance, the reformed money market in London aimed to circumscribe pro-cyclical risk.

The rise in the market for international bills and decline in the volume of inland bills was noted by King. This issue has been explored more thoroughly by Nishimura (1971), who has computed the volume of inland and international bills, showing that the former declined from a peak in the early 1870s, while foreign bills exceeded inland bills before the 1890s. He shows that inland bills were in decline well before the main period of bank amalgamations in the 1890s, which King argues was the main factor explaining the reduced supply of inland bills.

The role of the money market changed as the need for inland bills declined from 1870. The old pattern of surplus funds arising in agricultural counties being channelled into bills drawn by debtors in industrial counties was modified. Borrowing through the use of overdraft facilities grew at the expense of bill finance. Nishimura also attributes the reduced need for short-term finance in industry to economies in the holding of inventories made possible by improvements in transport. Meanwhile the rapid growth of world trade was the driving force behind the expansion of international bills.

There was a threat to the financial system from the failure of the City of Glasgow Bank in 1878. Its importance has been emphasized by Collins (1989), who argues that the failure of this major bank had a serious impact on the financial system. This view is not shared by all writers, including King. The bank failed during the economic downswing of the 1870s, rather than during a more risky phase of the cycle, and this may have reduced its systemic impact. In any case, the post-1866 reforms had successfully weakened interactions between the business cycle and the money market.

The stability of London's money market was assisted by closer cooperation between leading central banks over the operation of the gold standard. Continental central banks supported the Bank in the face of the US panic of 1907, as discussed by Eichengreen (1992), and there was no crisis in the City of London, but there was a sharp downturn in the British economy in 1908. On a number of occasions there was a need to protect the acceptance houses, in view of their systemic importance. The Baring crisis of 1890 was the first example, when the prospect of failure led to pre-emptive action orchestrated by the Bank. The outbreak of war in 1914 and the freezing of payments between belligerent countries likewise threatened the acceptance houses. In this case the Bank and Treasury intervened to protect the houses and the system as a whole. A similar threat emerged in 1931 due to the restriction of payments by short-term debtors in continental Europe. This was a serious threat to the money market, as argued by Accominotti (2012). It was averted by prompt action by the Bank, as discussed by Sayers (1976).

Although the bill on London had been the main security traded in the money market in the late nineteenth century, it was supplemented by the Treasury bill (short-term government paper). It was introduced in 1877, but the market remained limited prior to 1914. Treasury bills became much more important during the First World War and during the interwar period they became the main trading asset of the money market, providing higher security than prime international bills. The Macmillan Committee (1931) did not make recommendations for changing the money market. It recognized that there was an imbalance between Britain's short-term overseas liabilities and its liquid assets, but the international crisis of 1931 did not disturb the working of the market.

The Radcliffe Committee (1959) was similarly disinterested in liberalizing the money and banking markets after the Second World War. Post-war controls on foreign exchange and bank lending acted to repress the monetary system and restricted competition. The Euromarket, tapping non-UK resident depositors, nevertheless started to grow in London in the 1960s and with it an interbank market mainly in Eurodollars, including US$ certificates of deposit (CDs). A domestic interbank market started to develop in parallel, as well as a market for local authority deposits. The market for prime bank bills—those accepted by a bank of recognized standing—underwent a revival and Treasury bills lost their place as the dominant instrument of the market. The main high street banks—the London and Scottish clearing banks—continued to manage their domestic balance sheets conservatively, adhering to a liquid assets ratio of at least 28 per cent. Liquid assets comprised short-dated gilts, Treasury bills, money at call with the discount market, prime bank bills, and local authority bills. These assets could be relied upon to retain their liquidity in a crisis precisely because the Bank was willing to rediscount them, or accept them as collateral for loans. Interbank lending was not regarded as a liquid asset because it could not be rediscounted at the Bank (Bank of England, 1984: 8–9, 34).

3.3.7 Deregulation of 1971 and 1979/80

In 1971, a reform package, known as Competition and Credit Control, allowed the clearing banks to lend to each other directly, in addition to indirect lending via the discount market. This enabled the domestic interbank market to grow rapidly and a wider wholesale money market developed, including insurance companies, fund managers, and corporate treasurers. Competition and Credit Control provided a halfway house between the domestic London money market of the pre-1971 period and the Euromarket model. Quantitative ceilings on lending were lifted and credit expansion was supposed to be regulated by variations in Bank rate, and thence the level of short-term rates. The 28 per cent liquidity ratio was abolished and a 12.5 per cent reserve asset ratio put in its place. Broadly speaking, the definition of reserve assets followed the pre-1971 definition of liquid assets. Although the clearers could not simply match-fund their domestic sterling books, as they did in the Euromarket, the reduction of the liquidity ratio from 28 per cent to 12.5 per cent meant there was scope for them to economize on liquid asset holdings (Bank of England, 1984).

The breadth and depth of London's money market allowed the clearers and other banks to manage their liabilities more accurately, and they came to rely on the wholesale markets for funding. As a result, they felt able to adopt more aggressive lending policies and to expand their balance sheets rapidly. Expanded property-related lending led to a commercial property upswing in 1971 to 1973, the bursting of the property bubble in 1974, and a secondary banking crisis. Direct controls on banks' balance-sheet growth were re-imposed in 1973 and remained a tool of monetary policy until exchange controls were abolished in 1979 (Bank of England, 1984: 117–28).

Without exchange controls, limits on bank lending could be circumvented by booking (UK residents') deposits and loans with offshore banking entities. Lending controls were therefore abolished in 1980 to avoid offshore disintermediation. In the same year, banks were allowed to compete in the mainstream market for first mortgages, alongside building societies. Finally, the 12.5 per cent reserve asset ratio was abolished with a view to developing prudential requirements for bank holdings of primary liquidity (Treasury and Bank of England, March 1980). These deregulatory measures led to a sustained expansion in bank credit throughout the 1980s, a significantly larger mortgage-lending market and lower proportionate holdings by banks of primary liquidity (the new name for reserve assets).

The growing importance of property-related lending in banks' balance sheets gave a new dynamic to the relationship between the banks and the economic cycle, and in particular the property cycle (Goodhart, June 1989: 501). Domestic bank credit expanded during the 1980s, but there was no immediate domestic crisis. The Latin American debt crisis challenged the international banks—including UK ones—from 1982, but the problem was contained. The equity-market crash of 1989 was followed by recession and some negative equity problems in the UK housing market in the early 1990s. This led to increased mortgage loan impairments and some discussion about the cyclicality of the home loans market. Mortgage arrears and impairments in 1991 were high compared to past experience in the market, possibly suggesting an increase in pro-cyclical risk. Bank profitability was hit, but this did not lead to sustained problems like those faced by the Japanese economy and its banks.

The Asian and Russian banking crises of the 1990s and the bursting of the dot-com bubble in 2000 presented problems, but not intractable ones for UK banks. It took the downturn of the US residential housing market of 2006 and the collapse of Lehman in 2008 for the international money market, including London's, to face paralysis. To understand why this shock proved fatal while other financial disturbances did not, it is useful to trace developments in London's money and credit markets since the reforms of 1979/80.

3.3.8 London's Money and Credit Market since 1980

The discount market contracted during the 1980s and in the mid 1990s it was effectively disbanded. Trading in prime bank bills and Treasury bills had become too small for the Bank to conduct its day-to-day money market operations. In its place, the Bank instituted a gilts repo market: instead of discounting bills at the Bank, banks could sell gilt-edged stock (UK government bonds) to the Bank for cash and simultaneously agree to repurchase them at a fixed price at a future date (a sale and repurchase agreement, or repo). Gilt repos can be viewed as cash loans collateralized with gilts. The gilt repo system came to be an effective mechanism for the Bank's routine operations and it proved to be resilient during the credit crunch of 2007–8 (Tucker, 2004: 377). However, the credit system that replaced the traditional one for creating good-quality paper palpably failed.

The securities-market boom of the 1990s encouraged banks to move from strategies based on asset-led growth to ones based on the originate-underwrite-and-distribute model. Loans could be securitized so that the funding and credit risk could be borne by other parties and traded as asset-backed securities (ABS). ABS could be repackaged as collateralized debt obligations (CDOs) where senior tranches of CDOs bore very little credit risk and junior ones carried disproportionate risk. Credit default swaps (CDS) could be used to repackage the risks further and create synthetic CDOs. As a result vertically integrated banks could be unbundled so that different parties undertook origination, underwriting, funding (senior note-holders) and credit risk (junior note-holders). A number of leading US and European banks (mostly UK ones) ceded mortgage and other loans to off-balance-sheet special investment vehicles (SIVs) which issued ABS, which in turn were repackaged as CDOs and synthetic CDOs. ABS, and in particular residential mortgage-backed securities (RMBS), became an important new asset class traded in the money market. Senior tranche CDOs could be AAA-rated ranking alongside the best-rated sovereign and supranational credits.

The markets for ABS appeared to be liquid and senior securitized debt became the successor to prime bills as the asset of choice for bank liquidity. Securitized debt of all kinds—not just gilts—was also used extensively as collateral for the repo-funding of investment banks' proprietary trading units and their investment clients (Gorton, May 2009: 567–72). Repo loans were arranged at a margin or haircut below the value of collateral provided. The collateral was (and is) adjusted daily to allow for valuation changes of the collateral and for changes in margin requirements which are at the discretion of the lender. When the ABS markets were being promoted in the 1980s and 1990s, it was suggested that they would provide a means for the banking sector to cede risk to a wider pool of non-bank end-investors. However, the appeal of

ABS as a liquid asset, which could be used as collateral for repo-funding, was so great that traditional banks and shadow banks became dominant holders, and not much risk was shared with end-investors (Financial Services Authority, *Turner Review,* March 2009: 14–16).

3.3.9 Road to the 2007–8 credit crunch

The path that led to the panic of 2007–8 started with a downturn in the US residential housing market in 2006, leading to falls in subprime RMBS values (Gorton, 2008). Subprime RMBS had been repackaged into CDOs and it was not necessarily clear which CDOs would be affected and by how much. Asset complexity and lack of transparency led repo lenders to play safe and reject certain asset types as collateral and to insist on increased haircuts. Many of the assets were not actively traded and therefore collateral valuations relied on modelled prices (mark-to-model) which lenders subjected to greater scrutiny. A more discriminating repo market forced borrowers to value collateral more conservatively and apply larger haircuts. Borrowers were forced to realize long positions and sell assets. This in turn led to a vicious circle where lower asset prices reduced collateral values and encouraged lenders to seek even larger haircuts, which in turn necessitated further forced sales (Gorton and Metrick, 2010). There was no mechanism to protect collateral values.

Prime brokers and their shadow-banking clients had been undertaking bank-style maturity mismatching by using short-term repos to borrow and relying on being able to roll them over so that they could fund longer-term investments. Prior to the summer of 2007 the scale of maturity mismatching appears to have increased, but from the summer of 2007 repo lenders started to apply a more conservative approach. Repo rollovers stopped and large parts of the prime brokerage market shut down.

The process whereby contagion shifted from the repo market to the interbank market is not exactly clear and it may never be established unequivocally. Some commercial banks were known to have some dependency on repo-funding and there were rumours about commercial bank exposures to subprime RMBS. Some British banks had programmes for tapping wholesale funds swapped into sterling from US money market mutual funds. These funds were exposed to the repo market in the US and faced customer withdrawals, and part of their response was to cut their lending to UK banks. Once it became clear that aggregate interbank funding was contracting, the market started to assess which banks would face funding difficulties and problems contracting their balance sheets. In the UK, Northern Rock was seen as being exposed and, once it became evident that it was in trouble, the market started to assess the next most vulnerable institutions.

3.4 CONCLUSIONS

3.4.1 Limiting Pro-cyclical Risk

The traditional practices of the London money market sought to limit pro-cyclical banking risk. In the early 1960s, the Bank still asserted its responsibility for maintaining credit quality at the heart of the banking system:

> The Bank of England's general policy regarding commercial bills [is] . . . to maintain the standards of quality long associated with the London prime bank bill and hence its reputation as a liquid asset of undoubted security. (Bank of England, 1961: 28)

The idea that the market, rather than the Bank, should set credit standards developed in the late 1960s in London's Euromarkets. Euromarket practices had been partially adopted in the domestic London money market after 1971. From 1980, controls on the domestic balance sheets of UK banks were permanently discarded and banks started to place much greater reliance on collateralized lending, in particular property-related lending. The development of the collateralized repo market accentuated this trend. In many cases, assets values were sustained by the flow of credit, and rises in asset values provided apparent security for yet larger loans. The pro-cyclicality of bank risk shot up, eventually leading to the credit crunch of 2007–8. The virtuous circle of more credit and higher collateral values was finally broken and collateral values collapsed, leading to defaults and bank insolvencies.

Of itself, securitization was not the root of the problem. The ultimate liquid asset of the late nineteenth and early twentieth century was the prime bank bill on London. It was created by a securitization process in which an acceptance house enhanced the credit standing of a commercial bill so that it could be resold as a quality asset in the money market. It took a decade or so after the 1866 crisis for an effective credit system to be put in place in the London money market. It is far from clear whether the same timescale will be met across major financial centres post 2008.

3.4.2 New Terminology for Old Problems

A major part of the problem is a lack of historical perspective and this is not helped by subsequent generations inventing a new terminology for old problems. The historical literature has identified a number of abuses in the money market which resemble modern financial problems. The first type of abuse which recurs in contemporary nineteenth-century literature is overtrading. This refers to banks and other financial firms holding insufficient capital in relation to the size of their business. In the boom of the 1830s there were complaints that the new joint-stock banks were discounting excessively in relation to their capital. Hence a small impairment of their bill portfolio could wipe out their capital. This is similar to the modern practice of engaging in excessive leverage which has become a major issue in bank regulation.

The second type of then-and-now abuse is excessive off-balance-sheet risk. Endorsers of bills—latterly acceptance banks—could be tempted by short-term profits to overexpose themselves to the risk of default on bills. In addition to engaging in excessive discounting, banks were not always careful to check the quality of the debtors whose bills they were discounting. Accepted bills could readily be discounted in the London market, enabling the bank to take up further bills. The money market did not have expert knowledge about the bills it discounted and would purchase bills provided they had been endorsed by a bank. From time-to-time, one or more banks could fail as a result of defaults by drawers of bills leading to problems in the market for those holding discounted bills. Uncertainty across the market about the quality of bills could lead to disruption and ultimately panic. In modern markets, off-balance-sheet finance and asset-backed securities can give rise to analogous problems.

A third area of abuse has been excessive maturity mismatch between assets and liabilities, a persistent problem in nineteenth-century crises. Commercial bills were supposed to be self-liquidating; the tenor (maturity) of a bill was supposed to match the delivery time for the underlying consignment of goods. Payment for the goods upon their delivery should then broadly coincide with the due date for repayment of the bill. Frequently this was not the case as bills could be used to finance longer-term projects. The borrower might assume that the bills could readily be renewed so there would be no need to repay the debt at maturity. Finance bills were regularly rolled over and used to finance longer-term investments. This could work out well but there would be problems if lenders were not willing to reinvest at maturity. Matthews (1954) reports that bill discounting was used to finance fixed investment in Lancashire. In the money market, discount houses were accustomed to finance their holdings of bills by borrowing call money from banks which was repayable on demand. Heavy reliance upon call money underlay the financial crisis of 1857. When a major bank, the Borough Bank of Liverpool, failed, banks summoned back money at call, forcing the discount market to seek support from the Bank. Perhaps the most serious abuse occurred in the 1860s when finance companies used bills to finance long-term projects. It was because of a heroic mismatch between the term of its liabilities and assets that Overend Gurney got into difficulties in 1866. Fears about the viability of longer-dated assets made it impossible to raise short-term finance, so exposing the firm's lack of liquidity.

The failure of Overend raised a further issue on account of its dominant position in the London money market. The refusal of the Bank to bail out the leading firm in the market precipitated a severe crisis. The panic was only stilled by the free discounting policy of the Bank at a high rate of interest, which was in general accord with the recommendations of Bagehot (1873). However the Bank might have considered that Overend was too big to fail on account of its dominant position. While this might have shortened the crisis, it could have created a major issue of moral hazard. The money market might have been less cautious after 1866 had the leading firm in the market been bailed out. In 1890, when Barings faced a crisis due to excessive exposure in Argentina, the Bank orchestrated a rescue. In this case, it reasoned that a leading acceptance house could not be allowed to fail because of the consequences for the financial system. Hence the 'Too-Big-to-Fail' issue of the recent crisis was also present before 1913.

The development of the London money market after 1870 has an additional lesson, which may be relevant to more recent financial disturbances. The role of the acceptance houses in assuring a supply of good-quality bills to the money market reduced the risks involved in rediscounting and provided bills deemed eligible for rediscount at the Bank. Good-quality paper was essential for the Bank to be able to relieve stresses in the money market, as shown by the crises of 1857 and 1866.

Major international exposures came to be concentrated on the acceptance houses, also known as merchant banks and latterly investment banks. These banks specialized in the finance of long-term overseas investment and providing short-term credit for the finance of international trade. In contrast, London's deposit banks, also known as clearing banks, concentrated mainly upon domestic finance in accordance with the system described in the Report of the Macmillan Committee (1931) and later in the work of Truptil (1936) and Balogh (1947). In this way, the London market achieved a separation between investment and deposit banking which may have contributed to the improved stability of the financial system after 1870. This structure was not radically changed at the time of the Report of the Radcliffe Committee (1959) and it persisted until the reform of the City, known as the Big Bang, in the 1980s (Banks, 1999). One consequence of the reforms was to end the historic role of the merchant banks, as described graphically by Augar (2000).

APPENDIX: A BRIEF SURVEY OF MACROECONOMIC CYCLES AND FINANCIAL CRISES IN THE UK

This appendix reviews the course of cycles in Britain and the incidence of financial crises. Our starting point is the financial crisis of 1825, which was important on account of its severity and also because of the reforms to the financial system which followed it. These introduced the major institutional features of the financial system which lasted up to 1914 and beyond (Neal, 1998). Our period is broken down into distinct sub-periods. The first is the experience of cycles and crises up to 1870, the second is 1870 to 1914, followed by the interwar period 1920 to 1938. The post-war period is divided into three sections. The first is the Golden Age 1948 to 1973, followed by the disturbed 1970s and 1980s. The last sub-period is from 1992 to 2008, which corresponds with the Great Moderation and the financial crisis of 2007–8. Our survey can be regarded as an exploration of the background to Table 3.1. We are concerned with the contribution of the business cycle to the creation of conditions in which a financial crisis may occur and also the feedback of financial disturbances to the real economy.

We begin with the departure of Britain from the gold standard in 1797 at an early stage in the Napoleonic Wars. It was understood that at the end of hostilities the gold standard would be restored. The legislation was approved in 1819 and became effective in 1821. The resumption of gold payments involved a period of deflation and a temporary check to economic activity. It was not until 1822 that economic recovery started. There then followed a vigorous expansion to 1825, which was ended by an acute financial crisis. There was widespread speculation, which was sharply reversed as rising imports reduced the Bank's reserves and led to a contraction of credit. Output rose by 11 per cent from 1822 to 1825. The financial crisis of 1825 sent this expansionary process into reverse as output fell by 5 per cent in 1826. It recovered strongly in 1827 and also showed signs of recovery in 1830–1 before declining again in 1832. There was a sharp rise in prices in 1825, followed by a decline in 1826, which persisted throughout the following recession (Deane, 1979; Neal, 1998; Gayer, Rostow, and Schwartz, 1953; Broadberry and van Leeuwen, 2010).

There was no sustained recovery from the boom which ended in 1825 until 1833. The recession may have been lengthened by a succession of poor harvests, which necessitated high imports of wheat. The next recovery started in 1833 and continued until 1836 with output rising by 12 per cent (Matthews, 1954; Gayer, Rostow, and Schwartz, 1953). In 1837 there was a setback to exports and financial markets associated with a financial crisis in the US. Output fell by 0.6 per cent in 1837 followed by a temporary revival in 1838 and 1839. This was not sustained as the economy went into recession in 1840, due to harvest failure which necessitated higher imports of corn. Rising imports depleted the Bank's reserves, so that credit was tightened under the gold standard. Output declined by 4.5 per cent from 1840 to 1842. There had been a rise in prices of 5 per cent in the boom in 1836, while there was a decline in prices during the recession, which continued until 1843.

The next recovery started in 1843 and was followed by vigorous growth of output to 1846, associated with a boom in railway building. In this upturn, output rose by 19 per cent but it turned downwards in 1847, when output fell by 2.5 per cent and there was a financial crisis in the same year. It was followed by a period of slow recovery to 1850. During the boom of the 1840s there was a rise in prices, notably a spurt of 6.6 per cent in 1847, which was sharply corrected after the cyclical peak (Ward-Perkins, 1962; Deane, 1968; Gayer, Rostow, and Schwartz, 1953).

There was renewed growth in the economy in the early 1850s and from 1851 to 1856 output rose by nearly 14 per cent. The boom of the 1850s was associated with gold discoveries and rapid growth of world trade. In 1857 there was a renewed crisis in the US economy which affected British financial institutions involved in Anglo-American trade. This caused a crisis in the money market and checked the growth of output in 1857 and 1858. Despite the severity of the financial crisis, output stagnated for only two years but did not fall. There was a strong upsurge in prices which rose by 6 per cent per annum from 1853 to 1854, followed by a decline of 3 per cent in 1858 as the economy went into recession (Hughes, 1960).

Recovery came in 1859 when output rose by 4 per cent and growth then continued at a moderate pace in the early 1860s of less than 2 per cent per annum. The British economy was adversely affected by a shortage of raw cotton on account of the interruption of trade due to the American Civil War (Temin, 1974). From 1863 the pace of recovery increased and growth rose to more than 4 per cent in 1865. In 1866 there was a setback associated with the failure of the leading firm of bill brokers Overend Gurney. In 1866 growth was checked in the wake of the crisis and there was a decline in output of 1 per cent in 1867. The recession was short lived as output started to rise again in 1868 followed by a major boom in the early 1870s.

Recovery in the late 1860s was based on strong export growth from 1868 to 1871, which enabled output to rise at an annual rate of more than 4.5 per cent per annum. Output growth slowed in 1872 and 1873, which marked the cyclical peak. Supply side constraints may well have limited growth in the later stages of the boom as shown by the rise in prices of 5 per cent per annum in 1872 and 1873. The reduction in working hours during the boom may have contributed to the check to output. 1873 was a year of financial crisis in both Germany and the US, but not in the UK. There was a setback to the growth of output, but no financial crisis in London. The cyclical peak of the 1870s was the first upper turning point of the cycle which did not involve a financial crisis.

During the period from 1873 to 1914 there were reasonably regular fluctuations in the growth of output, but cyclical peaks were not generally associated with domestic financial crises as in the period before 1866 (Dimsdale, 1990; Hills et al., 2010). Following the international crisis of 1873, there was a revival in domestic investment, particularly in housing so that the growth of output was maintained fairly well up to 1875 (Cairncross, 1953). Thereafter the economy moved into recession due to a check to the growth of exports. Output grew at less than 1 per cent per annum from 1875 to 1878 and output declined by 2 per cent in 1879. This fall in output may have been related to the failure of the City of Glasgow Bank in 1878 and also to pressure on the Bank's reserves due to poor harvests. The importance of this failure has been emphasized by Collins (1989). Bank rate rose to 6 per cent, but not to the levels of previous crises.

Output recovered strongly in 1880 and reached a peak in 1883 having risen by 7 per cent. It declined by 1.5 per cent in 1884 and 1885, but there was no disturbance in the money market. The growth of output slowed down in the late 1870s and 1880s on account of the weak performance of exports. There was a reasonably strong recovery from 1887 to 1889, when the economy grew at more than 3 per cent per annum, but it went into recession in the early 1890s and output declined in 1892 and 1893.

The Baring crisis of 1890 was averted by the prompt action of the Bank, which prevented the failure from affecting the rest of the money market. The problems of Barings arose from its exposure to Argentina and not from involvement in the British economy (Pressnell, 1968). The downturn of 1892–3 which followed the crisis cannot be attributed to domestic forces, but rather to the decline in exports due to the contraction of world trade. This in turn was associated with financial problems in the US, Argentina, and Australia. After a decline in output of 3 per cent in 1891–2, growth revived strongly in the mid 1890s. From 1894 to 1899 output grew at an average rate of 3.7 per cent per annum due to a major boom in domestic investment, in particular in housebuilding. Expansion was checked in 1900 as output hit a cyclical ceiling and the economy then showed only weak growth with a fall in output of 1 per cent in 1903. Growth was weak in the early 1900s on account of the exhaustion of the domestic investment boom. There was faster growth from 1905 due to the rising demand for exports and from 1904 to 1907 output rose at about 2 per cent per annum. In 1908 there was a severe setback as output fell by nearly 4 per cent. This abrupt downturn was precipitated by the US financial crisis of 1907. The crisis affected British exports, but not the British financial system, as the Bank received support from the French and German central banks (Eichengreen, 1992). Growth was then resumed and continued up to the outbreak of the First World War in 1914 under the influence of booming exports and a high level of foreign investment. The coal strike of 1911 had temporary effects on growth, but not enough to affect its general course. From 1909 to 1913 output grew at an average annual rate of 2.9 per cent. The financial crisis of 1914 arose from the difficulties of creditors in making payments due to the outbreak of hostilities. This caused serious problems for the acceptance houses and could have threatened the money market, but it was not related to the level of economic activity.

We can conclude that after 1866 cyclical movements in the economy were not associated with domestic financial disturbances. This may require some qualification with respect to the failure of the City of Glasgow Bank in 1878, but not for the Baring crisis in 1890. Neither of these events disturbed the financial system as severely as the earlier crises of 1825, 1837–9, 1847, 1857, and 1866. A major question is what brought about this change, which is such a prominent feature of British financial history. This question is examined in our study of the money market after 1870 in Section 3.3 of this chapter.

We also find that the setback to growth following a financial crisis was typically quite short lived. The length of the recession which followed the crisis of 1825 was an exception as recovery did not start until 1833, but there was a temporary recovery in 1831–2. This also applies to the recession following the crisis of 1837–42, which was not ended until 1843. High wheat prices may have contributed to this outcome in both cycles. By contrast, the financial crises of 1847, 1857, and 1866 had only short-term effects on the real economy which recovered rapidly once there was an easing of financial pressures.

The price level shown in Figure 3.4 indicates that there were fluctuations in prices in 1825–6, 1836, and 1847–8, which were associated with cyclical downturns and financial crises. The sharp rise in prices in 1853–4 can be attributed to the effects of gold discoveries. After 1870 there was a marked reduction in price fluctuations over the trade cycle. This change may have been related to the growth of international trade which enabled wheat and other commodities to be imported to supplement domestic production. There was a sustained fall in prices from 1874 to 1879. While there were price rises at cyclical peaks, as in 1882 and 1890, these were soon reversed in the following downturn. The most prominent rise in prices occurred in 1900 when price levels rose by 5 per cent due partly to the Boer War, but this increase was reversed in

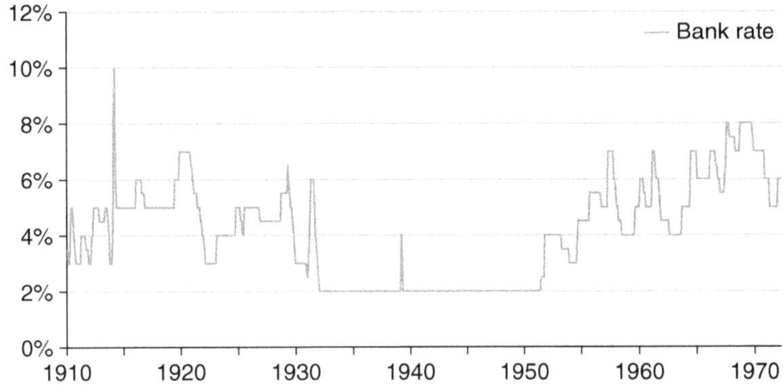

Figure 3.10. Bank rate, 1910–72 (Bank rate replaced by minimum lending rate on 16 October 1972)
Bank of England

the following year. There is evidence that the variance of changes in prices in the later nineteenth century was reduced compared with the higher volatility found in the period before 1870.

During the interwar period, there were severe fluctuations in the economy, but no major disturbances to the domestic financial system. There was a sharp contraction from 1919 to 1921 when output fell by 17 per cent. Output then recovered up to 1929 with an interruption due to the General Strike in 1926, which caused output to fall by 3 per cent. Even so, the growth of output averaged 3.3 per cent per annum from 1922 to 1929. During the Great Depression the economy experienced a downturn in economic activity with output declining by 5 per cent in 1931. There was a recovery from 1933 which enabled the previous peak of 1929 to be exceeded by 1934. The growth of output averaged 3.7 per cent per annum in the period 1933–8 (Figures 3.11, 3.12, and 3.13).

The domestic financial system remained stable throughout the interwar period despite wide fluctuations in output (Figure 3.10). The international financial crisis of 1931 could have affected the British financial system as the introduction of exchange controls by Germany threatened the solvency of British acceptance houses. This threat to the money market was averted by the Bank as discussed by Sayers (1976). The Report of the Macmillan Committee (1931) did not discuss the stability of the British financial system, which it appeared to take for granted. It did, however, draw attention to the UK's excess of short-term liabilities over short-assets, which contributed to the external vulnerability of sterling in the crisis of 1931.

During the period 1952–73 fluctuations in the economy were largely the result of government policy rather than endogenous economic factors. Successive periods of 'stop-go' policies produced fluctuations in the growth rate, but output did not generally fall in recessions. Cycles were typically cycles in the growth rate, rather than its level, with peaks and troughs approximately as follows: 1952–8, 1958–63, 1963–7. The fourth cycle was from 1967 to 1970/1 and was affected by the devaluation of sterling in 1967. These cycles were exceptionally mild and their timing is sensitive to subsequent revisions of the data (Figures 3.14, 3.15, and 3.16).

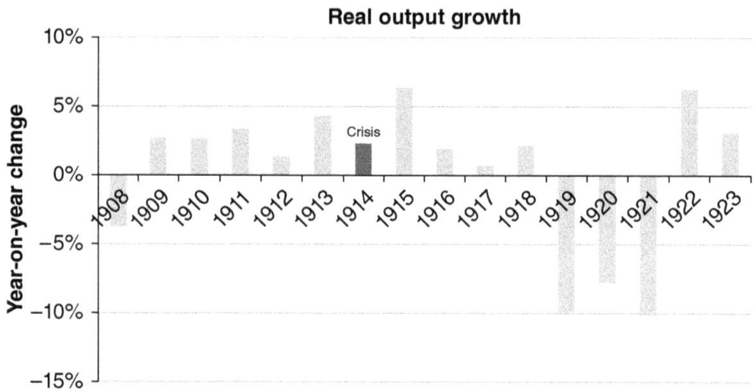

Figure 3.11. UK business cycles and financial crises, 1908–23
Broadberry et al. (2011); Hills et al. (2010)

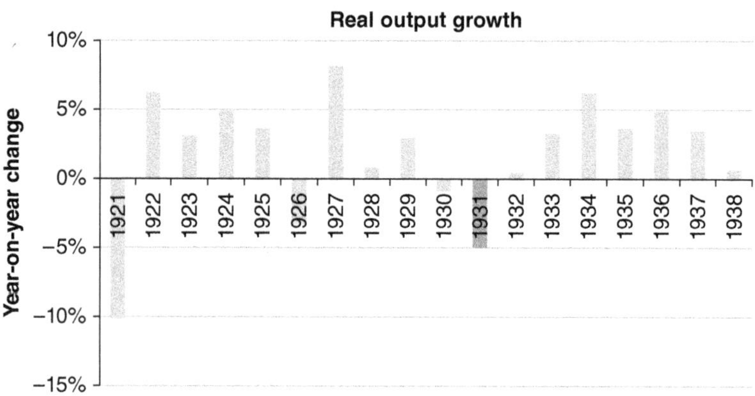

Figure 3.12. UK business cycles and financial crises, 1921–38
Broadberry et al. (2011); Hills et al. (2010)

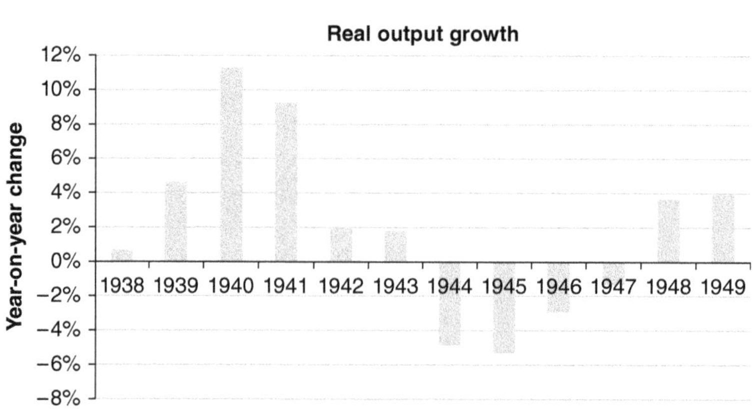

Figure 3.13. UK business cycles and financial crises, 1938–49
Broadberry et al. (2011); Hills et al. (2010); ONS (2013)

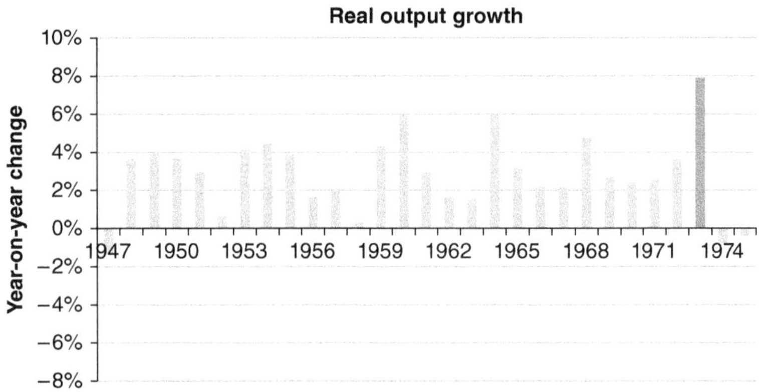

Figure 3.14. UK business cycles and financial crises, 1949–75
ONS (2013)

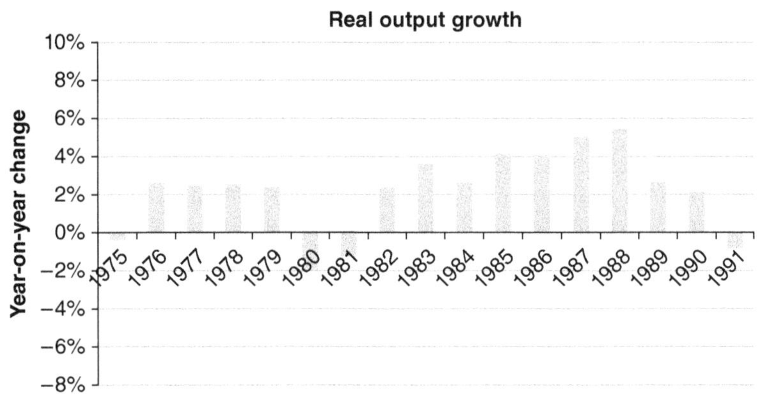

Figure 3.15. UK business cycles and financial crises, 1975–90
ONS (2013)

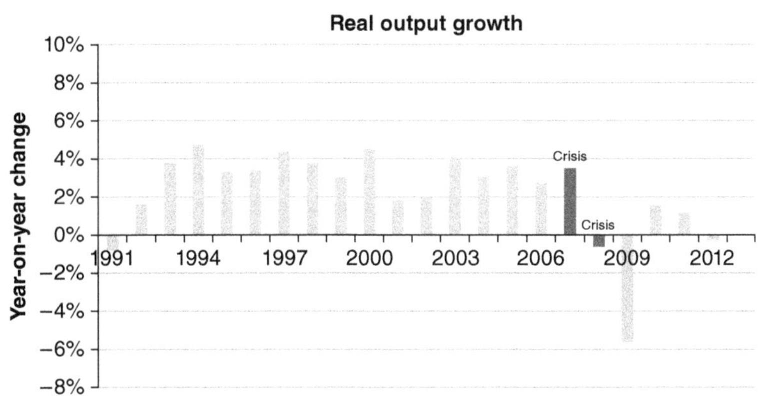

Figure 3.16. UK business cycles and financial crises, 1991–2013
ONS (2013)

The recessions which occurred in this period were mainly the result of measures taken to strengthen the balance of payments (Matthews et al., 1982; Dimsdale, 1990). As exchange rates were approximately fixed under the Bretton Woods system and capital mobility was restricted to some extent by capital controls, current account deficits could not be sustained for long by an economy, such as the UK, which had limited reserves and borrowing facilities. Hence it was necessary to curb balance-of-payments deficits even if this meant a temporary sacrifice of output and employment. Once the balance-of-payments problem was resolved, output could be encouraged to grow by expansionary demand-management policies, giving rise to the go phase of the cycle. The commitment to full employment policies meant that demand was stimulated if unemployment reached more than about 2 per cent of the labour force. As the response of the economy to a demand stimulus was lagged, there was a tendency for demand to exceed supply potential at the peak of the cycle giving rise to a balance-of-payments deficit.

During the early 1970s there was a strong boom which started in 1970 and reached a peak in 1973. In that year, output growth reached nearly 8 per cent and was not sustainable. The economy was hit by the first oil price shock (OPEC 1) in late 1973 and went into recession in 1974. Output declined by 1 per cent in 1974–5. There was a recovery from 1976 to 1979 with output rising at 2.5 per cent per annum. The cycle reached a peak in 1979, with a fall in output of 3 per cent in 1980–1. While there was a sterling crisis in 1976, which necessitated assistance from the International Monetary Fund, there was no threat to the banking system. From 1982 the economy recovered with an acceleration of the growth rate of output to 4 to 5 per cent per annum in 1985–8. Growth slowed abruptly in 1989 and the economy contracted by about 1 per cent in 1991 after Britain's entry into the European exchange rate mechanism (ERM).

Following Britain's withdrawal from the European ERM and the floating of sterling, there was a gradual rise in the growth rate to 3 to 4 per cent per annum to 2000. A steady growth rate was maintained throughout the period to 2007 before the economy moved into recession in 2008 and growth became sharply negative in 2009, when output fell by more than 5 per cent. The economy recovered weakly in 2010 and 2011 and has not shown strong evidence of an upturn until 2013. The steady growth rate achieved from 1993 to 2007 was without equal in the period we have reviewed since the 1820s. Growth was slower than in the Golden Age of 1952–73, but its variability was lower than in any comparable period. Both the sustained boom and the length of the post-2008 recession were unmatched in UK financial history.

Our review of cycles suggests that the Great Moderation before the financial crisis of 2007–8 and the subsequent downturn differed from past experience. It had some features in common with the cycles and financial crises of the 1820–66 period, but there were important differences. The Great Moderation lasted longer than previous upturns, the two years of financial turmoil in 2007–8 were exceptional, as was the persistence of the subsequent recession. The closest precedent was the 1825 crisis where the recession lasted until 1832, but the 1825 peak level of output was exceeded by 1827 and there was an incipient recovery in 1830–1. There has been no parallel in modern British financial history to the latest financial crisis and the subsequent recession. We conclude that 'This Time Things Really Were Different' in contrast to the claims of Reinhart and Rogoff (2009) in their well-known but controversial history of financial crises.

4

Government Policy during the British Railway Mania and the 1847 Commercial Crisis

Gareth Campbell

4.1 INTRODUCTION

During the 1840s, Britain experienced a period of financial turbulence. Railway share prices rose and fell dramatically during the railway mania, there was a surge and then crash in the price of corn, and a commercial crisis followed. The development of an asset price reversal, a commodity price reversal, and problems in the commercial and banking sectors within such a short period of time makes this a particularly interesting episode, and the variety and intensity of events makes it a useful study in how to deal with financial instability.

The turbulence began with the railway mania, which occurred between 1843 and the autumn of 1845, during which the prices of railway shares doubled, and thousands of new railway lines were projected. However, share prices then fell, and the railway industry endured a sustained downturn. The corn market also experienced a sharp price reversal soon afterwards, with prices rising rapidly between the summer of 1846 and June 1847, but then falling sharply thereafter. This exposed merchants who had speculated on prices remaining high, leading to the failure of a number of firms within the corn sector in August 1847. The problems quickly spread to other merchants and financial institutions, producing difficulties within the money market. The situation was compounded by the low reserve of the Bank of England, which restricted the ability of the Bank to supply credit. The panic was only relieved in October 1847 when the government relaxed the constraints within which the Bank operated.

The response of the British government to each of these developments can provide some insights into the challenges of legislating for stability. Parliament introduced several measures which could potentially have mitigated the extent of the difficulties, but these were generally ineffective. In some instances there was a conflict between stability and other goals, in other instances legislation had unintended consequences, whilst in most cases the focus was on small incremental changes which minimized opposition. The most effective policy was introduced in the midst of the crisis, when these considerations were less influential. Although this intervention may have increased moral hazard, by increasing expectations that similar policies would be pursued in future crises, the benefits almost certainly outweighed the costs.

The analysis in this chapter[1] suggests that designing legislation ex-ante, before the nature and extent of the instability is clear, can be challenging. Proposals for financial reform may have some marginal benefit, but measures which are stringent enough to prevent future crises are unlikely to be politically acceptable. This implies that it is probable that periods of financial distress will occur again, and the authorities should be prepared to intervene robustly when the next episode of instability arises.

This chapter also contributes to our historical understanding of the financial events of the 1840s, building on other literature which has discussed the development of the railway mania (Bryer, 2003; McCartney and Arnold, 2003; Odlyzko, 2010), and the commercial crisis (Andréadeès, 1909; Clapham, 1966; Gayer, Rostow, and Schwartz, 1953; Ward-Perkins, 1962; Dornbusch and Frenkel, 1984; Boot, 1984). In addition, it increases our understanding of specific episodes of bubbles and crises, adding to research on periods such as the Tulip Mania (Garber, 2001), the South Sea Bubble (Dale, Johnson, and Tang, 2005), the Mississippi Scheme (Velde, 2007: 276–9), and the Great Depression (Bernanke, 1983; Eichengreen and Temin, 2000; Romer, 1990; Grossman, 1994).

This chapter is structured as follows: section 4.2 explores the railway mania, section 4.3 considers the corn price reversal, section 4.4 examines the commercial crisis, and section 4.5 offers a brief conclusion.

4.2 RAILWAY MANIA

The British railway mania of the mid 1840s was characterized by a widespread enthusiasm for investing in railway shares. The industry had essentially begun in 1830, with the opening of the Liverpool and Manchester railway, but during the subsequent years many other lines were projected, and by 1842 there were 1,951 miles of railway track open in Great Britain (Mitchell, 2003: 674).

[1] An earlier version of this chapter was presented to the Winston Institute for Monetary History in Oxford. Thanks to Nick Mayhew, Nicholas Dimsdale, Luke Samy, and Anthony Hotson for their comments.

However, the early 1840s had been a period of poor economic growth, and the demands of paying for the construction of new lines had led to difficulties within the industry.

Railway share prices then began to rise rapidly, almost doubling between January 1843 and August 1845, as shown in Figure 4.1. Improvements in the economy, and a reduction in fares by the railways, led to higher passenger numbers, revenues, and profits, and an analysis of those railways established before the mania, suggests that their dividends rose steadily from 4.4 per cent of par value in 1843 to 7.0 per cent in 1847.[2] The projection of new railway schemes also increased dramatically during this period. The number of railway securities listed on the London Stock Exchange underestimates the extent of promotion as only a small proportion ever achieved a listing, but the number of listed securities appears to follow the pattern in prices with a lag (Figure 4.1). These new schemes offered payment terms which were initially very attractive to investors, as individuals could subscribe for shares by paying just a small deposit, rather than the total cost immediately.

In the autumn of 1845 railway share prices began to fall, declining by 18.2 per cent between their peak in August 1845 and the end of November 1845. After a brief recovery, prices continued to fall until April 1850, with a decline of 57.5 per cent from peak to trough. The initial declines coincided with the onset of economic difficulties associated with a poor harvest and the onset of the Irish famine (*The Economist*, 18 October 1845: 997). Perhaps of greater long-term importance was the unprecedented volume of railway promotions

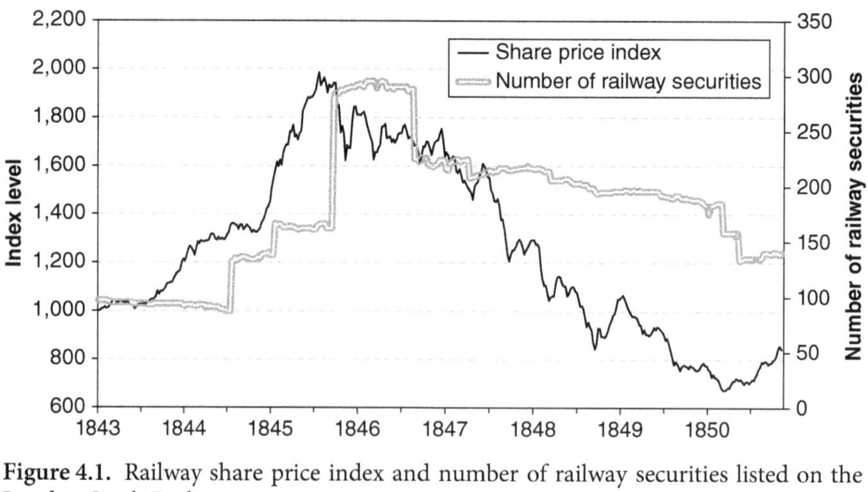

Figure 4.1. Railway share price index and number of railway securities listed on the London Stock Exchange

Calculated from weekly share price tables in *Railway Times*.

[2] Author's calculation based on dividend data from Wetenhall (1843–50).

which peaked in the latter half of 1845. During the downturn the railway industry struggled to complete many of the lines which it had attempted to construct, and many lines were abandoned or suspended (Lewin, 1936: 480–3). However, many other lines did open, trebling the size of the network to 6,123 miles by 1850 (Mitchell, 2003: 674), but they tended to earn lower returns and increased competition within the network, leading to the dividend/par ratio of the railway industry falling from a peak of 7.0 per cent in 1847 to just 2.4 per cent by 1852.[3] During subsequent decades there was a legacy of low returns on capital.

The key drivers of the mania were changes in dividends, the projection of new companies, and the instalment payment plans for shares. The government could have restrained the speculation, at least to some extent, by targeting any or all of these factors. Although it did make some attempts to do so, its policies were generally ineffective, as will be discussed in the remainder of this section.

4.2.1 Regulation of Profits

The initial increase in railway dividends during the mid 1840s was a major factor in the development of the railway mania, with investors bidding up share prices in response to the higher payouts which were expected. If the government had regulated how much profits the railways could have earned, and consequently how much of a dividend they could pay, speculation amongst investors about future returns could have been diminished. Many of the early railways were earning monopoly profits and, given the limited competition on the pre-mania network, such a restriction would not necessarily be unjustified.

A Parliamentary Select Committee investigation into the railways in 1844 suggested that the government should have certain rights over railways which were earning high profits. They proposed that the state should have the option to purchase a railway, or to revise its fares, if it was earning an annual profit greater than 10 per cent of its paid up capital in fifteen years (*Parliamentary Papers*, 1844: XI: 5). The purchase option would allow a railway to be purchased for 25 times profits, whilst the revision option would allow the government to lower fares if they compensated the railway company for any reduction in profits this caused. William Gladstone, President of the Board of Trade, went even further, and introduced a bill (*Parliamentary Papers*, 1844: IV) which proposed that any railway could be purchased, and stated that the rate of profit used in the calculation of the purchase price should be limited to

[3] Author's calculation based on dividend data from the *Course of the Exchange*.

10 per cent, even if the railway was earning much more than this. This reduced the expected price which the state would have to pay (Table 4.1).

However, opposition to the proposed Bill was vociferous. The *Railway Times* described it as the 'Railway Plunder Bill' (*Railway Times*, 1844: 713), whilst the *Economist* had seldom seen 'in any proposition such a mass of antiquated, exploded and objectionable principle' and objected to the desire to limit profits (*The Economist*, 1844: 962). A numerous deputation by the representatives of the various railway companies met the Prime Minister Robert Peel, and the proposer of the bill, William Gladstone, which may be regarded as the first large-scale campaign of the railway interest (Alderman, 1973: 16).

In the face of this opposition a revised bill (*Parliamentary Papers*, 1844: IV: 435) was published which had only 24 clauses, compared to the original 48. The time period of revision was extended from 15 to 21 years, and the calculations on how much shareholders would receive in the event of nationalization became much more favourable, as shown in Table 4.1. The maximum cap on profits of 10 per cent was removed, and any purchase of a company earning less than 10 per cent would be subject to arbitration. Cleveland-Stevens (1883: 109) remarked that 10 per cent had been the summit in the original bill, but had become the base in the revised bill. The *Railway Times* (1844: 825) was satisfied that 'the serpent is now robbed of its sting' and it passed the House of Commons as the Railway Regulation Act.

If Parliament had enforced a more severe version of this legislation it is possible that investor expectations of future profits would have been reduced, and the extent of the mania would not have been so dramatic. However, the opposition to the initial bill was such that a harsh limit on profitability was not politically feasible. Consequently, the conditions were moderated, and were considered to have placed no effective restraint on the railways, encouraging investors to believe that high profits could be attained.

Table 4.1. Implied purchase price of railways according to recommendations of different proposals

		Purchase price of a share, with a £100 par value, which was paying a dividend of:	
	Number of years before purchase considered	3%	15%
Select Committee	15	Not purchased	£375
Gladstone's Bill	15	£75	£250
Railway Regulation Act	21	Subject to arbitration	£375

Notes: Adapted from Cleveland-Stevens, E. C. 1883, *English Railways: Their Development and their Relation to the State*, Routledge, 110.

4.2.2 Restricting Expansion

The rapid expansion of the railway network was the most tangible consequence of the railway mania, and had a considerable influence on both the economy and the railway industry. The promotion of new railway schemes dramatically increased during the rise in share prices, with an estimated 1,238 projects seeking capital in 1845 (*The Times*, 17 November 1845: 4). If the government had strictly limited the number of projects which could be constructed it may have restrained the boom in company promotions. It would also have reduced the severity of the downturn, which was largely due to declines in profitability resulting from overexpansion, and the difficulties of financing the construction of the proposed railways.

Parliament had within its power the ability to impose such limits, as each new railway line had to be individually authorized, mainly because of the need to force property owners to sell their land along the chosen route (Kostal, 1994: 16). This ability to approve or deny every new track gave Parliament the ability to manage in fine detail how the network developed. However, the mechanism by which new lines were authorized meant that a national plan for the railways was not adopted.

Each year the proposed railways were grouped by region and allocated to individual Parliamentary committees, each of which worked in isolation, meaning that a broad overview of the development of the network could not be adopted. The fifth report of the Select Committee on Railways warned that 'local interests will be chiefly regarded' by these committees, making it 'almost impossible to hope that . . . there should issue any distinct system of sound general rules' (*Parliamentary Papers*, 1844: XI: 6). In response to this fear, the Railway Department of the Board of Trade was briefly asked to review all of the potential schemes and provide recommendations to Parliament, giving a national perspective. However, the suggestions of the Board were often ignored, and in July 1845, after just 11 months, the Railway Department was disbanded (Cleveland-Stevens, 1883: 134).

The focus on local provision tended to increase the likelihood that more railways would be constructed, as the competition between towns meant that each wanted its own railway connection (Casson, 2009a: 375; Casson, 2009b: 277). In the 1845 Parliamentary session there were 44 separate committees appointed to consider proposed schemes, each focusing on a particular area. Every committee, without exception, authorized at least one new railway (*Parliamentary Papers*, 1845: XXXIX). In the 1846 Parliamentary Session there were 64 committees appointed (Cleveland-Stevens, 1883: 65). Of the 516 Bills which were considered in this year, 81 were thrown out on Standing Orders, 83 were withdrawn, 106 were rejected based on the merits of the scheme, and 246 received Royal Assent (*Railway Times*, 1846: 1402). This implies that only a minority of projects were actually rejected, with a substantial proportion being approved.

The extent of new railway authorization led to construction representing 5.7, 6.7, and 4.7 per cent of gross domestic product in 1846, 1847, and 1848 respectively (Mitchell, 1964). The demands of railway companies for more capital to finance construction led to difficulties for many shareholders, and may have affected the wider economy. Many companies requested an extension to the length of time within which they were allowed to construct their lines, with railways requesting delays on the construction of a total of 3,650 miles of track (*Parliamentary Papers,* 1847–8: LXIII: 25). Those railways which did open often duplicated existing routes, increasing competition, or served less populous districts, leading to lower returns on capital. *The Economist* argued that all recent experience had shown that the new lines had shown little or no profit (*The Economist*, 21 October 1848: 1187).

By regulating which railway lines could be constructed, Parliament could have reduced the extent of the boom, and the difficulties of the downturn. However, rather than developing an overview of the whole system, Parliament conducted enquires on a district by district basis, leading to an oversupply of new railways. Political expediency suggested that particular areas should not be deprived of access to a railway, but this produced longer-term problems for the railways themselves, and for the wider economy.

4.2.3 Leverage Ratios

Part of the attraction of the new schemes for investors was the ability to purchase shares on an instalment basis. Individuals could subscribe for shares by paying a small deposit, and then pay the remaining amount when the companies made 'calls for capital' to finance the construction of their lines. The first effect of this payment plan was to make it easier for investors to find the money to subscribe to new schemes.

Another effect was to leverage the returns which investors could obtain. Subscribers gained exposure to the movements of the underlying asset for a small deposit. Small returns on an equivalent fully paid share were magnified by the effects of leverage to produce large returns on investors' deposits. *The Railway Investment Guide* described it as a 'peculiarity connected with this system, that a man possessed of very little capital to commence with, may at once treble or quadruple it' (*Railway Investment Guide*, 1845: 5).

Parliament could have prevented the use of partially paid shares by requiring new projects to collect a substantial fraction of the total cost of their lines before they could be considered for authorization. Investors would have been required to pay up most of the capital immediately, thus reducing the effects of leverage on their investments. To restrain a minor promotional boom in 1837,

Parliament had introduced a measure that moved in this direction, but set the required deposit at just 10 per cent (Francis, 1851: ii: 2). In the aftermath of this boom there was little further promotional activity, so the requirement was relaxed to 5 per cent in May 1844 (Francis, 1851: ii: 97), but with the increase in projected schemes thereafter, it was raised to 10 per cent again in July 1845 (Evans, 1849: 16).

This increase may be regarded as an attempt to reduce speculation, but it was largely ineffective. Evans (1849: 16) said that the increase in the deposit 'did not in the least repress the ardour of speculators'. In subsequent months the volume of new company promotion increased even further, reaching its peak in October and November 1845. A requirement of just 10 per cent provided little restraint, and the leveraged returns which could still be obtained by purchasing partially paid shares remained very appealing. Given the enthusiasm for investment, a requirement of at least 50 per cent is likely to have still resulted in many of the most valid schemes still applying for authorization.

The failure to impose stricter limits on leverage ratios during the boom meant that there was a process of painful deleveraging during the downturn. When the construction of lines began, shareholders struggled to make the required payments. *The Economist* (21 October 1848: 1187) said that 'every fresh call that was made upon exhausted shareholders was attended by one of two effects—either the shares themselves upon which the call had been made were sold in order to avoid payment, or some other shares were sold in order to raise the money for that purpose'. Calls for capital by the railways were also blamed by both a House of Commons and a House of Lords Parliamentary Committee for exacerbating the Commercial Crisis of 1847 (*Parliamentary Papers*, 1847–8: VIII, Pt. I; *Parliamentary Papers* 1847–8, VIII, Pt. III), as they diverted investment from other uses (Figure 4.2).

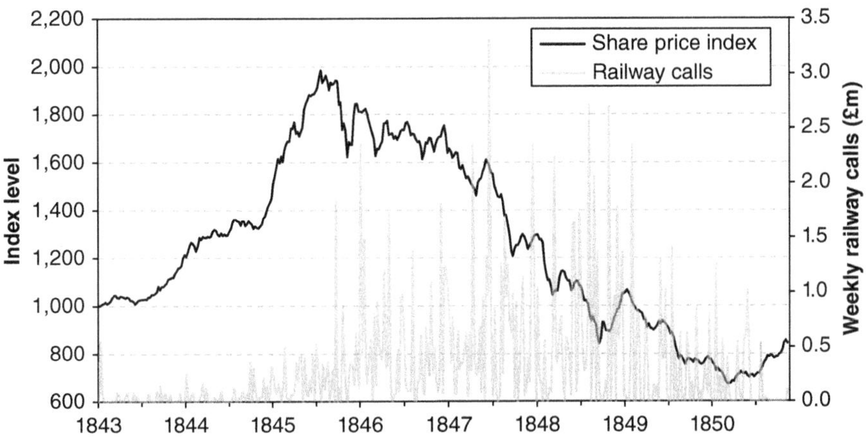

Figure 4.2. Railway calls on capital and share price index, 1843–50

Calculated from weekly share price tables in *Railway Times*.

The use of leverage played an important role in encouraging investors to subscribe to the new railway schemes promoted during the mania. The decision by Parliament to raise the required deposit can be interpreted as an attempt to restrain speculation, but it was largely ineffective. The introduction of a much higher rate, which would have required shareholders to pay the full cost of the share immediately may have reduced the volume of company promotion during the boom, and the difficulties which resulted from the continual payments of calls for capital during the downturn. However, Parliament did not take such a dramatic step, preferring an incremental approach which proved to be insufficient.

4.3 CORN PRICE REVERSAL

The British government was also largely unsuccessful in dealing with a boom in the price of corn. The problems had commenced with a poor agricultural harvest in 1845, and were worsened by another poor harvest in 1846. The price of wheat increased from 53 shillings per quarter in June 1846 to 61 shillings by the end of the year, reaching 77 shillings by March 1847, before peaking at 102 shillings at the start of June 1847 (Figure 4.3). However, prices then fell rapidly during the summer of 1847, reaching just 49.5 shillings in the middle of September, implying a fall of over 50 per cent in less than four months. The price declines led to a series of failures amongst corn merchants, who had speculated on prices remaining high, with the City Intelligence column of *The*

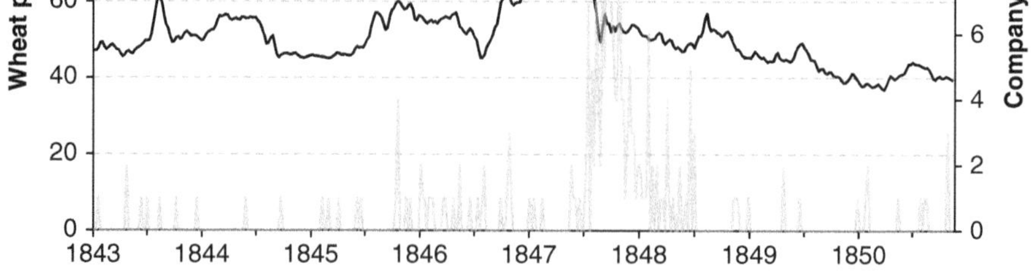

Figure 4.3. Wheat price and company failures, 1843–50

Wheat prices from the *London Gazette*. References to company failures in the 'City Intelligence' column of *The Times*.

Times indicating that 12 firms involved in the corn trade failed in August 1847, and others followed in subsequent months.

To have moderated the price reversal, policy could have been targeted at preventing the initial price increases, or at delaying the ensuing price declines. The British government focused its attention almost exclusively on minimizing the price rises, by using the standard mechanism for influencing the price of a commodity, namely the adjustment of import duties. The price of corn had traditionally been affected by the Corn Laws, but in June 1846 legislation was passed which led to their repeal. This Act reduced the corn import duties, which were then 17 shillings per quarter of wheat, to between 4 shillings and 10 shillings until February 1849, after which time a fixed duty of 1 shilling would be charged (*Parliamentary Papers*, 1846: I: 423). By liberalizing the market for corn, this should have led to an increase in imports, lower prices, and reduced volatility in the corn market.

However, as the reduction in tariffs was phased, there was still a duty of 4 shillings being charged in January 1847, when the price of wheat had risen to about 70 shillings per quarter (Figure 4.4). The navigation laws were also still in force, which restricted imports to ships which were either British or belonged to the exporting country (*The Economist*, 16 January 1847: 57). It was only with the opening of the new session of Parliament in January 1847 that both the duties and the navigation laws were suspended (*The Economist*, 23 January 1847: 85). This led immediately to a much higher volume of wheat being entered for home consumption, which had already been physically imported, during February, and a stabilizing of the wheat price at about 70 shillings.

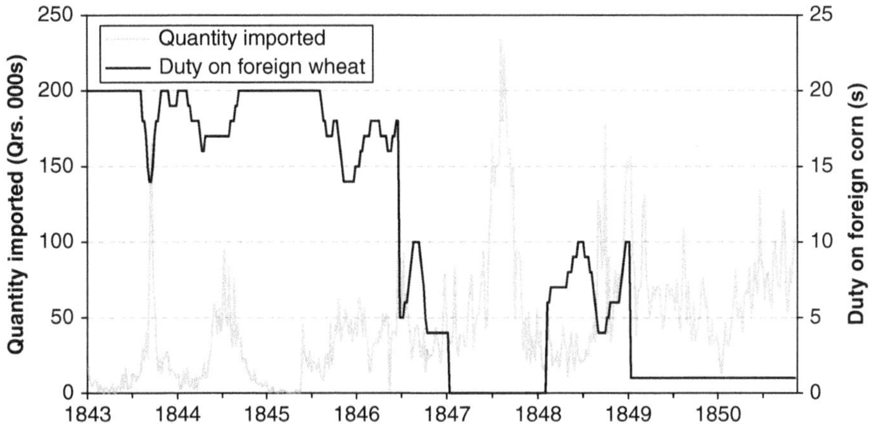

Figure 4.4. Wheat imports and duties on foreign wheat, 1843–50
Derived on a weekly basis from the *London Gazette*.

Despite the more liberal conditions, the volume of imports did not increase substantially thereafter, and the price of wheat began to rise again, particularly between the start of May, when it was 75 shillings, and the start of June, when it reached a peak of 102 shillings. With prices at such a high level, imports finally responded, and increased substantially. From July 1847 to the end of October 1847 weekly wheat imports exceeded 100,000 quarters for 15 weeks in a row, having exceeded this level in only one week during the previous four years, as shown in Figure 4.4. This led to sharp price declines and financial difficulties for corn merchants who had expected prices to remain high.

The policy pursued by the British government during this period attempted to avert the price rises by liberalizing the market for corn. When the gradual phasing out of the Corn Laws was deemed inadequate, all duties were suspended. They also opened the ports to allow imports on ships from other countries. However, the most dramatic price rises occurred after, and in spite of, the liberal policy. Given that they had been ineffective in preventing the price rises, the government could have attempted to manage the price declines, by reintroducing duties and quotas immediately. Such a policy may have delayed the crash in the corn price which occurred, and may have prevented the corn merchants from experiencing such dramatic losses. However, in June 1847, at the peak in prices, the suspension of duties had been extended to March 1848 (*Parliamentary Papers*, 1847: I: 205). The reversal of this policy may have improved financial stability, but it would have been deeply unpopular with the public who would have been forced to pay higher prices. It also conflicted with the long-term goal of revoking the Corn Laws, as the opponents of reform could have pointed to their usefulness at this time. Consequently, the price reversal was able to occur, and led to widespread problems in the corn sector which then spread to other merchants and some financial institutions.

4.4 COMMERCIAL CRISIS

After the initial mercantile failures, the difficult situation was exacerbated by legislation which the government had introduced several years before, namely the Bank Charter Act, which made it more difficult for the Bank of England to provide credit during a crisis. Under this Act the Bank had a limited reserve of notes and coin, and if it exhausted these resources it would have to suspend payment. In the year prior to the crisis, the reserve of the Banking Department of the Bank of England had declined steadily as gold was withdrawn for the payment of imports of corn. In April 1847 the low reserve had become a cause for concern, so to restore its position the Bank had rapidly reduced its holdings of securities, causing a 'pressure' for money. The reserve rose briefly, but remained at lower levels than in previous years.

This gave the Bank limited scope to respond when the failures in the corn sector were followed by difficulties amongst other merchants. In September there were failures amongst those involved with trade in East India, Mauritius, South America, coal, and wine (Evans, 1849: 74). Failures amongst some merchants contributed to difficulties amongst others with whom they had dealt and owed money to. For example, the failure of Gemmell and Co., a merchant based in Glasgow, was named as the immediate cause of the failure of at least three other firms. However, these other firms had pre-existing difficulties, with *The Times* noting that the position of Gower, Nephews and Co. had been doubtful for the previous two years (*The Times*, 13 September 1847: 6), Watson Brothers had insufficient capital for a considerable period (*The Times*, 22 September 1847: 6), and Lyall Brothers and Co. had extended their business beyond the amount warranted by their capital (*The Times*, 1 October 1847: 6).

As traders suspended payment, financial institutions began to experience problems. The failure of Lesley Alexander and Co., a corn merchant, and of some other smaller firms, led to the suspension of the major bill broker Sanderson and Co. in September 1847, who had held much of their paper. This gave 'rise to the utmost anxiety' (*The Times*, 15 September 1847: 3). The reluctance of other financial firms to provide credit led to a higher discount rate, as shown in Figure 4.5 for one of the other major money brokers, Overend and Gurney.

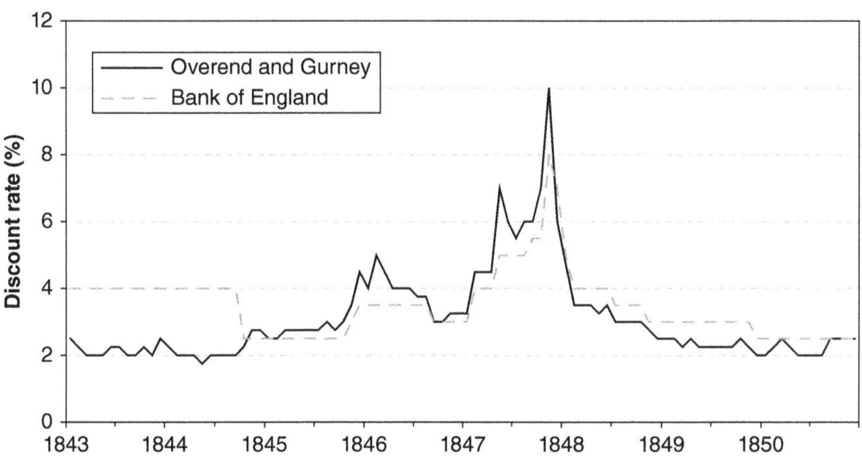

Figure 4.5. Discount rate for first class bills, 1843–50

Discount rate on first class bills for Overend and Gurney from *Parliamentary Papers* (1857, X: 475–6) and minimum rate of interest for Bank of England, *Parliamentary Papers* (1857, X: Appendix pp. 122–33).

These difficulties led to an increased demand on the Bank of England for discounting. Although the reserve of the Banking Department was already at relatively low levels, the Bank allowed its reserve to decline further in an attempt to provide credit. The level of the reserve fell throughout the summer, and with the payment of the October dividends to government bondholders, the notes in the Banking reserve fell to a perilously low level.

The Bank was forced to refuse any further advances on Exchequer bills or Consol warrants, leading to a 'panic'. Four joint-stock banks in Liverpool, Newcastle, and Wales stopped payment and numerous small country banks were declared insolvent (Evans, 1849: 77). Mercantile failures continued and Evans stated that the 'week of terror', ending October 23, would 'long linger in the remembrance of those who witnessed its career' (Evans, 1849: 83). The crisis was only relieved with the suspension of the Bank Charter Act, which had limited the reserve which the Bank could use for discounting.

4.4.1 Bank Charter Act

During previous decades the Bank of England had faced difficulties on several occasions, most recently in 1839 (Andréadès, 1909: 268). These problems had led some to conclude that crises were caused by an unsustainable overexpansion of notes which raised prices. This led to higher imports and an outflow of bullion in payment, much of which would be withdrawn from the Bank of England. If the decline in the reserve was not stopped by higher interest rates, it could lead to a monetary crisis as the Bank would not be able to convert notes to gold.

In an attempt to prevent these crises from recurring the British government introduced the Bank Charter Act in 1844 (*Parliamentary Papers*, 1844: I), with the intention of making the paper currency function like a metallic currency, thus restricting changes in the note supply. Under this legislation the note-issuing powers of the country banks were restricted, and the Bank of England was divided into two separate divisions, the Issue Department and the Banking Department (Andréadès, 1909: 289). The Issue Department was to hold £14 million of securities and a certain amount of gold and silver coin and bullion, and would allow anyone to exchange notes for gold at a fixed price. Only an increase in the holdings of gold in the Issue Department could lead to an increase in the note supply. The Banking Department of the Bank of England was to act in a manner similar to a private bank (Andréadès, 1909: 305). It held a reserve of notes and coin with which it could meet the needs of depositors, and it could advance funds by discounting securities. The interest rate which it offered on these securities would largely depend on its 'banking reserve'.

The Bank Charter Act ensured that the amount of currency outside the Issue Department moved in line with flows of bullion into and out of the country. If gold was needed for export, notes would have to be exchanged for it at the Issue Department, thus removing them from circulation. This should result in lower prices, increasing the exports of goods and the import of gold, thus providing automatic stabilization. However, the amount of currency in circulation outside the Bank, in the hands of the public, was also affected by the size of the reserve held by the Banking Department. If the banking reserve decreased, an outflow of bullion might be sterilized, and the amount of currency in circulation outside the bank remain unchanged (Dornbusch and Frenkel, 1984). It can be seen from Figure 4.6 that changes in the Issue Department were often offset by changes in the Banking reserve, and the notes in circulation outside the Bank remained fairly stable. This suggests that the circulation in the hands of the public did not fluctuate with the import and export of bullion, implying that the management of the Banking Department interfered with the operation of the stabilization mechanism. Whether this was beneficial or harmful to the economy is debatable, as discussed below, but it illustrates that legislation may not have operated as its authors intended.

The changes in both the Issue and Banking Departments were most pronounced in the year prior to the crisis. After the discovery of the poor harvest of 1846 there was a sustained outflow of gold, and the notes issued by the Issue Department fell from £29.9 million in September 1846 to £22.5 million in April 1847, as shown in Figure 4.6. However, the Banking reserve also fell, from £10.3 million to £3.1 million. The Bank had raised its discount rate from 3.0 per cent to 3.5 per cent, and then 4.0 per cent in January 1847, but it did not raise it further, even as its reserve steadily decreased. *The Times* commented that 'the extraordinary apathy of the Bank of the England from January last up to the stage we have now reached in our monetary affairs is beginning to excite universal comment, and to be regarded with universal apprehension' (*The Times*, 7 April 1847: 3).

It was not until the low point of April that the Bank responded by raising its discount rate to 5 per cent and by reducing the availability of discounting. Although the reserve increased, it remained lower than in previous years. With the beginning of the failures in August 1847 the Bank raised its discount rate to 5.5 per cent but did not raise it further, even though its reserve continued to decline. In an attempt to provide credit it actually reduced its rate on loans to 5 per cent in September 1847. With the payment of the dividends to government bondholders in October 1847 the Banking reserve fell to just £2.0 million, as shown in Figure 4.6.

The Bank of England had attempted to provide stability to the economy in the face of the substantial outflow of gold which had occurred, and the onset of commercial failures. It could be argued that such a policy was flawed as it hindered the automatic stabilization which had been envisaged in the Bank Charter Act. However, it is likely that allowing such rapid changes to have occurred without any response would have been even more damaging.

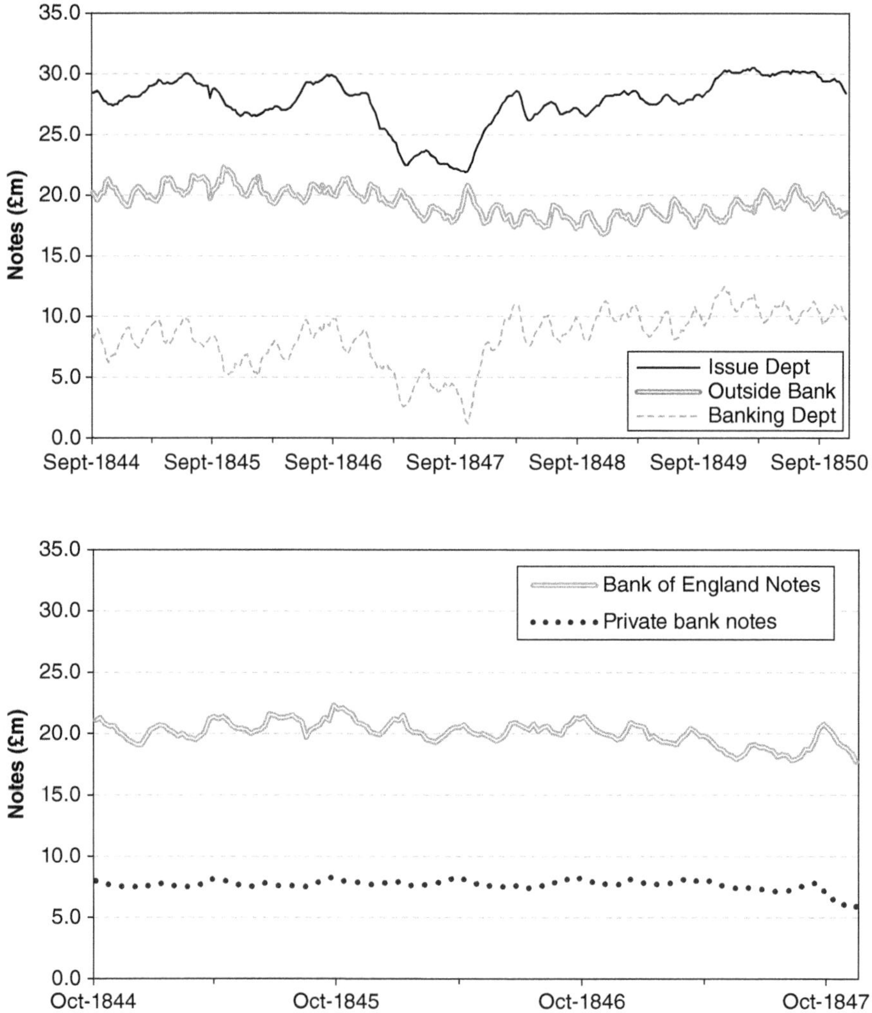

Figure 4.6. Bank of England notes issued, held outside the Bank, and held in the Banking Department, 1844–50

Weekly data on Issue Department and Banking Reserve obtained from *Parliamentary Papers* (1847–8, VIII, Pt. II: 16–21; 1850, XXXIII: 202–11; 1852–3, LVII: 328–35). Notes outside Bank calculated as Issue Department minus Banking Reserve.

The effect of the Bank Charter Act was to place the entire responsibility for counteracting this contraction with the Banking Department. Under the system prior to the Bank Charter Act, the Bank had to retain sufficient total reserves to ensure both the convertibility of notes to gold, and to cover its deposits. Under the new system the reserve in the Issue Department ensured convertibility, and the reserve in the Banking Department covered deposits.

The reserve of one department could not be used to meet the needs of the other. Tooke argued that the Act made the crisis more severe 'by diminishing the power of the bank to grant accommodation in consequence of the narrow limit of its banking reserve . . . There was no less than £6.25 million in the issue department, which was as little available as if it had been in China' (Parliamentary Papers, 1847–8, VIII: Pt. I: 435, q. 5310). Combining the bullion in both departments would have helped the Bank to continue discounting, but if the drain in bullion continued, the convertibility of the note would also have been at risk. Samuel Jones Loyd, who was regarded as one of the framers of the Bank Charter Act, argued that the Act had been successful in its aims, by preventing the Bank from allowing its bullion to fall so low that it also endangered the convertibility of the note (*Parliamentary Papers*, 1847–8 VIII: Pt. 1: 412, q. 5117).

The Bank Charter Act illustrates that legislation may have unintended consequences. The automatic stabilization which it was intended to provide was nullified by the management of the Banking reserve. The Act ultimately contributed to the panic because it shifted risk from one part of the monetary system to another, reducing the risk of inconvertibility of the note, but increasing the risk of the deposits held in the Banking Department.

4.4.2 Suspension of Bank Charter Act

To alleviate the crisis the Prime Minister, Lord John Russell, and the Chancellor of the Exchequer, Charles Wood, sent a letter to the Bank which recommended that the Bank of England 'enlarge the amount of their discounts and advances', but that the 'rate of interest should not be less than 8 per cent' (*The Times*, 26 October 1847: 4). The Bank would not be held liable for any infringement of the Bank Charter Act. This implied that the Bank would be able to use the reserve of gold held in the Issue Department to meet the needs of the Banking Department. The effect of this letter was to allow the Bank to extend credit beyond what would be possible with the existing Banking reserve, which stood at just £2.0 million on October 23.

The knowledge that the Bank could provide additional assistance was enough to allay the panic. Samuel Gurney, a prominent banker, said that 'the effect was immediate. Those [customers] who had sent notice for their money in the morning sent us word that they did not want it—that they had only ordered payment by way of precaution' (Evans, 1849: 86). From that date there was a gradual but progressive return to confidence (Evans, 1849: 90). The reserve fell to £1.6 million on October 30, but it recovered thereafter and the restrictions imposed by the Bank Charter Act were never infringed. It then increased steadily, to £2.3 million by November 6, to £5.6 million by November 27, and £8.4 million by December 25, as shown in Figure 4.6.

The policy pursued by the government in October 1847 was effective for at least three reasons. Firstly, it had a clear goal, secondly, it proposed a suitable remedy, and thirdly, that remedy was not opposed by interested parties. Each of these factors was only possible because the crisis was ongoing, suggesting that policy responses during a crisis are more targeted, and are more likely to be implemented, than any suggestions which are made in advance.

As the crisis was current, the goal of reducing instability was paramount. Attempting to frame legislation to prevent crises which may or may not occur in the future is inherently difficult, as there must be trade-offs between the likelihood of more stability and the restrictiveness which is imposed. However, during a crisis the focus is placed entirely on resolving the distress, and those measures which are most likely to be successful can be employed, with less regard to their longer-term consequences.

Government policy was also successful because it proposed an appropriate response to the problem. The suspension of the Act was not an inevitable decision, and the Bank of England Governor argued that 'as far as the Bank was concerned we did not require any relaxation' (*Parliamentary Papers* 1847–8: VIII, Pt. I: 271, q. 3237). The Bank could have attempted to sell some of its holdings of government securities to raise cash, or it could have refused all requests for discounting. However, Tooke argued that the former course was impractical as the securities could only have been sold at such a low price that it could not be contemplated (*Parliamentary Papers* 1847–8: VIII, Pt. I: 435, q. 5472). The latter course of action, of restricting discounting, may have ensured the Bank retained a reserve but would have intensified the panic. The path which was chosen by the government had fewer risks, and was repeated in future crises. Increasing confidence that the central bank would act as a lender of last resort during a crisis has since become a standard policy prescription (Bagehot, 1873; Kindleberger, 1978: 161–78; Bignon, Flandreau, and Ugolini, 2012).

The policy proposed by the government could be implemented quickly, and have an immediate impact, because it was not opposed. The crisis was having a detrimental effect on businesses, bankers, and the public, so there was almost universal support for some measure to relieve it. The Bank of England argued that they could have carried on without the issue of the government letter, but they were in no way opposed to it. Even Samuel Jones Loyd, a banker who had helped to frame the Act and defended it vigorously, agreed that 'circumstances may occur in mercantile affairs . . . that some interposition may be desirable for the purpose of alleviating the intensity of the pressure arising from destruction of confidence' (*Parliamentary Papers* 1847–8, VIII, Pt. I: 394, q. 5157).

However, the issue of the Government letter had one disadvantage. Even though it referred to the suspension of the Act as an 'extraordinary and temporary measure' (*The Times*, 26 October 1847: 4), William Cotton, a former Governor of the Bank of England, believed that it was likely to lead people to expect a similar letter in future (*Parliamentary Papers* 1847–8, VIII, Pt. I: 329, q. 4043). *The Economist* commented that 'it will be impossible to destroy a feeling which for many years must pervade the public mind, that the pressure must only be severe enough, and the demands loud enough, in order to procure a suspension of any restriction which may exist' (*The Economist*, 30 October 1847: 1241). Subsequent events proved these suspicions to be correct, with the Act again suspended in 1857 and 1866. Responding in the midst of a crisis thus met with much less opposition than any policies which could have been introduced prior to the difficulties, but it led to an increase in moral hazard. By increasing expectations that the Act could be suspended, it may have encouraged increased risk-taking as it was more likely that the Bank of England would always be available as a lender of last resort, regardless of the circumstances. Nevertheless, the benefits of the suspension were almost certainly greater than the costs.

4.5 CONCLUSION

The British government responded to the railway mania, corn price reversal, and commercial crisis of the 1840s in a variety of ways. The policies which were pursued before the crash in prices and the onset of financial distress were generally unsuccessful. However, this does not necessarily imply that the government should be strongly criticized for its actions. It was, like other administrations before and since, faced with the challenge of legislating in the midst of uncertainty. This meant that it had to balance the possible benefits of increased stability against the additional costs which this would impose, and there was a lack of clarity about the impact of the policies which it did introduce. The parliamentary system also ensured that legislation had to obtain broad support, so bold initiatives which may have been opposed by interested parties were not feasible. Government action was most effective in the midst of the crisis when these considerations were less of a concern.

The experience of the 1840s suggests that attempts to legislate to prevent future instability is challenging, so crises are likely to occur again. When they do, a vigorous response by government may help to mitigate the extent of the difficulties. The specific form of intervention will depend on the unique circumstances of the crisis. The commercial crisis of 1847 was relieved by increasing the ability of the Bank of England to act as a lender of last resort. However, it was successful because it targeted the particular problem at this time. In other periods of crisis a similar strategy has been successful, but each episode has unique characteristics and the response should target the particular constraint in that period. It may be impossible to eradicate crises, but intervention may be of some use when they do occur.

5

The Crisis of 1866

Marc Flandreau and Stefano Ugolini

5.1 INTRODUCTION

The so-called Overend Gurney crisis of 1866 was a major turning point in British monetary and financial history. Following the emergence of a modern financial system in the eighteenth century, the country had been plagued by recurrent panics. In every decade of the nineteenth century until the crisis of 1866 there had been a point when, following a phase of credit expansion and 'speculation', market conditions had deteriorated, and the money market seized. 1866 was just one more run in a series that included, among the most infamous, 1825, 1837–9, 1847, and 1857. Yet the run that began in May 1866 was to be the last of that variety to occur in the United Kingdom until the outbreak of First World War. The only two relevant episodes of financial stress that occurred between 1866 and 1914—1878 and the 'Baring crisis' of 1890—did not have much in common with previous financial shocks neither in virulence nor in nature, since—unlike the previous crises—they were not accompanied by dislocations of the money market.

This surprising feat has fascinated economists and historians alike, and they have sought to understand its reasons. All eyes have been rightly turned towards the Bank of England, but what exactly were the actions that planted the seeds of financial stability remains disputed. Following Fetter's (1965) characterization of the post-1870s decades as the era that saw the 'victory of the Bagehot principle', some scholars have argued that the newly acquired stability of the British financial system was owed to the Bank of England's new willingness to undertake lifeboat operations (also see Giannini 1999; Mahate, 1994). According to others, Britain's new financial resilience was owed to consolidations in the Bank's macro-policy, including its adherence to the gold standard (Schwartz, 1986, 1995): restrictions on the Bank's discretionary power over the issue of high-powered money (the gold standard's 'rule') would have stabilized the system by improving agents' ability to make forecasts. Still others have emphasized micro-prudential aspects of crisis management, such as the emergence of automatic, anonymous lending on recognizably good collateral. For instance, according to Capie's (2002: 310–11) frosted-glass discount window metaphor, the Bank's discount window was raised high enough to examine just the quality of the collateral, without revealing the identity of the discounter: the central banker 'does not know, nor does he care, who is on the other side of the window. He simply discounts good quality paper or lends on the basis of good collateral'. Arguments emphasizing micro-prudential features include Calomiris (2011), who claims that the Overend Gurney crisis served to establish the Bank of England's credibility and ability to act in a fully discretional way. The episode rebutted the principle of 'too big to fail' and signalled the Bank's decision to terminate 'the put option inherent in the Bank's willingness to accommodate demand'.[1]

This chapter discusses what really happened in 1866. For one thing, Bagehot (1873) never advised central bankers to engage in 'lifeboat operations'. He advised them to provide generous lending—essentially, to do away with credit rationing which had prevailed in previous crises. As recent research has shown, 1866 was indeed a watershed (something Bagehot himself had recognized). In 1866, the Bank had in practice—if not officially—acted as a lender of last resort, abstaining from credit rationing and as a result effectively becoming the place where the crisis was resolved (Bignon, Flandreau, and Ugolini, 2012). Using new statistical evidence from previous joint research (Flandreau and Ugolini, 2013) this chapter goes one stage further and provides a fuller characterization of the events in 1866 and of the revolution that occurred then. In contrast with Capie (2002), we argue that Britain's actual recipe for financial stability was the Bank of England's adoption of a principle of generous provision of *non-anonymous* lending. In other words, the Bank's discount window was fully raised so that the central banker could see the face of the discounter. The Bank was prepared to provide credit only to the extent that it liked what it saw. This meant that the counterparty had to abide by a number of behavioural norms: at the same time the Bank lent generously, it also performed strict monitoring over the banking system and thus protected itself against moral hazard. Tightened supervision and generous lending were the two sides of the new currency.

The remainder of the chapter is organized as follows. Section 5.2 reviews the structure of the English financial system on the eve of the Overend Gurney panic. Section 5.3 analyses in detail the Bank of England's actions during the crisis. In the light of this evidence, section 5.4 provides a characterization of

[1] Rejection of the too-big-to-fail principle is also a central theme of Capie (2002). One paper sceptical about the Bank of England's role in fostering financial stability is Batchelor (1986). He argues that after 1866 there was an increase in the amount of information available to the public concerning the quality of collateral held by the banking system.

Britain's newly formed approach to financial stability. Section 5.5 emphasizes the international aspects of the new policy adopted in 1866: we argue that the new policy helped entrench sterling as an unrivalled international currency. Section 5.6 sums up the findings and provides a comparison between the events in 1866 and the Baring Crisis of 1890.

5.2 THE STRUCTURE OF THE ENGLISH FINANCIAL SYSTEM ON THE EVE OF 1866

Since the early modern era, European financial systems had been developing around a particular form of money market instruments: bills of exchange. Bills were negotiable promissory notes bearing multiple guarantees: bound to be paid at maturity by one person (the 'acceptor' or insurer) who had agreed to certify the quality of the original debtor (the drawer), they were also secured by the signatures of all the people who had previously held and resold them (the endorsers). The bill market flourished in England during the Industrial Revolution, and specialized intermediaries (the bill brokers) started to emerge at the beginning of the nineteenth century.

If we are to believe King's (1936) classic account, the centrality of bill brokers within the system was established following the crisis of 1825 (initially known as 'The Panic'). During this crisis, rampant credit rationing by the Bank of England made major London banks—which were heavily invested in bills—experience a serious maturity mismatch, which forced them to suspend payments. Scared by this episode, commercial banks would have vowed never to find themselves in the same situation again. Instead of keeping all of their assets in bills, the banks started to deposit large amounts of money 'on call' with bill brokers, to whom the liquidity risk was shifted. This very episode transformed the English financial system into one which was unlike any other. Bill brokers (or 'discount houses', as they came to be known later on) evolved from being brokers to being money market funds, taking deposits from banks and investing them directly (on their own account) in the bill market. In normal times risks were limited, and so were margins, encouraging substantial leverage. According to King (1935), the ratio of total assets to capital hovered around 10 times in the mid nineteenth century, and this was larger than what a typical bank would do.

This is how Britain's variant of the modern 'shadow banking system' was born. Initially, the Bank of England looked favourably upon an evolution which was supposed to help it manage the money market at arm's length through the rediscounting system. However, relations gradually deteriorated. According to Wood (1939) this was caused by the Act of 1844, which sanctioned the private company character of the Bank. Encouraged to compete directly on the discount market, the Bank started to see bill brokers as challengers and its own rediscount facilities as a free lunch provided to these challengers.

Figure 5.1 summarizes the basic features of England's financial system as it had been evolving after the turning points of 1825 and 1844. In this system, credit seekers obtained funding by drawing bills which, once accepted by specialized merchant banks (or 'acceptance houses', as they came to be known later on), were sold (or 'discounted') on the money market. This was the hunting ground for bill brokers, who sought a profitable re-employment of the funds deposited with them by commercial banks—which, in turn, collected deposits from the general public. As Figure 5.1 shows, the Bank and the bill brokers competed against one another and it is plausible that this competition was one aspect of the tensions that grew steadily between the Old Lady of Threadneedle Street and the bill brokers—in particular the biggest and most 'prestigious' of them all, Overend, Gurney & Co.—setting the stage for the final denouement of May 1866 when the Bank refused to bail out 'Overends'.

Deteriorating relations between the Bank and the bill brokers (and principally Overends) cannot be solely explained in terms of commercial rivalry. Because bill brokers were money market specialists, the Bank of England could, to some extent at least, 'outsource' to them the screening of bills and just rely on the guarantee provided by them. Moreover, the generosity of bill brokers set the conditions of the money market: attempts by the Bank of England to, say, tighten money market conditions could be frustrated by bill brokers' expansionary policies. In other words, the bill brokers had both a prudential role and a monetary policy role. The Bank of England's need to make its rate 'effective' in order to protect the gold reserve (a big theme of the 1850s) ran against this circumstance, and contained seeds of discord.

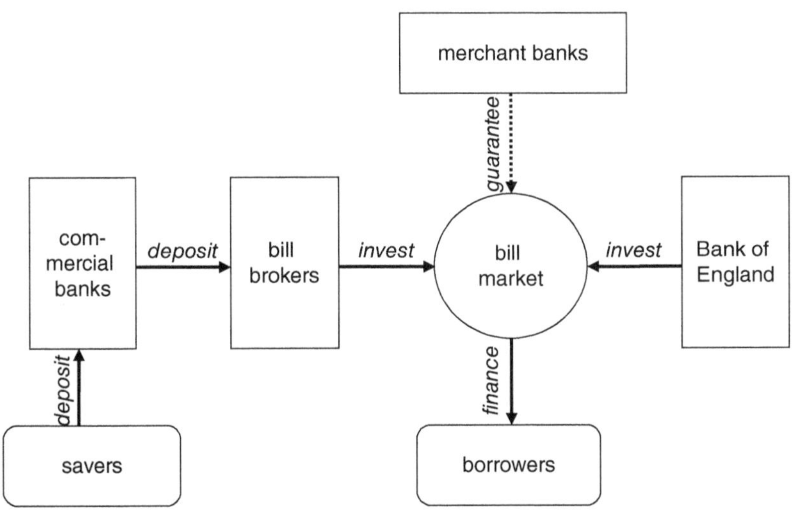

Figure 5.1. Stylized structure of England's financial system in the nineteenth century

The conflict between the Bank of England and Overend, Gurney & Co. became overt in the aftermath of the crisis of 1857. During this panic, bill brokers resorted extensively to the Bank's rediscounting facilities, and the Bank's directors started to think that the inherent inconsistency of the system had reached breaking point. By the end of November 1857, the Bank held £1.2 million in bills rediscounted to Overends, which amounted to 3.37 per cent of its total portfolio of commercial securities.[2] This number might look unimpressive, but it reflected a broader pattern among all bill brokers, and this is what was perceived as unbearable. The argument was that, had the bill brokers refrained earlier from reckless lending, the crisis would have been avoided. Bill brokers should have reduced leverage by keeping higher cash reserves and it was their automatic access to the Bank's discount window that created moral hazard. To provide incentives in this direction, in March 1858 the Bank issued a public statement which announced its willingness to shut down rediscounting facilities to bill brokers, except in exceptional circumstances. The press personalized the move as directed against Overend, Gurney & Co., and commented unfavourably (King, 1936: 202–3). Overends felt strong enough to indulge in retaliatory action: in April 1860, they launched a mini-run on the Bank of England by abruptly withdrawing a £3 million deposit they had previously accumulated at the Bank. However, according to Bagehot (1873: 299) the attempt failed to achieve its probable objective of strengthening the bill brokers' case by exposing the vulnerability of the Bank of England; instead, he says, the attack had the effect of 'exciting a distrust of Overends' while the 'credit of the Bank of England was not diminished'.

5.3 BANK OF ENGLAND LENDING DURING THE OVEREND GURNEY CRISIS

The aftermath of the crisis of 1857 saw a considerable expansion of discount houses and joint-stock banks, which King (1936: 217) associates with the Companies Act. Another relevant aspect of the boom was the internationalization of the bill market (Hughes, 1960). The massive expansion in international trade during the 1850s contributed to London's comparative advantage in trade finance and encouraged the multiplication of originators (merchant or joint-stock banks) and money market funds (bill brokers). Those with foreign connections and a London base could make large profits because they could

[2] Authors' computations on Bank of England Archive C25/3 and *The Economist* (21 November 1857).

take advantage of local information and London facilities. Figures provided by Roberts (1992) for Schroders, a merchant bank with contacts with the Continent and the US, suggest that in the early 1860s the profitability of acceptances was enormous—between 4 and 6 per cent of the amounts accepted. Figures quickly declined afterwards, possibly reflecting the effects of competition.[3] The result was the internationalization of the London money market—sterling acceptances becoming a funding and investing vehicle of choice.

As was bound to be the case, not all those joining the craze were prudent: many sought to enhance returns by investing short-term resources in long-term or illiquid resources. Overends ('the model instance of all evil in business' says Bagehot (1873: 275)) bucked the trend, and in the early 1860s they invested increasingly in speculative-grade bills and, as one investment after the other failed, they ended up with non-performing assets and their liquidity declined.[4] In an attempt to attract fresh capital, the partnership was transformed into a limited liability company and floated on the stock exchange in 1865. Bagehot (1873: 274–5) saw this move as the real cause of the firm's eventual fall, because henceforth losses became public knowledge and its reputation got irremediably tarnished. Further shocks included a long period of high interest rates in London, which exacerbated the company's refinancing difficulties (Figure 5.2), the stock market collapse of late 1865 and early 1866, and the failure of a number of customers. Calls to other bankers were unsuccessful and, in a last ditch effort, the Bank of England was approached in early May, but the 'Governor took the view that the Bank could not assist one concern unless it was prepared to also assist the many others which were known to be in similar plight' (King, 1936: 242). This was decided after a confidential report was commissioned to investigate whether assistance by the Bank or a consortium of London commercial banks was an option. At 3:30 p.m. 10 May 1866, Overend Gurney & Co. suspended payments. The immediate reaction was described as the 'wildest panic'. Contemporaries compared the event to an 'earthquake'. From King (1936: 243): it is 'impossible to describe the terror and anxiety which took possession of men's minds for the remainder of that and the whole of the succeeding day'.

How did the Bank react to the panic? In the months preceding the crisis, market interest rates had almost constantly coincided with the Bank's discount

[3] Figure computed using data provided by Roberts (1992: 527, 532). Acceptances were for a few months (typically 90 days), so that to compute the annual rate of return, one must compare annual revenues from acceptances and acceptances outstanding on the balance sheet at the end of the year (assuming they were essentially rolled over). Data for the early 1860s also include consignments made by Schroders: controlling for these on the basis of later proportions gives the lower bound reported. Note that technically, acceptances appeared for the same amount on the asset and liability sides of the balance sheet, and it was understood that some capital had to be set aside to meet contingencies.

[4] See Xenos (1869) for an informed—but not fully impartial—account of Overends' unhappy Greek investments.

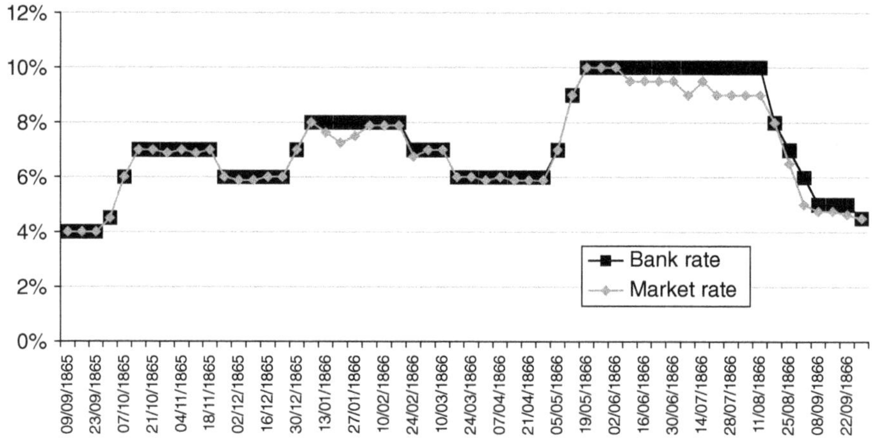

Figure 5.2. Bank and market interest rate in London

Source: *The Economist* (1865–6).

rate. This was evidence of money market tension, which the Bank was nonetheless accommodating (Bignon, Flandreau, and Ugolini, 2012). After the announcement of Overends' suspension, the official discount rate was raised from 7 per cent to 9 per cent and then 10 per cent, but again, the market rate never exceeded this threshold (Figure 5.2). In other words, the Bank continued to meet the considerably increased demand for cash. Both channels through which the Bank provided liquidity to the banking system—discounts of bills and advances on securities (including 'parcels', i.e. bundles, of bills)—were heavily resorted to, and very few demands for cash were rejected (Figure 5.3). In other words, the Bank was not losing its cool and continued to inject liquidity in the system.

Who was coming to the Bank's standing facilities? There comes an interesting finding: in spite of the official ban of March 1858, bill brokers dominated the stage. They were, by far, the biggest users of the discount window (Figure 5.4a) and they resorted heavily to the advance facility (along with commercial banks who took the lion's share: Figure 5.4b). The notable feature of the episode is that bill brokers and commercial banks were *not* usual customers of the Bank, which in 'normal' times used to have only merchant banks and trading houses coming to its discount window (Flandreau and Ugolini, 2013).[5]

[5] It is interesting to note that following its going public and diversification of its business into a financial conglomerate in the 1860s, Overend, Gurney & Co. had no longer been considered by the Bank as a 'bill broker'—its account being transferred to the commercial banks' ledger since 1865 (Bank of England Archive, C24/1). This means that, already by this time, Overend was formally outside the scope of the 1858 rule, implying that the reason for refusing support had nothing to do with the rule itself.

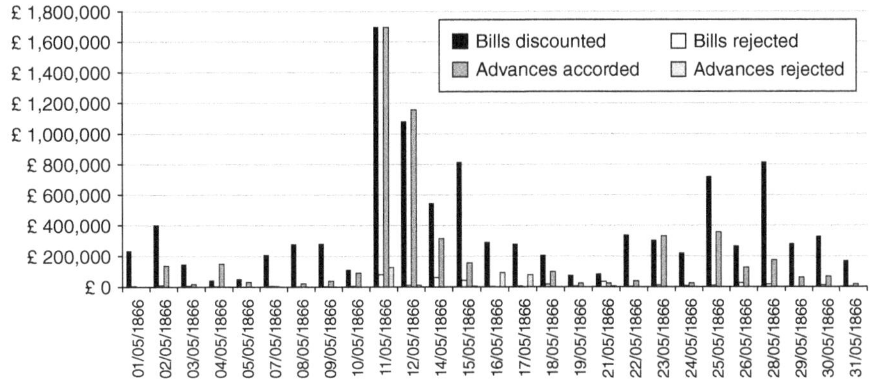

Figure 5.3. Daily discounts and advances by the Bank of England in May 1866

Source: Flandreau and Ugolini (2013).

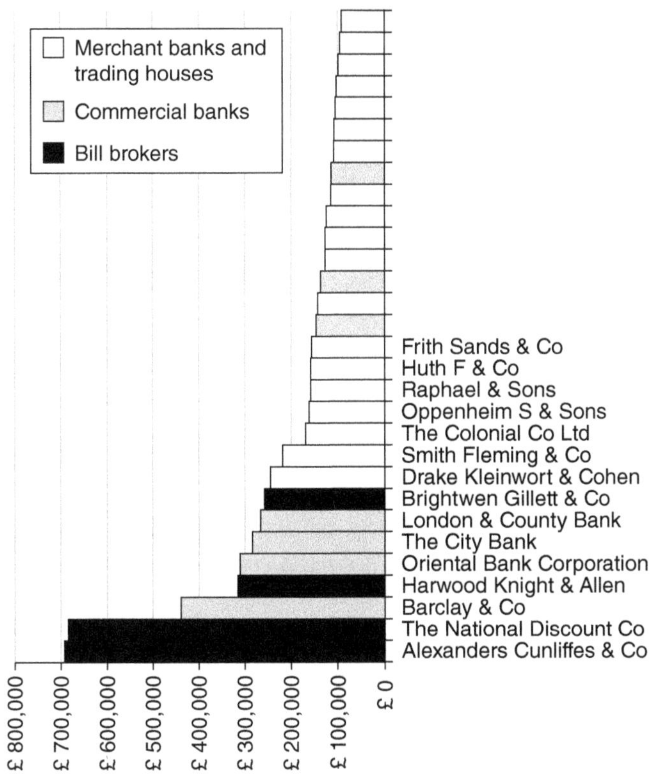

Figure 5.4a. Top 30 discounters from the Bank in May 1866

Source: Flandreau and Ugolini (2013).

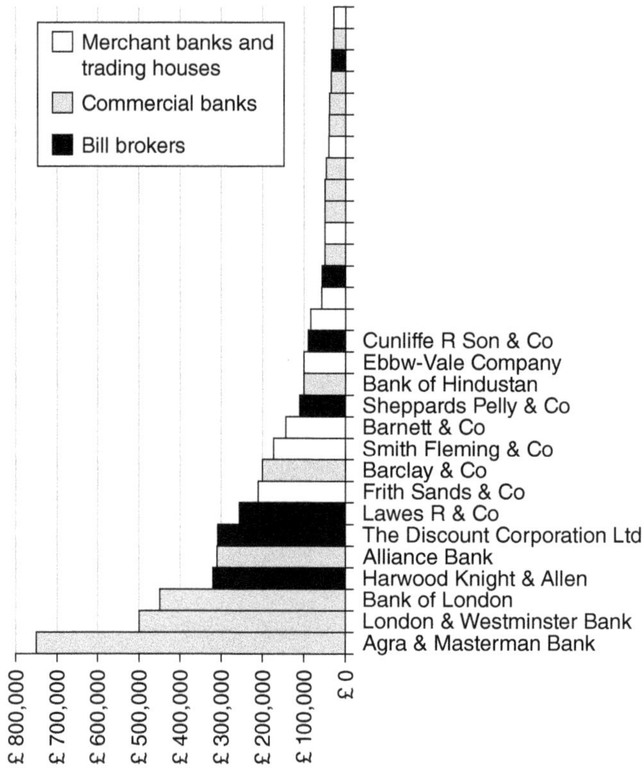

Figure 5.4b. Top 30 advances from the Bank in May 1866

Source: Flandreau and Ugolini (2013).

What were applicants bringing to the Bank in exchange for cash? The composition of discounts, for which precise information is available, provides some elements of an answer, which is broadly the same material as usual. If we sort out the paper discounted by the Bank in May 1866 according to acceptors (i.e. the firms which, after having been drawn upon, had underwritten the bills and thus bore the 'initial' responsibility) and then compare it to the situation one year earlier, we get a very stable composition of the underlying material. To the extent that acceptors had to be rated for their paper to be recognized by the Bank of England, this implies that the underlying quality of the material they accepted was very stable. Tables 5.1a–b illustrate this. They give the Bank's 25 biggest exposures to acceptors (amounting to 39.5% of the total) in May 1866 as well as one year before the crisis. The shares and ranking of acceptors did not change considerably. Paper that was discounted by the Bank in normal times could be expected to be discounted during crises.

To summarize, it appears that when the panic erupted, the Bank merely continued to do its 'usual' business—although on a much grander scale. It kept lending, only it did much more and met demand for liquidity from all sides (despite the 1858 ban of bill brokers from the discount window). Next, underlying this 'continuity' of operation, the nature (and thus quality) of the instruments considered eligible for refinancing operations did not change during the crisis. Guarantors (acceptors) deemed reliable before the crisis remained so during the crisis. In fact, as we also found, even in those cases in which the guarantee turned out to be dubious later (when the acceptor failed as a result of the crisis, as in the case of the Agra & Masterman Bank or the Consolidated Bank), the Bank of England adhered to the principle whereby it sustained its earlier policy. This supports the notion that a key aspect of crisis-lending was indeed the question of the instrument upon which it lent, perhaps more than the identity of those to whom it lent. Indeed, it turns out that, among the discounters who received the biggest volumes of Bank's liquidity, were some of the main casualties of the crisis (such as Agra & Masterman or the Bank of London). At first sight, this is consistent with Capie's (2002) idea that the important question for lending of last resort is 'What do you accept?'—not 'From whom?'. However, as the next section shows, the 'what' and 'from whom' issues are more intertwined than a superficial reading of the crisis of 1866 would suggest.

5.4 THE RAISED EYEBROW: FROM LENDING OF LAST RESORT TO BANKING SUPERVISION

Although generally originated in the course of commercial transactions (such as for the finance of physical commodity shipping), bills of exchange were not backed by physical security. In case of default of the acceptor, the holder of the bill had the right to turn to previous endorsers, but in no case could they seize (say) the bales of cotton collateral that might have been mentioned on the bill (Seyd, 1868: 81–3). Hence, the 'value' of a bill of exchange consisted of the names written on it and of those names alone. Exposure was exposure to names, and this meant that—willy-nilly—the Bank actually *had to know and to care about* who was on the other side of the discount window: 'what' and 'whom' were the two sides of the same coin.

This helps explain the sophisticated system the Bank of England developed in order to monitor discounting risks. First, not anybody could be a discounter. This was a privilege and admittance in the discounters' list required being presented by other members of the club and the provision of material

Tables 5.1a–b. Top 25 acceptors of the bills discounted by the Bank in May 1865 and May 1866

May 1865

1	**London Joint Stock Bank**	166,862.66	7.75%
2	**Union Bank of London**	84,419.34	3.92%
3	**London & County Bank**	69,317.37	3.22%
4	**City of Glasgow Bank**	52,555.49	2.44%
5	Imperial Ottoman Bank	42,580.81	1.98%
6	**Frühling & Goschen**	42,560.03	1.98%
7	**The City Bank**	39,170.67	1.82%
8	**Drake Kleinwort & Cohen**	29,261.21	1.36%
9	Bank of London	26,359.61	1.23%
10	**Agra & Masterman's Bank**	24,504.00	1.14%
11	**Baring Brothers & Co**	21,635.55	1.01%
12	**Finlay Campbell & Co**	19,216.32	0.89%
13	**F Huth & Co**	19,029.89	0.88%
14	**The National Bank**	15,793.46	0.73%
15	**Finlay Hodgson & Co**	14,456.01	0.67%
16	NM Rothschild & Sons	12,853.00	0.60%
17	Union Bank of Australia	12,498.68	0.58%
18	Dadalhai Naoroji & Co	12,000.00	0.56%
19	**Glyn Mills Currie & Co**	11,956.26	0.56%
20	**Merchant Banking Co of London**	11,264.87	0.52%
21	**Oriental Bank Corporation**	11,139.60	0.52%
22	Moses Brothers	10,200.00	0.47%
23	Colonial Bank	10,179.34	0.47%
24	Alliance Bank	9,101.34	0.42%
25	JH Schroder & Co	8,421.57	0.39%
	TOTAL	*777,337.08*	*36.13%*

guarantees.[6] Second, risk management took the shape of a system of ledgers that permitted a real-time control of exposure: each bill that the Bank took into its portfolio gave rise to two entries—one for the acceptor who had underwritten the bill, and one for the discounter who had presented it.[7] By examining its ledgers, the Bank could see at a glance its exposure to any given signature. The quality of acceptors was periodically reviewed and recorded in so-called 'rating books'. The evidence from the rating books also suggests that there were thresholds for exposure to any single risk (Bignon, Flandreau, and Ugolini, 2012).

This arrangement, which—if we are to believe ledgers—was developed from 1844, allowed the Bank to implement a close monitoring of the financial system. This monitoring was hardly anonymous. It enabled the Bank to keep a close eye on both the origination and the distribution of bills of

[6] 'Membership' shrank dramatically throughout the nineteenth century (Bignon, Flandreau, and Ugolini, 2012). However, it seems that this owed to the consolidation of the banking system, not to the Bank striking out previous customers.

[7] It also recorded information on drawers. See Flandreau and Ugolini (2013) for details.

May 1866			
1	**London Joint Stock Bank**	637,028.01	6.21%
2	**Union Bank of London**	474,520.92	4.62%
3	**The National Bank**	321,824.83	3.14%
4	**Frühling & Goschen**	279,321.03	2.72%
5	**Agra & Masterman's Bank**	191,511.83	1.87%
6	**The City Bank**	188,088.95	1.83%
7	North Western Bank	175,129.64	1.71%
8	**London & County Bank**	150,793.66	1.47%
9	**Baring Brothers & Co**	147,425.16	1.44%
10	Royal Bank of Liverpool	146,905.89	1.43%
11	**Drake Kleinwort & Cohen**	144,033.20	1.40%
12	**F Huth & Co**	125,467.88	1.22%
13	**Finlay Hodgson & Co**	123,896.58	1.21%
14	**City of Glasgow Bank**	96,051.60	0.94%
15	JS Morgan & Co	95,764.03	0.93%
16	Bank of Liverpool	85,577.62	0.83%
17	Ebbw-Vale Company Limited	80,771.80	0.79%
18	Smith Fleming & Co	80,741.91	0.79%
19	Consolidated Bank	80,253.50	0.78%
20	R & J Henderson	77,485.63	0.76%
21	**Oriental Bank Corporation**	77,025.64	0.75%
22	**Finlay Campbell & Co**	75,030.05	0.73%
23	**Merchant Banking Co of London**	72,484.53	0.71%
24	Dickinson W & Co	62,141.31	0.61%
25	**Glyn Mills Currie & Co**	61,882.74	0.60%
	TOTAL	*4,051,157.91*	*39.5%*

Source: Flandreau and Ugolini (2013).

Note: Institutions in the top 25 at both dates are shown in bold characters. That makes 16 out of 25.

exchange across the system (Flandreau and Ugolini, 2013). Critically, this allowed the Bank to observe when potentially speculative positions were in the course of being built by abnormal drawing or accepting of bills. Suppose for instance that an acceptor relaxed its standards and began accepting more paper than its capital permitted. The signature, thus indiscriminately thrown upon the market would have flowed back to the Bank of England, who would have immediately noticed the problem. For instance, in 1890 the Bank realized long before the crisis that Barings were getting into trouble because the amount of Baring-accepted bills flowing into its portfolio through third-party discounts had become unusually large. This resulted in exchanges whereby the Bank of England pressured Barings to fall into line.[8] The strategy

[8] While in October 1889 the Bank had had in its portfolio no more than £80,000 in bills accepted by Baring Bros., in early October 1890 its exposure had climbed to £500,000. At this

may not have worked, but such monitoring made sure that the Bank would not be caught sleeping at the wheel (more on this in the conclusion).

This sheds light on the Bank's attitude towards the financial system and in particular, towards Overend, Gurney & Co. during the crisis of 1866. By controlling its exposure, the Bank limited the amount of credit that could be granted to any single individual. As a matter of fact, not too much of the same paper could actually be presented to the Bank by the same discounter: if for any reason one financial agent had excess exposure to another, it would find itself on the hook for the excess. If such rules were understood by all participants, then in principle no single failure could be a serious threat for the system at large. On the other hand, all those who had behaved 'well' (by the Bank of England's standards, which meant—among other things—being properly diversified) were eligible for assistance—assistance of the 'ordinary' variety, through the discount window.[9] Under the new 'regime' that was definitively established with the crisis of 1866, the Bank was happy to discount proportionate amounts of bills guaranteed by all those signatures which were considered eligible in ordinary times (including those whose solvency might be at risk afterwards). Given the detailed knowledge that the Bank had of the money market, the multiplicity of guarantees that it took from acceptors and discounters, and the extreme division of risks in a system where the biggest exposure remained limited (as seen, the top acceptor was only 6 per cent of the Bank's portfolio), the Bank's policy involved a very narrowly calculated risk. And this does not even include the strong interest discounters had in doing whatever they could in order not to lose access to the discount window.

Thus, the sophisticated supervisory system put in place by the Bank of England around the mid nineteenth century allowed it to extend lending-of-last-resort operations without provoking an increase in moral hazard. As a matter of fact, throughout the nineteenth century the amounts-at-risk for the Bank experienced a secular decline, and by the late 1860s they had become basically negligible (Bignon, Flandreau, and Ugolini, 2012). This, we argue, was Britain's nineteenth-century recipe for financial stability. It consisted neither in reliance on abstract market discipline, nor on automatic and anonymous lending of last resort. It had little to do with the gold standard,

date, George J. Goschen, then Chancellor of the Exchequer, noted in his diary: 'Went to the Bank, things queer! Some of the first houses talked about' (Clapham, 1966: 327–8). At the peak of the crisis (18 November 1890), the Bank's exposure to Barings would reach £715,000 (Bank of England Archive, C22/43). The 'anomalous' supply of acceptances by Barings is also manifest from the figures reported in Chapman (1984: 121).

[9] It is crucial to note that the Bank never refused 'ordinary' assistance to Overend, Gurney & Co.: because they were probably short of eligible securities, Overends never showed up at the discount window in the period preceding the crash, and only went to Threadneedle Street—when things were already beyond repair—to ask for 'extraordinary' assistance (Bank of England Archive, C24/1).

and nothing at all with rescue operations. Rather, it rested on a strict monitoring system or, if one prefers, *de facto* central bank regulation. To this *de facto* regulation banks and money market participants had to submit, if they wanted to be on good terms with the central bank. Such good terms were valuable when crisis hit and the Bank was the last lender around—literally, the lender of last resort.

This qualifies the oral tradition that in the late nineteenth century, supervision was minimal and dealt with the 'Bank of England Governor's eyebrow'.[10] According to this view, it was enough for the Governor of the Bank to raise an eyebrow for bankers to put their house in order. There was, of course, much more to the raised eyebrow than the inconvenience of a stern look. There was detailed information held by the Bank, and there was the Bank's power to act by denying discounting facilities. For those needing a reminder, the corpse of Overends could be shown.[11]

5.5 TWIN SUCCESS: INTERNATIONAL ASPECTS OF THE CRISIS OF 1866

But the panic of 1866 did not have solely domestic significance. As already indicated, the London market was relied upon by non-residents. London was a place where international supply and demand for short-term credit were cleared.[12] Foreign balances were held and funding was sought, notably—as indicated—trade finance. Figure 5.5 illustrates this, showing the breakdown of the Bank of England's portfolio of bills according to the geography of drawers: it shows totals drawn by domestic ('inland') versus foreign drawers (i.e. foreign and colonial). We see the predominance of foreign originations (65 per cent of the bills discounted by the Bank in May 1866). As a result, both the crisis and the Bank of England's actions to handle it were bound to have a significant impact on sterling as an international currency.

The crisis translated into increased risk aversion on behalf of international investors, and contemporaries pointed to what is today known as a 'sudden stop' (Calvo, 1998). The mechanism they had in mind is today known as that of twin crises: in this instance, a credit crisis that became a currency crisis. The sterling confidence crisis that developed was triggered by the surge in credit

[10] For a printed variant, Withers (1910: 56) has an intriguing digression on the Bank of England being the 'final arbiter' when the credit of a house came under suspicion.

[11] Another interesting case discussed in Bignon, Flandreau, and Ugolini (2012) is that of the House of Vagliano, who after a dispute with the Bank of England was excluded from the discount window and had to leave banking (Chatziioannou and Harlaftis, 2007: 38–9).

[12] For an account of the international foreign exchange market in the mid nineteenth century, see Ugolini (2012).

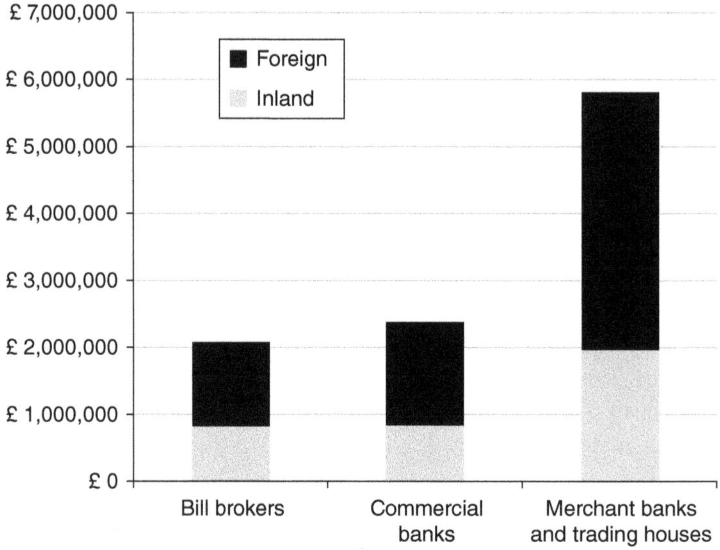

Figure 5.5. Geographical origin of the bills discounted by the Bank in May 1866 (per kind of discounter)

Source: Flandreau and Ugolini (2013).

risk associated with the failure of Overends (Patterson, 1870: 227–8 is perhaps the most articulate illustration. See also Juglar, 1889: 368; Wirth, 1890: 434–5; Macleod, 1891: 833–4). Unsure about the prospects of the London market, some foreign investors liquidated positions and repatriated balances. The consequence was, in the immediate aftermath of the crisis, a weakening of sterling in spite of the exceptionally high interest rates the Bank maintained. In fact, if we use market rate differentials to compute the 'forward' sterling-franc exchange rate and compare it to the gold points (Figure 5.6), we see that the credibility of sterling—which was already under (mild) suspicion before the crisis—came under serious doubt during the panic (a 'forward' rate below the gold export point suggests that sterling suffered a credibility crisis and indeed, in April, the 'forward' exchange rate raced away from the gold points). As for the spot rate it stayed discouragingly close to the gold export point following the Overend collapse, despite a baffling 6 per cent interest rate differential between London and Paris.[13]

[13] Hawtrey (1919: 149–50) argues that foreign investors were questioning the viability of the gold standard. This may be exaggerated: after losing £1.3m in the first two weeks after 11th May, the gold reserve surpassed its pre-crisis level in June, and never sank below it in spite of the fact that an additional drain took place in July (Figure 5.6). Thus, the case for a confidence crisis is strong (Ugolini, 2010).

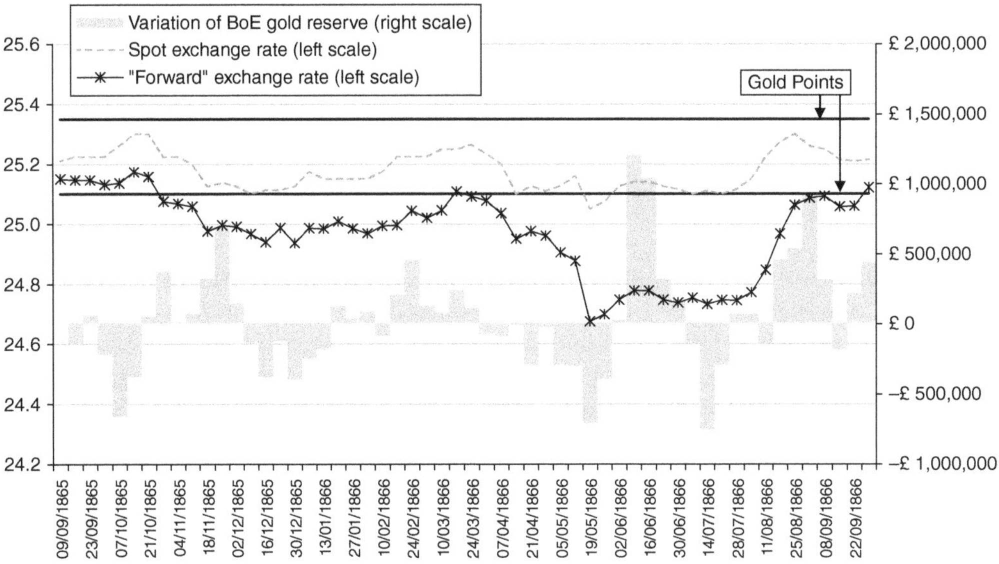

Figure 5.6. International aspects of the 1866 crisis: variation of the Bank of England's gold reserve, and spot and 'forward' franc-pound exchange rates

Sources: Ugolini (2010); *The Economist* (1865–6); Seyd (1868).

Thus the 1866 crisis was also a currency crisis. It was arguably the worst experienced by sterling during the whole 'classical' gold standard period (1821–1913), at least if we are to evaluate this from the length and extent of the 'high rates' period. Faced with reserve losses, the Bank of England had to keep the interest rate at a record level (10 per cent) for more than three months, the longest period ever (Clapham, 1966: 429–32). Many observers saw the crisis as a blow to the reputation of London as an international money market. The shock was deterring foreign creditors from investing in English money market instruments despite the high rates. This opinion was taken seriously by the British Foreign Office, which felt it was necessary to send a circular to all diplomatic representations reassuring foreigners about the solidity of the English financial system (the text of the circular is found in Patterson, 1870: 234–5). Indeed, the policy followed by the Bank of England resulted from the same reading of the crisis—that is, that the currency crisis would be resolved if the credit crisis was resolved. Such was also the logic of Bagehot's exhortations for generous lending against good collateral, while the 'high rates' he also advised would take care of the currency crisis.

The consequences of this policy were equally important. At the end of the day, those investors who had not panicked and kept their money in London fared very well compared, say, to a counterfactual investment in Paris. Consider for instance an investor who would have converted his sterling into

French franc bills with short maturities one month before the crisis (mid March 1866) and then reinvested the bills as they matured, say week after week, during 6 months (until mid September 1866) and then converted the proceeds in sterling again, and compare this investment with a similar one this time in sterling all the way through. At the end of the period the difference in yield between franc and sterling was 2.14 per cent in favour of sterling, or an annualized differential of 4.28 per cent.[14] This is one measure of the extent to which the more versatile—those who had fled to seek safety abroad—were encouraged to be faithful in the future. We conclude that the Bank of England's adoption of lending-of-last-resort policies in 1866 was one aspect of the process through which the role of sterling as a key reserve asset was established.[15] In successfully dealing with the financial shock, the Bank of England acquired enormous financial clout, and this cannot have been an irrelevant aspect of its subsequent triumphs.

5.6 CONCLUSION

Relying on new statistical evidence (Flandreau and Ugolini, 2013), this chapter has surveyed crucial elements of the management of the crisis of 1866. First, our assessment sheds new light on how Britain found her path towards financial stability in the second half of the nineteenth century. By investigating the structure of the money market and the central bank's actions during the crisis, we have shown that Britain's recipe for financial stability consisted of a combination of generous liquidity provision and strict monitoring, made possible by the credible threat of exclusion from the central bank's standing facilities. The Bank's decisive adoption of this approach in 1866 reflected the end of credit rationing that had characterized crisis management until 1857 (Bignon, Flandreau, and Ugolini, 2012) and paved the way for the establishment of a more resilient financial system in the following decades.

Second, we have emphasized the significance of the new policy beyond Britain and the British financial system. The successful handling of the situation by the Bank of England, we argued, had implications at the international level. The Bank had dealt with a twin crisis: the seizure experienced by the London money market in the few hours that followed the collapse of

[14] Authors' computations from data in Ugolini (2010). Details available from authors.

[15] The fact that a central bank should be expected to behave in such a way could not have been taken for granted at the time: for instance, the Bank of France's inability to do so after the events of 1870 seriously compromised the fate of the franc as an international currency. Bagehot himself noted this with satisfaction, but not without preoccupation: high-minded concern about the increased responsibility falling upon the Bank of England after the French debacle was a key motivation for *Lombard Street* (Bagehot, 1873: 31–2).

Overend, Gurney & Co. tested both the resilience of British trade credit institutions and the stability of sterling. Therefore, the Bank's eventual success contributed to establishing the role of sterling as an international currency.

Last, in a volume devoted to British financial crises, it seems natural to end this chapter on the crisis of 1866 with a comparison. We suggest one with the Baring crisis of 1890. One major difference between the two crises is that, while the Bank let Overends fail, it did organize a rescue of Barings—although it made sure that the bankers paid dearly for it. We can think of one main difference between the two crises that may account for the contrasted behaviour. The fall of a bill broker was bound to inflict losses to commercial banks but, since bill brokers did not play a first-stage role in the origination of money market instruments (see Figure 5.1), there was nothing in Overends' fall that would impair the operation of the money market. If cash was needed, the Bank could always provide it, and no large amount of information would be destroyed. By contrast, the fall of a first-order merchant bank such as Barings shattered the foundations of the London money market. Barings, unlike Overends, were large acceptors whose paper was 'normally' received by the Bank of England. Refusing Barings' paper would undermine the London money market and send shockwaves throughout the system.[16] There was this, and there was also the large exposure that the Bank of England had to Barings—in contrast with the lack of exposure it had to Overends.

[16] The systemic importance of merchant banks will again be proved by another crucial event in British financial history—that is, the crisis of 1931 (Accominotti, 2012).

6

'How We Saved the City'

The Management of the Financial Crisis of 1914

Richard Roberts

6.1 INTRODUCTION

The financial crisis of 1914 was by no means a 'typical' financial crisis that unfolded along the lines of Kindleberger's 'Anatomy of a Typical Crisis' (Kindleberger and Aliber, 2011: 26–38).[1] There was no preceding credit expansion, euphoria, speculative mania, or asset bubble. However, there was a clear 'displacement' event or 'Minsky moment'—Austria's belligerent ultimatum to Serbia delivered in Belgrade at 6 p.m. on Thursday 23 July—which transformed risk perceptions of the likelihood of a major European war. This prompted panic across Europe including the rapid breakdown of London's financial markets with the prospect of wholesale failure by City firms and a general run on the banking system that threatened the country's credit and payments mechanisms. Market participants, the Bank of England and the Treasury responded with a variety of 'containment' measures, as emergency expedients are known in recent writing on the financial crisis management, against the backdrop of an unfolding diplomatic and then military crisis, with Britain at war from 11 p.m. on Tuesday 4 August (Honohan and Laeven, 2005: 7–17; Gelpern, 2009: 493–548). Major financial crises frequently feature a subsequent 'resolution stage' in which institutions that have been assisted are restructured. However, institutional failure and restructuring were not features of London's 1914 crisis and 'revival' is a more appropriate term. Revival measures comprised initiatives to revitalize financial activity and to remove the restrictions imposed by containment initiatives. These overlapped with the beginning of the mobilization by the authorities of Britain's financial

[1] I am grateful to Anders Mikkelsen for research assistance.

system to meet the requirements of the war effort, such 'financial repression' being typical of wartime.

David Lloyd George, Chancellor of the Exchequer, entitled his recollections of the financial crisis of 1914: 'How We Saved the City' (Lloyd George, 1938: 61–74). Following the series of stages outlined above, this account examines the challenges faced by the Chancellor and colleagues and their responses. What measures were adopted and why? How appropriate and effective were they? Overall, how successful was the management of the financial crisis of 1914?

6.2 BREAKDOWN

The assassination of Austrian heir-apparent Archduke Franz Ferdinand in Sarajevo on 28 June had no perceptible effect on London's financial markets. After all, there had been international tensions the previous three summers and the Balkan War of 1912 had remained localized. But war risk perceptions were transformed by the Austrian ultimatum on 23 July. 'Markets have rarely, if ever, had a worse week, a worse account or a worse Saturday', declared *The Observer's* City editor on Sunday 26th beneath the headline, 'War Clouds Over the Markets' (*The Observer*, 26 July 1914). But there was yet worse to come: over the course of the following week—Monday 27 July to Saturday 1 August—the City's key markets—the foreign exchanges, the discount market, and the stock market—broke down.

Under the gold standard, demand for foreign exchange facilities arose principally from international trade. The foremost means of making international settlement in 1914 was the sterling bill of exchange (Sonne, 1915: 102; Michie, 2007: 66–8). Sterling bills were widely held abroad constituting what merchant banker Hans Sonne called an 'international currency' that was bought and sold by banks around the world, providing recipients of bills with the means to obtain local currency and those wanting to settle a debt in London with a sterling instrument to do so. War risk fear prompted a scramble for sterling bills in foreign centres, 'a kind of international "Hoard of Sterling"' (Sonne, 1915: 106–7). The explosion of demand for sterling produced 'absolutely grotesque' departures from its gold standard parities: for instance, the sterling-dollar exchange rate soared from \$4.88 on 24 July to a nominal \$6.50, 'a level never seen before' (*Sunday Times*, 'City Chatter', 2 August 1914; *Financial Times*, 'American Markets', 28 and 29 July 1914; *The Times*, 1914: 170). Sterling bills quickly became unobtainable, bringing international remittance to London to a halt early in the week beginning Monday 27 July. International remittance could also be made by the shipment of gold or goods, but this took time to arrange and was heavily disrupted by war risk turmoil in shipping and insurance arrangements.

6.3 DISCOUNT MARKET TURMOIL

The creation and trading of sterling bills of exchange was the function of the London discount market (money market). Bills, typically with a three-month maturity, financed international trade (commercial bills) but were also used for short-term funding by banks (finance bills). The unique scale and liquidity of the sterling money market, a continuous over-the-counter interbank market, was a key factor in London's pre-eminence as an international financial centre before 1914 and had led 71 foreign banks to open London branches by 1913 (Michie, 2007: 51, 65).

The participants in the discount market were banks and the discount houses, specialist intermediaries that acted as brokers and market makers for bills. They enjoyed privileged access to discounting (purchase) of their holdings of bills at the Bank of England. The discount houses funded their bill portfolios by short-term call loans from domestic and foreign banks, collateralized by the bills. The negotiability of a bill of exchange was enhanced by its endorsement by an 'acceptor'—a guarantor of payment upon maturity in case of default by the debtor in a trade transaction. This was the business of a set of City firms known as accepting houses (merchant banks) whose outstanding acceptances (guaranteed bills) on the eve of war aggregated £80–120 million (Roberts, 1992: 131; Chapman, 1984: 106; Sir Robert Kindersley, evidence to the Macmillan Committee, 1931: I: 76; Spring-Rice, 1923: 426). The accepting houses had modest capital relative to their acceptance obligations, totalling some £20–30 million in 1914.[2]

The discount market was beset by several difficulties. The market quickly became moribund because there were no buyers, just sellers. The discount houses were hit by the calling of loans by banks, obliging them to raise funds from the Bank through sales of bills or advances. Acceptors were also in trouble because of the breakdown of remittance from foreign debtors in respect of maturing acceptances, which meant that they were obliged to honour bills when they became due. On Wednesday 29 July, Frederick Huth Jackson, senior partner of leading accepting house Frederick Huth, confided to Sir George Paish, editor of *The Statist*, a financial weekly, that his own firm and seven others—a third of the sector—were on the brink of insolvency (London School of Economics Archives [henceforth, LSEA]. Coll. Misc. 26/2. Sir George Paish, 'My Memoirs', typescript n.d. *c.*1950: 59). The failure of an acceptor would render worthless its guarantee of all bills that it had endorsed,

[2] Author's estimate. Aggregate capital of £20 million was suggested during a meeting between the Chancellor and a delegation from the accepting houses on 12 August 1914, but this was challenged as too low by Frederick Huth Jackson, the firms' leading representative. The National Archives [henceforth, TNA]. T172/134. Conference: Between the Chancellor, members of the cabinet and representatives of Accepting Houses, p.13.

devastating the liquid assets of discount houses and banks. The scale of failure foreseen by Huth Jackson conjured the prospect of the destruction of the infrastructure of the City and endangered the banks.

6.4 CLOSURE OF THE STOCK EXCHANGE

The London Stock Exchange was the largest and most liquid securities market in the world. A 'frantic outpouring of stock from the Continent' sent prices plummeting from Monday 27th (*Financial News*, 'Early General Demoralisation', 28 July 1914). Activity was minimal, reported *Financial News*, because 'jobbers refused to buy; there was no market' (*Financial News*, 'Shut the Stock Exchange', 28 August 1914; *Financial News*, 'All Stock Exchange Business Now a Matter of Negotiation', 30 July 1914). Stock market firms funded their businesses by call loans from banks, with £80 million outstanding in summer 1914 (*The Economist*, 'The Loan Positions of the Stock Exchange', 17 October 1914; *Bankers' Magazine*, 'The Great Crisis IV', December 1914). The loans were collateralized by the securities they funded, plus an element of margin. The collateral securities were regularly marked to market and if the price went down firms had to provide increased margin or repay the loan (raising funds by selling securities). London firms conducted substantial international business and were owed large sums by foreign clients that were unable to pay because of the breakdown of remittance and the imposition of payments moratoria abroad. Seven firms failed on Wednesday 29th and four more on Thursday 30th, including the major firm, Derenberg & Co. (*Financial News*, 'Stock Exchange Transactions', 31 July 1914; *The Economist*, 'The Financial Crisis of 1914', 24 October 1914). That evening 40 large firms lobbied the Stock Exchange Committee for closure of the market, maintaining that they were on the verge of failure (*Financial News*, 'Curious "Street" Reports', 31 July 1914; Lawson, 1915: 54–5). At 10.15 a.m. on Friday 31 July, for the first time ever, the Exchange closed (London Metropolitan Archive [henceforth, LMA]. London Stock Exchange, Committee of General Purposes, 24 March 1915. Reprint in minutes of diary entry of Chairman Sir R. E. W. Inglis; *Financial News*, 'London Stock Exchange Closed as a Precautionary Measure', 1 August 1914; *The Economist*, 'The Financial Situation at Home and Abroad', 1 August 1914). Closure protected firms by postponing the completion of settlements and halting mark-to-market pressure since there were no official prices (*Financial Times*, 'Unprecedented Day in the City: Reason for the Suspension', 1 August 1914; Withers, 1915: 18–20).

6.5 CRISIS CONTAINMENT—BANK OF ENGLAND MEASURES

The Bank of England was the City's foremost institution. It had handled the financial crises of 1847, 1857, 1866, and 1890, and leadership in 1914 fell naturally to the Bank. The Governor was Walter Cunliffe, 'a big, brave, sporting English man of affairs, experienced in the City but not a financial thinker', who conducted the Bank's handling of the crisis 'almost blatantly alone' ('Sir John Clapham's Account', in Sayers, 1976: Appendix 3: 32–3; Sayers, 1976: 67). On Wednesday 29th Cunliffe told the Treasury that 'the Bank of England was in a very strong position' and 'had the situation in hand' (TNA. T170/14. Sir John Bradbury. Visit to Bank as to Mr Joynson-Hick's Question, 29 July 1914). By 1914 the established approach to the management of a financial crisis was, following Bagehot, for the Bank to lend liberally against sound collateral, charging a penalty rate. If pressure on the Bank's resources became too great, it could seek a suspension of the 1844 Bank Charter Act.

Cunliffe unhesitatingly fulfilled the Bank's expected role of lender of last resort to the discount market in the opening days of the crisis, with discounts and advances trebling from £12 million to £37 million between Friday 24th and Wednesday 29th. 'The Bank of England, with its traditional coolness in times of great crisis, advanced without stint at normal rates', stated *Truth* approvingly, while the *Financial Times* praised 'the splendidly cool policy it has adopted throughout the crisis' (*Truth*, 'Mammon: The City and the Crisis', 5 August 1914; *Financial Times*, 'Unprecedented Day in the City', 1 August 1914).

On Thursday, the normal day for Bank rate changes, Cunliffe raised the rate from 3 to 4 per cent, coolly ignoring Bagehot's penalty rate prescription. The *Financial Times* welcomed this decidedly modest advance as 'reassuring since the decision shows that in the opinion of experienced advisers to the Old Lady of Threadneedle Street the situation is not yet so serious as to necessitate the adoption of abnormal methods to protect the gold reserve of this country' (*Financial Times*, 'The Money Market', 31 August 1914).

While Cunliffe kept his cool, the banks and the public were losing theirs. The banks were worried about a run since, as Sir Edward Holden, chairman of the London City and Midland Bank, told the Chancellor, almost seven-eighths of banks' assets were 'frozen up', while much of the liabilities side comprised footloose demand deposits (TNA. T170/55, Conference between Chancellor of the Exchequer and Representative Bankers and Traders, 4 August 1914. Sir Edward Holden: 4).

On Thursday 30 July Henry Bell, general manager of Lloyd's Bank, the largest British bank of the day, told Paish that a general run on the banks was underway (LSEA. Paish, 'My Memoirs', 59). To conserve their gold holdings the banks began to pay depositors making withdrawals mostly in Bank of England notes rather than gold sovereigns (£1), the everyday circulating currency. But the smallest denomination Bank of England note was £5 (*c*.£400 in 2014 money), 'an unwieldy instrument for small people', noted *Financial News* ('Crisis in Real Earnest', 1 August 1914). The banks claimed that they were preventing hoarding, one customer who asked for £1,000 in sovereigns but received only £10 plus £990 in notes, being told, 'if there is any hoarding to be done, we will do it ourselves' (*Financial News*, 'Decisive Precautionary Steps Are Taken by the Great Banks', 1 August 1914).

Paish recalled that after his conversation with Bell: 'I hurried round to the Bank of England and there found an immense queue waiting to cash their notes . . . Hundreds and hundreds of people waiting as patiently as possible to see if their money was still safe!'(LSEA. Paish, 'My Memoirs', 59). Discount house Smith St Aubyn's business diary for the day recorded that: 'People are getting really alarmed and are flooding the Bank of England to change notes for gold. Discount business has practically ceased' (LMA. Smith St Aubyn Business Diary, Ms. 14,894, vol. 24, 30 July 1914). In the three days from Thursday 30 July to Saturday 1 August 5,000 people took £5 notes to the Bank of England to be cashed into sovereigns forming long queues that gave the unfortunate impression of a run on the Bank (Bank of England Archive [henceforth, BEA]. 'Bank of England, 1914–1921', iii). They contributed to an alarming drop in the Bank's stock of sovereigns, which fell from £26 million on Tuesday 27 July to £14 million on Saturday 1 August (BEA. C1/62. Daily Accounts, 1914). 'All over the country a heavy run was made on the Banks', recorded Hoares Bank partners' memorandum book, 'everybody wishing to hoard gold' (Hoare's Bank Archive. HB/2/E/3. Partners' Memorandum Book, September 1914).

6.6 THE BANK AND THE BANKS

Closure of the Stock Exchange heightened banks' anxieties, since it created a 'serious congestion in credit' by rendering illiquid their loans to stock exchange firms and holdings of securities put up as margin ('The Financial Crisis', *Morning Post*, 1 August 1914). The banks focused immediately and remorselessly on calling loans to discount houses, driving them into the Bank on a massive scale: on Friday 31 discounts and advances leapt from £38 million to £63 million, a staggering 62 per cent jump in a single day (BEA. C1/62. Daily Accounts, 1914). Being 'virtually overwhelmed' with bills the Bank's discount office steadily pushed up the rate at which it would discount bills to 10 per cent, making retention of the 4 per cent official rate impossible and around 4 o'clock Bank rate was raised to 8 per cent bringing it 'more or less into agreement with the rate at which the Bank was doing business' (*Sunday Times*, 'City Chatter', 2 August 1914; 'Bank Rate 8 Per Cent', *Morning Post*, 1 August 1914). 'Needless to say this sensational step is without parallel', observed the *Sunday Times*, 'but last week has smashed so many records that the announcement caused no panic' (*Sunday Times*, 'City Chatter', 2 August 1914). Indeed, it was taken as 'indicating the determination of the Bank of England to protect the national stock of gold' and greeted as 'inevitable' (*The Times,* 'Position of the Bank', 1 August 1914). But this was no comfort to the discount houses, the City editor of *The Observer* reporting that 'many bill brokers and others were so excited on Friday afternoon that they were often incoherent'(*The Observer,* 'The Story of the Crisis', 2 August 1914). 'A bad day', recorded Smith St Aubyn's daily diary. 'Looks like panic. All business ceased' (LMA. Smith St Aubyn business diary, Ms. 14,894, vol. 24, 31 July 1914).

Mid afternoon on Friday the Governor visited the Chancellor and requested suspension of the 1844 Bank Act to relieve the Bank from the requirement to exchange its notes for gold and to allow it to print notes in excess of its statutory limit to meet financial intermediaries' craving for liquidity, as had been granted in three previous crises. Leading bankers were then summoned to join the Chancellor and Governor, resulting in heated exchanges with Cunliffe who was furious at the banks' conduct in forcing the discount houses and depositors to turn to the Bank; in the early evening the company moved to 10 Downing Street for a two-hour meeting with the Prime Minister Herbert Asquith. With much else to deal with, this appears to have been Asquith's only formal engagement with the financial crisis. Cunliffe, Edwin Montagu, Treasury Secretary, and Sir John Bradbury, Permanent Secretary, tried to persuade the bankers to pay out gold, but they resisted pressing instead for the suspension of the Bank Act and the adoption of their long-standing scheme to place their private gold reserves with the Bank in exchange for 1-for-3 allocations of Bank notes; the meeting broke up without agreement.

Saturday saw further extraordinary developments. The bank run claimed a victim, National Penny Bank, a London savings bank with 14 branches. And Cunliffe went to war with the banks, refusing facilities to the discount houses which meant they were unable to meet the banks' demands for the repayment of call loans. 'The experiences of the bill brokers, thus crushed between the upper and nether millstones of finance, were extraordinarily unpleasant', observed Hartley Withers, future editor of *The Economist*, 'but the Bank of England relented at last' (Withers, 1915: 29). Indeed, despite the initial boycott the day saw a further substantial increase in the Bank's discounts and advances from £63 million to £72 million, approaching the estimated £100 million of discount house call loans outstanding before the crisis (Sykes, 1915: xxvi (2): 73). 'The Joint Stock banks panicked and it was only at ¼ to 1 that we were able to get anything [meaning funds from the Bank]', recorded Smith

St Aubyn's daily diary. 'A truly fearful Saturday. Clearing kept open till 2 o'clock & we just managed to get home [enough money] in time to pay our clearing. The worst day we have ever had since the business began' (LMA. Smith St Aubyn business diary, Ms. 14,894, vol. 24, 1 Saturday 1914). While yet again long queues of note changers and discount brokers besieged the Bank, Cunliffe returned to the Treasury to collect the letter authorizing the suspension of the Bank Act, which he received signed by the Prime Minister and the Chancellor. Following what they understood to be the precedent set by previous crises, the politicians stipulated that Bank rate should be raised to the crisis level of 10 per cent, which was promptly put into effect (Lloyd George, 1938: 63). Cambridge economist John Maynard Keynes, who was an unofficial adviser at the Treasury during the crisis, was scathing about the 'violent movement' in Bank rate, as was Withers who condemned the 'sky-rocket' rises at the height of the crisis as being 'quite ineffective for all purposes for which the Bank rate is usually raised' and having counter-productive 'evil effects . . . a most untimely shock to the public's nerves . . . merely for the sake of blindly following a mouldy old precedent' (Keynes, 1914: 481; Withers, 1915: 11–12). With the Bank in entirely unchartered waters as regards its financial ratios, the Governor at loggerheads with the banks, and the Treasury setting Bank rate and in direct contact with the bankers, the management of the crisis moved from Threadneedle Street to Whitehall.

6.7 'THE SAVIOURS'

Although he had been Chancellor for seven years and had presented six budgets, at the beginning of the financial crisis Lloyd George, 52, had 'never seen a bill of exchange and knew little or nothing of the delicate and complicated mechanism by which international trade is regulated' (Jones, 1951: 50). But he rose to the crisis, impressing advisers by his rapid assimilation of complex detail and responsiveness to guidance. William Lawson, an editor of the *Financial Times*, observed that the City and the nation were fortunate to have an 'unconventional and free-handed Chancellor of the Exchequer to deal with', instead of an orthodox finance minister who might have been 'very slow indeed' to take bold measures to confront the emergency (Lawson, 1915: 86).

The Chancellor's closest advisers during the crisis were: personal confidants Sir George Paish and Lord Reading; Treasury Secretary Edwin Montagu and Treasury officials Sir John Bradbury and Basil Blackett; ministerial colleagues Walter Runciman, President of the Board of Trade, Reginald McKenna, Home Secretary, Lord Crewe, Lord Privy Seal, and Lord Harcourt, Colonial Secretary; and Walter Cunliffe, Governor of the Bank of England, who was made Baron Cunliffe in recognition of his contribution. Paish, 47, had acted as Lloyd

George's informal economic adviser since 1909 being knighted for his services in 1912, an exceptional honour for a financial journalist (LSEA. Paish, 'My Memoirs'; Offer, 1983: 124–9; Middleton, 2004–10). Reading (Rufus Isaacs), 54, worked in the Stock Exchange as a young man before embarking on a brilliant career in the law that led to his appointment as Lord Chief Justice in 1913. With an office in the Treasury during the crisis he was 'a spare Chancellor', helping particularly to draft emergency legislation (Sayers, 1976: 68). A banker praised his 'clearness of mind and decisive action', while Lloyd George called his advice 'invaluable', recalling how 'his knowledge of finance, his mastery of figures, his dexterity and calm and sure judgement helped at many turns' (Matthews, 1969: 80; Lloyd George, 1938: 68). Montagu, 35, served as parliamentary private secretary to Asquith both as Chancellor in 1906–8, and Prime Minister in 1908–10, and was appointed Financial Secretary to the Treasury in February 1914 (Waley, 1964; Kaul, 2004–10). He was later described as Lloyd George's 'right-hand man' during the crisis, but that was not how it appeared to him at the time, writing to his mother late at night on Sunday 2 August that: 'My position is only that of scullery maid to the Government and the City. Panic follows panic, foreign office telegrams come hourly, hopes vanish and revive only to be dashed again—nothing but blackness ahead' (*The Times*, 'Obituary: Mr Edwin Montagu', 17 November 1924; Waley, 1964: 63).

6.8 CRISIS CONTAINMENT—THE MORATORIA

From Saturday 1 August the Chancellor and his advisers were in continuous crisis session at the Treasury for more than a week, calling in bankers and businessmen as required. Monday 3 August happened, providentially, to be the annual summer bank holiday so the banks and financial markets were closed. The first crisis containment measures were several moratoria that deferred liability for payments in a variety of ways, all without precedent. The closure of the Stock Exchange, instigated by market participants, was the first such firebreak. The government followed with three official moratoria. Anxieties about the solvency of the accepting houses when the markets reopened, because of interruption to remittances from abroad, prompted the proclamation of a one-month moratorium on the payment of bills of exchange on Sunday evening. Then on Monday, responding to 'considerable pressure' from bankers and businessmen, Tuesday, Wednesday, and Thursday were declared further bank holidays, creating an unprecedented four-day public holiday (bank moratorium) that provided time for 'reflection and wise counsels' (Hansard, HC, Postponement of Payments Bill, Lloyd George, vol. 65, col. 1807, 3 Aug. 1914; *Bankers' Magazine*, 'The Great Crisis VI', January 1915).

The priority was to prevent a run on the banks when they reopened on Friday 7 August. This was the foremost objective of the 'general moratorium' which provided that repayment of any debt or deposit made before 4 August could be postponed for a month. Exceptions included wages and, inevitably, taxes. Cunliffe considered the general moratorium an unnecessary hindrance to commercial activity, but the bankers insisted: 'they wanted security and more security', observed Bank of England historian Sir John Clapham, 'and it was given to them' (Clapham in Sayers, 1976: Appendix 3). It enabled them to refuse to pay out to depositors should a run develop, as well as relieving other businesses under pressure because of financial disruption. 'At the end of July, 1914, any citizen of London who was asked what a moratorium meant would probably have answered that there was no such word', mused Withers. 'Possibly he might have said that it was a large extinct woolly beast with big tusks. If he was exceptionally well-informed in matters of finance he would have replied that it was some sort of device used in economically backward countries for blurring the distinction between *meum* and *tuum*' (Withers, 1915: 1).

6.9 CRISIS CONTAINMENT—TREASURY NOTES

The other major crisis containment measure was the issue by the Treasury of currency notes with small denominations. The Treasury note issue was an alternative to the suspension of the Bank Act, which, despite the provision of the letter to Cunliffe, was never implemented. They were alternative ways of creating paper substitutes for sovereigns and increasing the supply of currency. 'We came to the conclusion after a very anxious discussion', Lloyd George told the House of Commons on Wednesday 5 August when he announced the emergency measures, 'that, on the whole it had better be a Government note on the security of the Government, and convertible at the Bank of England' (Hansard, HC Deb. State Financial Provisions, vol. 65 col. 1993, 5 Aug. 1914). A key difference was that suspension of the Bank Act meant suspension of the convertibility of Bank notes into gold, which was unnecessary if Treasury notes were issued. Indeed, the Treasury notes were made convertible into gold at the Bank, enhancing their acceptability to recipients. There were several further reasons for the preference for Treasury notes: (1) seignorage revenue—as Lloyd George observed, there was 'an advantage to the Government from a revenue point of view'; (2) Treasury notes were acceptable in Scotland and Ireland; and (3) the Bank's printing department was unable to meet the deadline (TNA. T170/56. Conference between the Chancellor of the Exchequer, Members of the Cabinet, and Representatives of the Bankers, Treasury, 5 August 1914). Nevertheless,

Cunliffe was not at all happy about 'this arrangement of yours' as he referred to the Treasury notes to Lloyd George, who recalled his 'deep resentment' (TNA. T170/57. Adjourned Conference between the Chancellor of the Exchequer, Members of the Cabinet, Representatives of the Bankers, Treasury, 6 August 1914; Lloyd George, 1938: 68).

The Chancellor told the House that he was 'proud to say' that after 'very careful consideration' it had been decided that 'it was not necessary to suspend specie payments'. In fact, Lloyd George was initially in favour of the suspension of sterling's convertibility into gold, which was advocated by the bankers to enable an expansion of the Bank note circulation and to prevent an external gold drain. Briefing notes on suspension were written by Paish and Keynes, the 31-year-old don arriving from Cambridge at the Treasury on Sunday 2 August in his brother-in-law's motorcycle sidecar (TNA. T171/92. Miscellaneous Memoranda by G. Paish and J. M. Keynes, 1–5 August 1914). Keynes argued forcefully and effectively against the suspension of convertibility. 'I've just heard that they consider I played an important part in preventing the suspension of specie payments', he wrote to his father on 6 August, 'as it was my memorandum [which] converted Lloyd George' (Skidelsky, 1983: 289).

6.10 TREASURY CONFERENCES AND RE-OPENING OF THE BANKS

Having determined the strategy—the moratoria plus the Treasury notes—Lloyd George sought comment and practical guidance from bankers and businessmen at a series of 'conferences' at the Treasury. At the invitation of the Chancellor, Austen Chamberlain MP, 51, Chancellor in the previous Conservative administration, joined the conferences and took the chair when Lloyd George was called away (Sir Austen Chamberlain, 1935: 105; Hansard, HC, State Financial Provisions, vol. 65, col. 1991, 5 Aug. 1914). On Tuesday 4 August, the Chancellor and his entourage met 'representative bankers and traders' (merchants and businessmen) (TNA. T170/55. Conference between the Chancellor of the Exchequer and Representative Bankers and Traders, Treasury, 4 August 1914). Discussion addressed the proposed general moratorium and its impact on the conduct of banking, commerce, and manufacturing. At 11 p.m., a few hours after the meeting broke up, Britain went to war with Germany.

The conferences on Wednesday 5 August and Thursday 6 August were with bank and City representatives and focused on the Treasury notes, the Chancellor stating at the outset that the decision to issue government notes had been taken and was 'too late to alter' (TNA. T170/56. Conference between the

Chancellor of the Exchequer, Members of the Cabinet, and Representatives of the Bankers, Treasury, 5 August 1914). Lloyd George mollified the bankers by announcing that Bank rate, which was to be lowered to 6 per cent on Friday 7 August, would be cut to 5 per cent 'if things go all right'. During an interlude when the bankers were conferring out of the room, Lloyd George expressed concern that 'lame duck' banks would 'exploit' the Treasury currency notes facility by borrowing more than they should. 'If there are lame ducks, it does not matter to us', Cunliffe responded. 'We have to help them over the stile. We cannot afford to let one bank go—not the smallest in the country' (TNA. T170/57. Adjourned Conference, 6 August 1914: 9).

During the long bank holiday politicians and the press campaigned against 'the folly of hoarding', which was denounced as 'foolish and unpatriotic', and even 'wicked' (*The Times*, 'The Folly of Hoarding', 4 August 1914). By the time the banks reopened public panic had subsided. 'When the banks reopened their doors there were no signs of anxiety on the part of the public', reported the *Globe*, a London evening paper, on the day. 'The public which was demanding gold for notes on Friday, is today demanding notes for gold' (*Globe*, 'Banks Re-Open', 7 August 1914). The moment featured in a popular contemporary novel by H. G. Wells, *Mr Britling Sees It Through*: 'When the public went to the banks for the new paper, the banks tendered gold—apologetically. The supply of the new notes was very insufficient, and there was plenty of gold' (Wells, 1916: 208). That afternoon Lloyd George reported to the House that returns from banks all over the country were 'perfectly satisfactory' (Hansard, HC Deb. vol. 65, cols. 2195, 2197, 7 Aug. 1914). 'I think congratulations are due to the Chancellor of the Exchequer', responded Chamberlain, as well as to 'our countrymen generally. I ventured to say two days ago that if the public kept its head the public would be safe. The public has kept its head'.

6.11 REVIVAL—RESTORING THE FOREIGN EXCHANGES

With the banks open and safeguarded, Lloyd George and his advisers turned their attention to the revival of the financial markets, focusing initially on the foreign exchanges and the discount market. A Foreign Exchange Committee of the English and Foreign Banks was formed on Saturday 8 August which provided expert advice to the authorities and led to the reappearance of published foreign exchange rates on 25 August. A new arrangement to overcome the difficulty of shipping gold in wartime was launched by the Bank of England on Monday 10 August (BEA. 'Bank of England, 1914–1921', Ch. V, ii: 246–51). Depositors of gold at the Canadian Finance

Ministry in Ottawa received a sterling credit with the Bank with which they could meet obligations in London. Similar arrangements soon followed with South Africa, India, New Zealand, and Australia (BEA. *Bank of England 1914–1921*: Ch. V, ii: 309–85; Ally, 1991: 221–38). Between 12 August and the final consignment on 16 December, the Ottawa facility received 286 consignments of gold totalling $105 million (£21 million).

Yet at first there was little movement in the sterling-dollar exchange rate, leading to the despatch in October of Paish and Blackett to Washington to negotiate the restoration of Anglo-American payments. 'Meanwhile', noted Lawson, 'natural causes, combined with a little patience, brought sterling back to a normal level' (Lawson, 1915: 268). Various factors, principally remittances via Ottawa, the resumption of cotton exports to Britain, and the beginning of Allied war purchases, propelled the sterling-dollar exchange rate towards its gold standard parity of £1 to $4.86. With the sterling exchange rate with the US and the major countries of the Empire 'nearly normal', on 16 January the Treasury issued a statement that the foreign exchange situation required 'no further government consideration' (Morgan, 1952: 22).

6.12 REVIVAL—DISCOUNT MARKET 'COLD STORAGE' SCHEME, 12 AUGUST 1914

A key objective, explained an official announcement, was to 'terminate the present deadlock in the discount market' whose revival would 'enable the trade and commerce of the country to resume its normal course... providing traders in this country with all the banking facilities they need' (official announcement in the *London Gazette*, 12 August 1914, quoted in *Bankers' Magazine*, 'The Great Crisis I', September 1914). The foremost problem, as it was perceived in early August, was the large volume of 'derelict' bills that had lost their negotiability, because of the war and the moratorium, which cluttered the balance sheets of banks and discount houses (*Daily Telegraph*, 'Financial Situation greatly Relieved by Bank's Action', 14 August 1914). It was estimated that there were £350 million of outstanding 'pre-moratorium' (pre-war) bills with the most problematic—those for which remittance was due from German, Austrian, and Russian clients—amounting to £100–140 million (TNA. T172/134. Conference between the Chancellor of the Exchequer, Members of the Cabinet and Representatives of the Accepting Houses, 12 August 1914). But it was anticipated that the war would be brief and that the problem was principally one of liquidity not solvency. 'Most of these bills are good and were the machinery of credit to be restarted the means of meeting them would soon be forthcoming', Paish told Lloyd George on

Thursday 6 August. 'All that is needed is the machinery for and the means of holding the bills until the money is received to pay them' (TNA. T172/183. Memorandum by Sir George Paish, 6 August 1914).

An original and audacious scheme to 'set the market going . . . to get rid of this tremendous incubus', as the Chancellor put it, was launched on Thursday 12 August to remove pre-moratorium bills—the 'troubled assets' of the day—from the money market (TNA. T172/134: 3; Announcement in the *London Gazette*, 12 August 1914, quoted in *Bankers' Magazine*, 'The Great Crisis', September 1914: 333). The plan was 'simplicity itself', breezed the *Financial Times*—the Bank of England, acting as the government's agent and indemnified by it against loss, would buy (discount) bills from their holders (*Financial Times*, 'Restarting the Credit Machine', 14 August 1914). Established practice was that the Bank would discount only the 'finest' commercial bills, but eligibility was thrown wide open encompassing 'also good trade bills and the acceptances of such foreign and Colonial firms and bank agencies as are established in Great Britain' (official announcement: 12 August 1914, quoted in *Bankers Magazine*, September 1914). 'Practically', commented Lawson, 'the Bank lowered its standard from first-class to second, and even third-class bills' (Lawson, 1915: 117). An attractive feature for sellers—principally the banks and discount houses—was that under the scheme the Bank waived the normal right of recourse to holders (meaning that the government relieved sellers totally of risk).

Lloyd George's 'cold storage scheme', as he called it, 'staggered' the City and was hailed 'almost ecstatically' by the press as a 'stroke of financial genius' (*Bankers' Magazine*, 'The Great Crisis', September 1914; Lawson, 1915: 118; *Sunday Times*, 'City Chatter', 16 August 1914). 'A dazzling example of how the solidarity of the government with finance, trade, and industry can be given practical expression in an emergency', was the verdict of the *Financial News*, while the Chancellor himself had become 'quite a national asset' (*Financial News*, 'Effect of Step Taken by Government to Enable Country to Carry on its Business', 14 August 1914). Yet there were a few dissenting voices. 'There is no doubt that the Chancellor of the Exchequer has become exceedingly popular in the City', observed the ever-sceptical 'Magpie' in the *Sunday Times*, but, he added presciently, 'it would be better to reserve extravagant praise until final success is assured, and in the opinion of the highest banking authorities further action may yet become necessary . . . To say that this measure is without precedent does hardly full justice to its unique character. For it is conceived on absolutely novel lines, never before adopted in this or any other country. In effect, it practically makes the nation responsible for financing its international business' (*Sunday Times*, 'City Chatter', 16 August 1914). The potential burden for taxpayers was a major reservation for *The Economist*, which warned that Lloyd George's 'extraordinary measure', taken in the interests of the banks and discount houses 'in the hope of indirectly reviving trade and credit', might, it calculated, cost the public purse from £50 million to £200 million depending on the length of the war (*The Economist*, 'The War, Trade and Finance', 22 August 1914).

Bill holders rushed 'pell-mell' to the Bank, £9 million worth of bills being discounted the first day (*The Statist*, 'Restoring Credit', 12 September 1914). 'So great was the pressure on the Bank that it became almost a physical impossibility to deal each day with the mass of bills presented', reported *Bankers' Magazine* ('The Great Crisis', September 1914). 'It was not simply to obtain the necessary financial accommodation, but to get rid of all liability on the part of the holder'. At the final reckoning, Bank purchases totalled £133 million—around a third of the discount market. This was state intervention in the financial system on an undreamt scale—72 per cent of 1913 central government expenditure; 5.9 per cent of GDP (Mitchell, 1988: 836).[3]

6.13 REVIVAL—ADVANCES TO ACCEPTING HOUSES, 4 SEPTEMBER 1914

Despite the Chancellor's 'heroic intervention', the discount market remained moribund. 'After a while it became manifest that merely enabling the holders of pre-moratorium bills to get those bills discounted was not sufficient', recounted *The Statist*. 'Those who had been in the habit of accepting were so alarmed by the great war which had suddenly been sprung upon them that they were afraid to perform their functions properly' (*The Statist*, 'Restoring credit', 12 September 1914). Montagu quickly recognized the flaw, writing to Lloyd George just three days after the launch: 'If I may be allowed to express an opinion, I think that you will have to amend your scheme, and that you will have to put endorsers in the same position as holders if you want the banks and Acceptance Houses to move' (TNA. T170/28, Edwin Montagu, Treasury Secretary, to David Lloyd George, Chancellor of the Exchequer, 15 August 1914). By leaving the accepting houses liable for unknown losses at an uncertain point in the future, the cold storage scheme did nothing to enable them to endorse new bills.

The Chancellor's answer was state-underwritten loans to that part of the banking sector, another unprecedented intervention. An 'enlarged scheme of assistance', as *Bankers' Magazine* called it, was launched on 4 September (*Bankers' Magazine*, 'The Great Crisis IV', December 1914). The Bank of England would advance funds to accepting houses enabling them to repay outstanding

[3] Total government expenditure in 1913 was £184 million, p. 590; gross domestic product at current prices in 1913 was £2,244 million, in 1914 £2,278 million, p. 836.

pre-moratorium bills on maturity, with the government guaranteeing the Bank against loss. The advances would cost borrowers 2 per cent above Bank rate, a steep premium relative to prevailing market rates, but repayment was deferred until one year after the end of the war. Through the provision that new endorsements would rank ahead of the advances from the Bank as claims, it was anticipated that firms would be able to resume acceptance business.

Reporting of the 'enlarged scheme' in the financial press was subdued, strikingly so when compared with the enthusiasm for the cold storage scheme three weeks earlier. 'Whatever may be said as to the wisdom, or otherwise, of this action on the part of the state', observed *Bankers' Magazine* guardedly, 'there can be no question that its unusual character and the prompt and courageous manner of its application will go down in financial history as one of the most remarkable features of the worldwide financial crisis occasioned by the war' (*Bankers' Magazine*, 'The Great Crisis II', October 1914). Holden's jaundiced view, recorded in his diary, was that the government had been captured by 'Huth Jackson and that other gang round the table of the Bank of England who have put the Chancellor in their pocket' (HSBC Group Archives. Holden Diary, 24 September 1914).

In total £74 million was advanced to acceptors under the enlarged scheme—40 per cent of 1913 government expenditure; 3 per cent of GDP (BEA. 'Bank of England, 1914–1921', i: 364). In aggregate, the two schemes meant taxpayer support for the banking system of £207 million, an astounding 9.2 per cent of 1913 GDP. The loans to accepting houses were used to pay off cold storage bills that had been bought by the Bank; by November 1914 the Bank's holding of pre-moratorium bills was down to £12.5 million (from £133 million) (Hansard, HC Deb. Mr Lloyd George, vol. 68, col. 1545, 27 Nov. 1914). Having initially eagerly taken up the offered funds, the accepting houses found that it was significantly cheaper to borrow from a bank than pay the Bank 7 per cent interest. Hence there were substantial pay-offs of the Bank's pre-moratorium bills advances. By August 1915, thanks to the resumption of remittances from abroad, the outstanding aggregate of funds provided under government guarantee—both (1) pre-moratorium bills bought by the Bank; plus (2) advances by the Bank to acceptors to pay off pre-moratorium bills—was down from a total of £207 million of payments to £39 million outstanding (Hansard, HC Deb. Statement by the Prime Minister, vol. 80, col. 448, 21 Feb. 1916). Thereafter, the outstanding bills for which remittance was awaited were mostly from enemy debtors.

Despite the Treasury's twin schemes to revive the discount market, in October commercial bill business was just 5 per cent of the pre-war level (*The Economist*, 'The Joint Stock Banks', 24 October 1914). By 1915 the expectation was that 'restoration to normal activity' would have to wait until the end of the war (*The Economist*, 'The Money Market', 23 January 1915;

Lawson, 1915: 122). Initially the fall was attributed to the 'drastic curtailment of home and foreign trade due to war conditions . . . the difficulties of the bill market have been rather a symptom than a cause. The bill market cannot *make* trade which does not exist, and the absence of bills merely testifies to the absence of trade' (Kirkaldy, 1921: 90; *The Economist*, 'The Banks and the Accepting Houses', 12 September 1914; Morgan, 1952: 303–14). As world trade adjusted and revived after the initial war shock, foreign merchants and bankers found means of finance other than the bill on London. This applied to British trade as well, it being reported as early as October 1914 that mostly it was 'now being done without the assistance of the bill on London' (*The Economist*, 'The Money Market', 3 October 1914). Moreover, more and more the government became 'the principal buyer of everything' conducting transactions not by bills of exchange but on a 'cash basis' (Spring-Rice, 1923: 427; Lawson, 1915: 122–35). Bold and imaginative as the cold storage and enlarged schemes certainly were, they addressed the perceived requirements of a pattern of activity that was rapidly being overtaken by new realities.

6.14 REVIVAL—LIFTING THE MORATORIA

'Of all the emergency experiments made in the first excitement of the financial crisis, the moratoria caused the largest amount of disturbance to business', stated Lawson (Lawson, 1915: 101). Potentially, the general moratorium was so restrictive that if stringently applied economic activity would have ground to a standstill, but in practice, banks and businesses exercised restraint in invoking it (Peters, 1993: 142–7). Nevertheless, it caused significant cash flow problems for firms because they were obliged to pay wages and taxes but had to await payments owed. The Treasury received a stream of complaints about the moratorium, but also about the conduct of the banks. 'I have had some complaints that the Banks are not quite playing the game so far as traders are concerned', Chamberlain told Lloyd George. 'I hear of builders and other trades who see their way to give employment but are checked by refusal of the facilities usually given to them' (TNA. T170/28. 'The Conduct of the Banks 1914'. Austen Chamberlain to Chancellor of the Exchequer, 11 August 1914).

On 19 August the government sent questionnaires to firms asking: (1) 'are the banking facilities now available reasonably comparable to those available before the war?' and, (2) whether they favoured lifting or retention of the moratorium when it expired on 4 September? Perhaps surprisingly, 86 per cent of respondents expressed satisfaction with banking facilities. As regards the future of the moratorium, 4,653 favoured lifting and 3,603 retention. Analysis of the results shows that manufacturers, merchants, and retailers wanted the moratorium lifted, while financial interests and exporters wanted it kept (TNA. T172/162. General Summary of Remarks). Despite the poll result, under pressure from the banks the Chancellor extended the moratorium twice, expiring finally on 4 November without difficulties (Lloyd George, 1938: 67; *The Times:* 'Moratorium Proclamation: The Final Extension', 1 October 1914).

6.15 REVIVAL—REOPENING THE STOCK EXCHANGE

'Though not the largest problem which the Treasury and the City bankers had to tackle', observed Lawson, 'that of the Stock Exchange was by far the most complicated' (Lawson, 1915: 124). An array of tortuous issues meant that the simplest course was to keep the Exchange closed, while pursuing government assistance. The biggest problem was the outstanding short-term debts of exchange firms, which after 'exhaustive investigation' were found to total £92 million nationally (*Bankers' Magazine,* 'The Great Crisis IV', December 1914; Morgan, 1952: 26). The lifting of the general moratorium threatened wholesale failure among stock exchange firms because with the market closed they were unable to sell securities to raise funds to discharge their debts. However, 'negotiations revealed that the Government was very unwilling to grant direct assistance to the Stock Exchange', noted *The Times,* 'presumably on the grounds that it would be giving help to a body of speculators who had only themselves to blame for the position they found themselves in' (*The Times,* 'The Stock Exchange: An Unprecedented Year', 22 January 1915).

Instead, the Treasury applied pressure on the banks for a *quid pro quo* for Treasury note drawings. Accordingly the bankers determined, as one of them put it, 'to behave like angels to their Stock Exchange customers' (Lawson, 1915: 125). The loan issue was resolved through a 31 October undertaking by the major banks not to call loans until one year after the end of the war—without any government guarantee against loss. Smaller banks that had not taken Treasury notes, which were owed half the outstanding loans, became eligible for advances from the Bank against the loans and were guaranteed by the state against 60 per cent of any ultimate loss. 'The Treasury', commented *The Economist,* 'has done as little as possible, and now leaves the Stock Exchange to work out its own salvation' (*The Economist,* 'The Stock Exchange Scheme', 7 November 1914). It turned out to be the least availed of the government schemes with Bank advances totalling just £520,000.

Agitation for reopening mounted among members who were frustrated by the growth of outdoors cash dealing in Throgmorton Street—'the trench' as it was known—and alternative forums for trading securities, including auction rooms and the small-ads columns of the *Daily Mail* (*The Times,* 'Stock Exchange: Scenes at the Re-opening', 5 January 1915; Michie, 1999: 148). With Treasury backing the Stock Exchange Committee proceeded on

18 November with the 'critical' settlement of the suspended mid-August account, succeeding 'with infinitely more ease than anyone had expected' (*The Economist,* 'The Critical Stock Exchange Settlement', 14 November 1914 and 'The Stock Exchange Settlement', 21 November 1914). Early December saw a marked advance in curb market prices, lifting them to around the level at the time of the exchange's closure. The recovery mitigated the danger to the banks from a premature re-opening stemming from significantly depreciated securities pledged as collateral for loans. On 23 December it was announced that the Treasury had sanctioned re-opening, but trading was to be subject to 'drastic' restrictions with minimum prices for transactions to forestall the threat to the banks as well as to make it easier and cheaper for the government to borrow. Hailing the reopening of the Stock Exchange on 4 January 1915, *The Times* declared that 'in the financial history of the war a new period begins today' (*The Times,* 'The Stock Exchange Reopens', 4 January 1915 and 'Stock Exchange: Scenes at the Re-opening', 5 January 1915).

6.16 CRISIS MEASURES AND WAR FINANCE

The effect of the authorities' 'benevolent operations'—the Treasury notes and the cold storage scheme—was a rapid accumulation of cash by the banks. But instead of providing credit to business, the banks placed the funds on deposit with the Bank of England. Lloyd George and his advisers had not expected this outcome. 'The last thing that they had wished for was an abnormal accumulation of money in Threadneedle Street', stated Lawson. 'There might easily have been a fresh crisis if the Chancellor of the Exchequer had not intervened once more as *deus ex machina*. This time he did not come as a saviour but as a borrower' (Lawson, 1915: 118). With mobilization costing £1 million a day the Chancellor urgently needed funds and 'the Bank of England and the Treasury suited each other admirably. The abnormal needs of the one fitted exactly into the abnormal resources of the other'. 'There will shortly be plenty of credit available for fresh business', wrote Edward Hilton Young, City editor of the *Morning Post* and one of the most astute crisis commentators (as well as a future Financial Secretary to the Treasury), 'that makes it an ideal moment for the Government to begin to borrow what it needs to finance the war' (*Morning Post,* 'A Time for Treasury Bills', 15 August 1914). Indeed, within days of the launch of the cold storage scheme on 12 August the Treasury invited tenders for £15 million of Treasury bills. The banks were eager buyers and the offer was three times oversubscribed allowing the government to secure the funds at the 'extraordinarily low' price of 3.65 per cent, 'so that in this direction alone the Government reaped a very great advantage from its bold policy in coming to the assistance of the money market' (*Bankers' Magazine*, 'The Great Crisis I', September 1914).

The outcome of the dearth of new commercial bills along with the government's hunger for funds, was the domination of the wartime money market by the Treasury bill: the volume of outstanding Treasury bills rose from £15 million in August 1914 to £1.1 billion at the end of the war in November 1918 (£1.2 billion at the peak in mid 1921) (Spring-Rice, 1923: 430–1). In fact, the absence of competition from commercial bills suited the government's war finance requirements very well.

While the Stock Exchange was in the throes of its 'anxious settlement', on 17 November the government launched a £350 million War Loan, 'the largest loan ever raised in the history of the world' Lloyd George told the Commons (Hansard, HC Deb. Mr Lloyd George, vol. 68, col. 1553, 27 Nov. 1914). Despite the shut Exchange, the loan was, according to the Chancellor, oversubscribed by applications from banks and small savers. 'Wonderful' exclaimed the *Daily Express*, but, in truth, the issue was a fiasco with the Bank of England covertly purchasing £113 million of the bonds (*Daily Express*, 'War Loan Letters of Allotment', 28 November 1914; Wormell, 2000: 82–3).

6.17 SAVING THE CITY

The management of the financial crisis of 1914 was a notable success and 'Saved the City'. Faced by an unprecedented systemic breakdown, the containment and revival measures effectively safeguarded the banks and City firms and restarted the stalled financial markets. Remarkably, there were no failures among major financial institutions, casualties amounting to just a dozen stock exchange firms, a minor discount house, and a small savings bank. The failure of prominent firms in financial crises generates panic and, if the house is systemically significant, may have serious contagion effects, as demonstrated by Overend Gurney in 1866 and Lehman Brothers in 2008. The avoidance of significant failures was an important achievement of the authorities' measures.

Crisis containment measures began along established lender-of-last-resort lines, with liberal discounting by the Bank of England initially without applying a penalty interest rate. But as discounting soared and the Bank's stock of sovereigns plummeted, it hiked Bank rate to crisis levels and sought the suspension of the Bank Act signalling to the Chancellor that it was time to take control of the escalating emergency. The Treasury's further containment measures—the moratoria and Treasury notes—were unprecedented in Britain, but had been used previously in other centres. For instance, moratoria were introduced in France in 1870, New York in the panics of 1873 and 1907, and in

Vienna in 1873, while government note issues had been used by France, Italy, and elsewhere at moments of fiscal stress. But the opening of the overseas gold depositories, the cold storage scheme, and the advances to acceptors scheme were imaginative and original.

Individual measures varied in soundness of judgement and effectiveness in the promotion of containment or revival. The bank holiday extension, the decision not to suspend sterling convertibility, the establishment of the overseas gold depositories and the Treasury note issue were well judged and effective, though the notes fuelled inflation later in the war (Morgan, 1952: 68). The general moratorium was more problematic, being arguably unnecessary and borne by business and the public for the benefit of the City and the banks, which did not live up to their responsibility to provide struggling customers with credit. So too the cold storage scheme, which was ineffectual in reviving the commercial bill market and characterized by *The Economist* as 'more remarkable for its boldness than for clearness of vision in those who advised it' (*The Economist,* 'The Financial Crisis of 1914', 24 October 1914). However, the scheme may well have forestalled failures among the discount houses and even the banks. Likewise the advances to acceptors scheme appears to have assisted the survival of accepting houses, both measures helping the avoidance of significant institutional failures. The unprecedented hike in Bank rate from 3 per cent to 10 per cent in three days was a traumatic experience for financial firms and unhelpful to crisis containment. So, unsurprisingly, a mixed record, but positive overall.

The foremost motive for the authorities' actions was to save the financial system, rather than to finance a war in which Britain was not even involved when the initial measures were introduced. However, the preservation of the City's established structure allowed the state to make use of its financial intermediaries and financial markets to meet its war finance needs: the Bank of England for Ways and Means advances; the discount market for sales of Treasury bills; the Stock Exchange for the issuance of War Loans; and the banks as buyers of government bills and bonds. As in wars since the late seventeenth century, Britain's financial robustness was a strategic strength.

Many of the containment and revival measures involved an increase in state intrusion into the financial and economic system: crisis management moved from the privately owned Bank of England to the Treasury; the state became an issuer of currency notes; state-proclaimed moratoria governed contractual relations; and the state (taxpayers) became guarantors of two major and several minor schemes of assistance to financial institutions, with risks of significant potential losses. These were fundamental departures from pre-war practice, though as it turned out they were not out of line with the advance of the state across the board in the conduct of a total war.

6.18 SAVING TAXPAYERS

How did taxpayers fare? Lloyd George warned the Commons in November 1914 that government guarantees might cost £50 million, observing that 'the total losses upon the whole of these transactions will not be equal to the cost of a single week of carrying on the War, and it saves British industry and commerce from one of the worst panics' (Hansard, HC Deb. Mr Lloyd George vol. 68, col. 1546, 27 Nov. 1914). *The Economist* was more pessimistic, putting the downside at potentially £200 million (9 per cent of gross domestic product), depending on whether the war lasted for a short or long period (*The Economist,* 'The War, Trade and Finance', 22 August 1914). In fact, no public account of the cost to the taxpayer of the 1914 government guarantees was ever presented. During the war the matter was secret; afterwards there were other concerns.

In 1915, the Treasury paid the Bank £39.5 million in respect of its holdings of outstanding cold storage bills and advances to acceptors. Thereafter, when the Bank received payment in respect of a discounted bill or an advance to an acceptor, the Treasury received a reimbursement. By 1916 outstanding cold storage and advances had fallen to £31 million (Hansard, HC Deb. Statement by the Prime Minister, vol. 80, col. 448, 21 Feb. 1916). On 31 August 1921, the 'official' end of the war, they were down to £15 million. Provisions of the Versailles Peace Treaty facilitated repayment of the bulk of outstanding German and Austrian pre-war debts (plus interest) (*Bankers' Magazine,* 'Pre-Moratorium Bills', 1921). A year later, when advances to acceptors became repayable, £197,000 was written off on account of 16 failed banks or financial firms (BEA. 'Bank of England, 1914–1921'). By then the total outstanding had been reduced to £4 million, most of which was recovered in subsequent years (BEA. C92/110, 'Advances O/A Pre-Moratorium Advances').

In December 1926, prompted by an inquiry from a leading City editor, the Treasury conducted an internal study. It calculated that it had received repayments (including interest) from the Bank totalling £46 million (against its payment to the Bank of £39.5 million in 1915) (TNA. T160/998, Letter from Sir Otto Niemeyer, Treasury, to Arthur Kiddy, City Editor, *The Morning Post*, 28 December 1926). Thus in the final reckoning, taxpayer support for the financial system, via Bank discounts and advances under government guarantee, during the financial crisis of 1914, netted the Treasury a nominal profit of £6.5 million. So a happy ending for taxpayers too as well as the banks and the City.

7

The Financial Crisis of 1931 and the Impact of the Great Depression on the British Economy

Nicholas Dimsdale and Nicholas Horsewood

7.1 INTRODUCTION

There is currently a revival of interest in the economic history of the interwar period and in particular in the Great Depression of the 1930s. This is exemplified by the recent collection of papers edited by Crafts and Fearon (2010). The last upsurge of interest occurred during the early 1980s, when unemployment emerged as a major problem facing most advanced economies. It is not surprising that the recent financial crisis and the severe recession, which followed it, have led to renewed interest in the 1930s. The impact of the international financial crisis which resulted in Britain's suspension of the gold standard needs to be reconsidered. In addition the effects of the Great Depression on the British economy need to be examined again.

In this chapter we examine the financial crisis of 1931, which led to Britain's departure from the gold standard and had widespread consequences for the international economy, as shown by Eichengreen (1992). Our focus here is on the British experience. First, we examine carefully the events which led up to the decision to leave the gold standard in September 1931. We provide an explanation for the crisis and the reactions of policymakers, which differs in some respects from the interpretation Eichengreen and Jeanne (2000), which is the most thorough recent assessment. We follow these authors in attempting to interpret the speculative attack which led to suspension in terms of the recent literature on currency crises.

The second question which we consider is the impact of the Great Depression of 1929–32 on the British economy. While the suspension of the gold standard insulated Britain's financial system from the crisis, it did not prevent this open economy from being exposed to the impact of the world recession of the early 1930s. We examine this issue by carrying out some simulations of the economy using an econometric model. The main question which we are seeking to address is why the effects of the downturn in Britain were relatively mild compared with international experience. Crafts and Fearon (2010) refer to this issue, which suggests that it may be useful to re-examine British experience, which was so different from that of other leading economies, such as the United States and Germany. We then examine how the economy was able to recover from the downturn of the early 1930s. This is an issue which has been extensively discussed by economic historians in terms of individual sectors, such as the recovery in housebuilding. The use of an econometric model enables us to make a broader assessment of the contributions of a number of elements in the recovery.

We carry out the simulations using an updated version of the macroeconomic model, which appeared in Dimsdale and Horsewood (1995). Eichengreen and Jeanne (2000) comment that the model is 'state of the art' and it has not yet been superseded. Its results are also assessed in Middleton (2010). By contrast with our earlier paper which was concerned with the possibilities of fiscal expansion, as advocated by Henderson and Keynes in *Can Lloyd George Do It?* (1929), we are now looking at the response of the economy to forces resulting from the international depression. We are focusing on macroeconomic behaviour rather than seeking to assess the effects of economic policy which is the concern of much of the literature, such as Howson (1975), Dimsdale (1981), and Middleton (2010). The main area of the economy in which we are interested is consumers' expenditure, since this was the main component of demand which showed resilience in the downturn. The role of consumption in the explaining the recovery of the1930s has been strongly advocated by Richardson (1967). Using our model we are able to explore its contribution more rigorously.

7.2 THE FINANCIAL CRISIS OF 1931 AND SUSPENSION OF THE GOLD STANDARD

Our starting point is a review of the British balance of payments in the 1920s as a background to the 1931 crisis. First we consider the issue of the overvaluation of sterling implicit in the decision to return to gold at the pre-war parity of \$4.86 to £1. Keynes claimed in 'The Economic Consequences of Mr Churchill' (1925) that sterling was overvalued by about 10 per cent, when the gold standard was reinstated in April 1925 at the old parity of \$4.86 to the pound. Keynes's choice of index numbers in his purchasing power parity calculations was later criticized. Nevertheless, subsequent writers using improved data have generally supported Keynes's view that sterling was overvalued by 10 to 14 per cent when

Britain returned to the gold standard in 1925 (Moggridge, 1972; Redmond, 1984; Dimsdale, 1981). A discordant note has been sounded by Matthews (1986) who has questioned whether sterling could have been overvalued, since the economy in the mid 1920s was close to the natural rate of unemployment. According to this view the level of benefits was the major factor contributing to the higher unemployment rate rather than the overvaluation of sterling.

Contemporary opinion was divided on the question of the degree of overvaluation of sterling in 1925 (Moggridge, 1972: 94–7). It was expected that in the event of sterling being overvalued, there would be a correction through either a reduction of British costs or alternatively by a rise in US prices relative to prices in the UK, brought about by an inflow of gold into the United States, leading to an increase in the money supply and a rise in prices (Moggridge, 1972: 91–2). There was, however, little evidence of an improvement in the UK's competitiveness relative to the US in the period 1925–1931, as shown by a comparison of British and American prices in Eichengreen and Jeanne (2000: 12, Fig 1.2). By 1931 there was a growing acceptance that sterling was overvalued relative to the US dollar. The most authoritative examination of this issue was in the Report of the Macmillan Committee (1931), which concluded that sterling was overvalued and examined a number of remedies for this problem. These included the raising of international prices or reductions in money wages, (Sayers, 1976: 390). Addendum I to the Report, which was signed by both Bevin and Keynes, rejected reductions in wages and argued for a tariff on imports, which would be used to subsidize exports. This was in effect a form of devaluation through the backdoor, while retaining the existing exchange rate (Macmillan Committee, 1931: Addendum I: 194–200). Devaluation itself was ruled out in the Majority Report, which favoured promoting a rise in world prices, but did not suggest how this might be achieved (Macmillan Committee, 1931: paras. 266–73).

The lack of competitiveness of sterling under the restored gold standard contributed to the high level of unemployment in the UK through both discouraging exports and forcing the Bank of England to adopt a relatively restrictive monetary policy, as indicated by an average short-term interest rate of about 5 per cent. In view of the downward trend in prices this implied a burdensome real rate of interest of about 8 per cent. Nevertheless the UK balance of payments showed a relatively comfortable current account surplus, which was lower in real terms than the surpluses achieved before 1914. According to Feinstein (1972) from 1927 to 1929 the surplus on the current account averaged 2.3 per cent of gross domestic product. There was a problem in that overseas long-term lending tended to exceed the surplus on the current account, implying that the basic balance (current account surplus less long-term capital outflow) was negative, which led Keynes to propose measures to make overseas investment less attractive. This meant that the UK's short-term liabilities were rising as the excess of long-term lending over the current account surplus had to be financed by short-term borrowing from overseas (Sayers, 1976: Appendix 32, Table C).

In the appendix of its report, the Macmillan Committee showed that sterling short-term liabilities exceeded short-term assets (Macmillan Committee, 1931: Appendix I, Table 9). As Sayers (1976: 389–90) pointed out, Britain was suffering from external illiquidity, which could make it vulnerable in a financial crisis. This was reinforced by a weakening of the balance of payments in 1931. The trade in services normally showed a surplus, which was sufficient to offset the deficit on visible trade (Feinstein, 1972; Sayers, 1976: Appendix 32). As the world economy fell into depression in 1931, international trade contracted, which had a damaging effect on trade in invisibles. As a result, the current account of the balance of payments recorded a deficit during 1931. The fundamentals of the British balance of payments showed signs of weakness, which would make sterling vulnerable in the face of an international financial crisis.

The European financial crisis began with the failure of the Austrian Credit Anstalt in August 1931 and failures among German banks occurred as financial contagion spread on the Continent. Both Germany and Austria imposed exchange controls, which restricted the freedom of short-term capital movements. This meant that British banks which had short-term claims on Austrian and German banks had their assets frozen. The institutions which were most seriously affected were the acceptance houses and particularly those which had a large business accepting Austrian and German bills. These acceptance houses faced the prospect that the bills which they had discounted would not be paid off at maturity. The houses were major providers of international bills to the discount market, many of which were later purchased by the clearing banks. There was, therefore, a risk of a crisis at the heart of the British financial system, as shown by Accominotti (2012).

The threatened crisis of 1931 was similar to the crisis which affected the London money market at the outbreak of war in August 1914. Richard Roberts assesses the latter crisis in this volume, and therefore there is no need to describe it in detail here. Suffice it to say that London's discount houses and acceptance houses faced the prospect of failure because some of their foreign bills remained unpaid due to the outbreak of hostilities. Thanks to a joint effort on the part of the Treasury and the Bank of England, a moratorium was introduced and enhanced market assistance was provided. In addition, an emergency paper currency in the form of Currency Notes was introduced and a run on the banks was avoided (Morgan, 1952: 9–19).

In August 1931, it was the introduction of foreign exchange controls rather than the outbreak of war which impeded the settlement of short-term debts, but the situations had marked similarities. Learning from its previous experience, the Bank recognized the threat which the freezing of chiefly German bills posed to the discount market. The Bank kept the frozen assets under close review and encouraged the view that these claims could be held in the money market, although the prospects for repayment were uncertain (Sayers, 1976: 509). In this way the threatened crisis in the London money market was avoided. The subsequent history of the frozen bills and the arrangements with debtors is discussed in Sayers (1976: 503–12) and Balogh (1947). The shortage of Treasury bills in the early 1930s due the Bank's funding policy may have made the discount market more willing to hold Continental bills (Clay, 1957).

Accominotti (2012) argues that the narrowly averted crisis in the London money market was a major factor weakening confidence in sterling and so contributed to the exchange rate crisis in September 1931. The main point which we wish to make here is that the threatened banking crisis did not occur, thanks to the response of the Bank. Hence Britain experienced only an exchange rate crisis in 1931, which was not combined with a banking crisis as in Germany.

The main events leading up to the suspension of the gold standard can be briefly summarized. The crisis began with the failure of the Austrian Credit Anstalt Bank on 11 May. It then spread to the German banking system and resulted in failure of the important Danat Bank on 13 July. The Berlin stock exchange was closed and exchange controls were introduced in Germany. On the same day the Report of the Macmillan Committee was published. This showed that the Britain had short-term liabilities which exceeded its short-term assets, thus revealing the potential vulnerability of Britain in the event of a speculative attack (Macmillan Committee, 1931: Appendix I, Table 9). In addition the short-term lending of British banks to Austria and Germany was effectively frozen as a result of the introduction of exchange controls in Central Europe, immobilizing Britain's short-term assets and aggravating the problem of sterling's illiquidity.

Bank rate which had been reduced to 2.5 per cent in May 1931 was raised by one point to 3.5 per cent on 23 July, but losses to the reserves persisted. Sayers (1976: 392) records that discussions took place in the Bank about whether to respond to gold losses by raising Bank rate or alternatively by seeking to negotiate credits, that is short-term loans, from co-operative central banks. The first policy was favoured by the traditionalists, while the international school favoured the use of credits from other central banks. It was agreed to raise Bank rate further to 4.5 per cent on 30 July and that credits would be sought from the Federal Reserve and the Banque de France. Both lenders recommended that pressure should be put on the Labour government to reduce the budget deficit. The Federal Reserve required assurance that sufficient gold would be available to repay the credits it was granting. This assurance required a rise in the Bank's fiduciary issue of notes to release additional gold reserves. Although it helped the negotiation of credits, this relaxation did not provide any assurance to those who had doubts about the commitment of the Bank to the gold standard. The announcement of the credits from New York and Paris coincided with the publication of the Report of the May Committee (1931) on public expenditure on 25 July. The Report called attention to the size of the budget deficit in an alarming way and argued for reductions in public expenditure, including a cut in the dole, that is unemployment benefits. It shocked financial markets, overshadowing the announcement of the credits, and there were renewed losses to the reserves (Sayers, 1976: 394–5).

On 5 August the Bank withdrew support temporarily from sterling, which fell below the gold export point and resulted in a heavy loss of gold. The Banque de France was critical of the Bank's tactics and urged strongly that credits should be used to support the exchange rate (Sayers, 1976: 395–6). The advice from Paris and New York was that Bank rate should not be raised, but both central banks looked for reductions in the budget deficit. The Bank also emphasized the need for 'self-help' and put increasing pressure on the Labour government to take action on the budget deficit. Between 10 and 23 August Sir Ernest Harvey, acting as Governor on account of Norman's illness, had eight meetings with Prime Minister Ramsay MacDonald on the issue of the budget deficit in addition to meetings with leaders of the opposition parties. On 13 August there were heavy losses of gold and the first instalment of credits was almost exhausted. Further assistance was sought from New York and Paris. The Bank was informed that further credits could be extended, but there must be a firm assurance over the reduction of the budget deficit. Morgan's who were the Bank's agents in New York urged that action on the deficit was a requirement, if they were to be able to raise funds from a syndicate of US banks (Sayers, 1976: 398). This is also confirmed by Morgan's records (Burk, 1989: 146–56).

From 22 to 23 August the Cabinet discussed the issue of Budget cuts urgently. No agreement could be reached, in particular on the issue of a reduction in the dole, and Prime Minister Ramsey Macdonald resigned (Sayers, 1976: 398–9). A National Coalition government was formed with Macdonald as Prime Minister and Snowden continuing as Chancellor. The new administration had the support of the Conservatives and the Liberals, but not of the bulk of the Labour Party. On 10 September Snowden introduced an emergency budget which included proposals to cut the Budget deficit. This enabled the additional credits from Paris and New York to be secured, but losses of reserves persisted at an increasing rate, such that the new credits were virtually exhausted by 18 September. Between 26 August and 16 September the losses to the reserves came to approximately £80 million, which implied the exhaustion of the recently negotiated credits. There were continuing losses in the following two days (Sayers, 1976: 399, 404–5). At this point the Bank decided to cease defending the exchange rate and the suspension of the gold standard was announced on 19 September. Throughout the final stages of the crisis Bank rate was held unchanged at 4.5 per cent, but it was agreed to raise the rate to 6 per cent after the departure from gold was announced.

There are number of unresolved issues in this account of events leading up to the suspension of the gold standard. The first issue was the failure of the fiscal measures introduced by the Coalition government to reassure the foreign exchange market. It had been expected that the Coalition would include all the major political parties, but in the event Labour, which was the largest party in Parliament, did not participate. It was believed by some market participants that Labour would win a majority in the approaching General Election and after regaining power would reverse the restrictive measures introduced by the Coalition. In the event this expectation was ill-founded as the Conservatives emerged as the dominant party in the election on 27 October.

Eichengreen and Jeanne (2000) provide an explanation of the crisis in terms of a second-generation model of currency crises, which makes the timing of crises unpredictable, provided certain conditions are satisfied. We argue that an alternative model of currency crises provides a better insight into the causes or the speculative attack on sterling.

The second issue, which we consider, is the failure of the Bank to use Bank rate to defend sterling in the final stages of the crisis. This was the traditional weapon for checking gold outflows as advocated by Bagehot (1873). The Bank's tactics in the 1931 crisis were strongly criticized by Sir Otto Niemeyer for not using a rise in Bank rate to strengthen sterling. He argued that sterling could and should have been defended by appropriate use of Bank rate (Sayers, 1976: 406). Eichengreen and Jeanne (2000) suggest that the Bank did not use the traditional weapon on account of the high level of unemployment, which stood at 20 per cent of insured employees in 1931. The Bank was well aware of this issue, having been criticized in the 1920s for raising Bank rate to strengthen sterling at a time of high unemployment. It had also been attacked over its reluctance to admit the connection between the Bank rate and unemployment in its evidence to the Macmillan Committee (1931). A similar view is expressed by Janeway (1995–6) who points to the growing political element in decisions over Bank rate compared with the operation of the pre-1914 gold standard. There is, however, another consideration which could help explain decisions on Bank rate policy. As we have seen, the Bank was heavily dependent on support from Paris and New York throughout the crisis. Neither source of support wanted Bank rate to be raised, but they urged action over the budget deficit with which the Bank concurred. A rise in Bank rate in 1931 would not have been helpful to other central banks, which were seeking to combat rising unemployment in their own economies. Within the Bank, Bank rate was coming to be seen as being less important than complying with the terms required to secure credits. Discussions which Sayers (1976) records relate largely to the negotiation of credits and efforts to secure budget cuts, but not to movements in Bank rate. These appear to have been downgraded in an era in which central bank cooperation was the main consideration. Clarke (1967) points to the importance of joint action by central banks in the crises affecting Austria and Germany. The Bank does not appear to have been much concerned about the high level of unemployment in its discussions before the suspension of the gold standard. Its chief concern was with the budget deficit. It brought unremitting pressure on the Labour government to tighten budgetary policy, which would have increased unemployment. A rise in Bank rate was generally preceded by losses of gold. When the Bank allowed sterling to drop below the gold export point in early August, this could well have prompted a rise in Bank rate. At this stage the Banque de France intervened to urge the use of credits in the form of holdings of foreign currency to support the exchange rate rather than allowing gold reserves to be depleted (Sayers, 1976: 395). Providers of credits were concerned that gold reserves should be retained to ensure that the borrower was able to repay the credit in due course. Central bank cooperation through provision of credits made traditional manipulation of Bank rate secondary. Such cooperation did not achieve its objectives on account of the failure of the Bank to secure cuts in the budget deficit.

We argue that neglect of the traditional use of Bank rate in the sterling crisis of 1931 is to be explained by the growth of international cooperation among central banks which made compliance with the terms of credits the main consideration for borrowers. These terms did not call for the use of the traditional Bank rate mechanism to induce gold flows between financial centres. They did, however, assume the ability of the central bank to influence decisions over budgetary policy. This assumption could not be satisfied by the Bank in the 1931 crisis, because of the priorities of the Labour government. Eichengreen and Jeanne argue that the high level of unemployment deterred the Bank from raising Bank rate to crisis levels. However the Bank was keen to reduce the budget deficit, even if this involved cuts in unemployment benefits and higher unemployment. The condition for receiving credits was curbing the budget deficit rather than a rise in Bank rate. The Labour government refused to curb the budget deficit which was growing largely on account of the rise in expenditure on benefits. From 1929 to 1931 expenditure of central government on national insurance benefits and other grants to persons rose from £190 million to £264 million, an increase of 39 per cent. At the same time the current budget recorded a deficit of £82 million in 1931, which was 2.1 per cent of gross domestic product at factor cost (Feinstein, 1972: Table 12). It is not surprising that the budget deficit caused concern as the ratio of public debt to nominal gross domestic product was 172 per cent in 1931, largely as a result of the massive accumulation of debt during the First World War. Action by the incoming Coalition to reduce the budget deficit was not sufficient to save sterling.

Eichengreen and Jeanne make an interesting attempt to interpret the events of 1931 in term of the modern theory of currency crises. The first generation crisis proposed by Krugman (1979) attributes crises to an inconsistency between the domestic monetary and fiscal policies of a government and its external objectives. Expansionary domestic policies can force a government to abandon its peg for the exchange rate. The foreign exchange market can anticipate this inconsistency in economic policy and so precipitate an exchange crisis. In the second-generation crisis the change in the exchange rate is precipitated by expectations which are self-fulfilling. Expectations of a crisis among agents are sufficient for an exchange rate crisis to occur. Fundamentals do not necessarily need to be weak, since at any time the foreign exchange market can decide to attack a currency and force the abandonment of its pegged exchange rate. This is the type of model which is used by Eichengreen and Jeanne to explain the sterling crisis of 1931.

Morris and Shin (1998) propose an intermediate model in which both fundamentals and self- fulfilling expectations play a part. They point out that the second-stage model leaves the timing of crises as indeterminate, whereas in their model the incidence of a crisis is at least theoretically predictable. They focus on situations in which there is common knowledge about the state of fundamentals and contrast this when such common knowledge does not exist and agents are confused about fundamentals. In such circumstances agents will start inferring the knowledge of other agents from their behaviour, leading to joint action which may force abandonment of the peg. This situation in which agents become confused about fundamentals can occur at a time when fundamentals may be improving.

This analysis provides some useful insight into the 1931 crisis. In the final days of the Labour government the fundamentals of sterling were generally agreed to be weak. This was due to the generally acknowledged over-valuation of sterling, the budget deficit, the deficit in the current account of the balance of payments and the excess of short-term liabilities over short-term assets on capital account. These facts were common knowledge among agents in the foreign exchange market. When the Coalition government came to power following the fall of the Labour government, the budget deficit was reduced and fundamentals had therefore improved in some respects.

There was, however, a widely held belief that a Labour government could soon be re-elected and the cuts in public expenditure would be reversed. This belief was reinforced by the fact that Labour was the largest party in Parliament and did not participate in the Coalition. There was an approaching election in which there were good prospects of a Labour victory. It was difficult for agents to form a view of the outlook for sterling. Fundamentals became confused and agents switched to acting interactively, so precipitating a crisis as analysed by Morris and Shin (1998). The critical factor leading to a change of market opinion in their model is confusion about fundamentals. This occurred under the Coalition government. Some agents may have accepted that the budget cuts introduced by the new government might strengthen sterling. Others may have expected that Labour would be re-elected at the forthcoming general election and that the budget cuts would be reversed. This gave rise to conditions in which a speculative attack could well occur as agents acted in accordance with what they believed other market participants thought about fundamentals.

7.3 THE IMPACT OF THE GREAT DEPRESSION OF THE 1930s ON THE BRITISH ECONOMY

The suspension of the gold standard as a result of the 1931 exchange rate crisis gave policymakers a greater degree of freedom. The depreciation of the exchange rate enabled Bank rate to be reduced after an interval. Lower interest rates helped to cushion the effect of the international downturn on domestic investment in Britain. Credit conditions could be relaxed as Britain had avoided the threat of a banking crisis following the suspension of the gold standard. Nevertheless the economy was exposed to the effects of a major contraction in world economic activity. In order to explore these issues in a quantitative way, we use an econometric model to examine the effect of the Great Depression on the British economy. This makes it possible to examine the effects of a number of influences on the economy. What we have to explain is how, despite a major setback to exports, Britain managed to avoid the worst effects of the world slump. Britain suffered less than other major economies, such as the US and Germany, despite its vulnerability to a major contraction of world trade as shown by Crafts and Fearon (2010).

In order to explore the effects of the Great Depression on the British economy we employ the model used in Dimsdale and Horsewood (1995), which has been updated in some respects. At that time the model was state of the art in that it reflected current applied macroeconomics. The model included an error-correction consumption of the form developed by Hendry (1983), which has been widely used in macroeconomic modelling employing the general-to-specific method of estimation. Investment was modelled using the approach of Bean (1981), which was an application of the Hendry methodology to investment. The supply side of the economy applies the model developed by Layard, Nickell, and Jackman (1991), which has been widely used in the analysis of labour markets. The emphasis placed on sticky wages and prices in the labour market makes the model consistent with a New Keynesian approach to macroeconomics. The short-term interest rate is set exogenously rather than by the Bank following a feedback rule of the kind proposed by Taylor (1993).

The approach to modelling which we employ represents only one of a number of ways of doing empirical macroeconomics. There is, as pointed out by Pagan (2003), a trade-off in empirical macroeconomics between models which emphasize the empirical data and those which emphasize consistency with economic theory. The approach used here is only one of several now available to researchers. It represents the middle ground in the trade-off between the empirical and the theoretical approaches to modelling. The model represents an intermediate position between a purely empirical approach to macroeconomics and an approach based on consistency with theoretical principles. These choices in modelling are conveniently discussed in Pagan (2003: 228). It should be noted that macroeconomic models of this intermediate type continue to be widely used by policymakers and forecasters, such as the National Institute and the Bank of England. They may also be useful to economic historians, but they may not be of interest to time series analysts or those seeking to calibrate theoretical models for reasons explained by Pagan.

The model is used to examine the effects of the Great Depression on the British economy and factors making for recovery in a series of simulations. Before reporting these results we look at some figures which show some of the features of both the data set and the relationships in the model.

Figure 7.1 shows GDP and unemployment. There was a decline in output in 1931–3 followed by recovery and the associated fluctuation in unemployment, which remained at a high level throughout the interwar period compared with both pre-1914 and post-1945 experience. The main feature of the course of gross domestic product is the mild decline of 5 per cent, which occurred in 1929–32. Figure 7.2 shows the relative stability of consumers' expenditure in the slump compared with the wider cyclical fluctuation in fixed investment. This stability is one of the main features of the British interwar economy and needs to be explained.

The main shock to the British economy came from the decline in exports which was closely related to the contraction of world trade 1929–32. Figure 7.3 examines the relationship between the volume of UK exports and the imports of major industrial economies. This indicator of international trade is computed in Andrews (1987). It suggests that the collapse of international trade in the depression had a major effect on British exports. By contrast UK imports showed much more resilience in the downturn, while there was a marked improvement in the terms of trade, due largely to the fall in import prices in the slump. This occurred despite the weakening of the exchange after the suspension of the gold standard Figure 7.4. Fixed investment is plotted in the next two figures. The revival of private sector housebuilding shown in Figure 7.5 was a major feature of the early stages of the recovery between 1932 and 1934. Investment in housing was sensitive to interest rates, here represented by the Treasury bill rate (TBR), which is a major feature in the

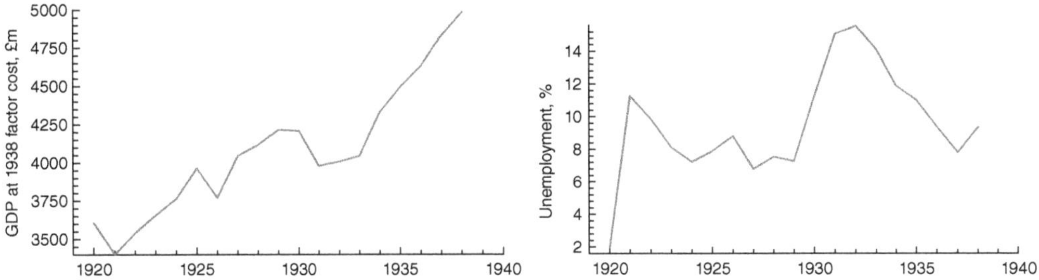

Figure 7.1. GDP and unemployment

Feinstein (1972), Table 5.

Feinstein (1972), Table 57.

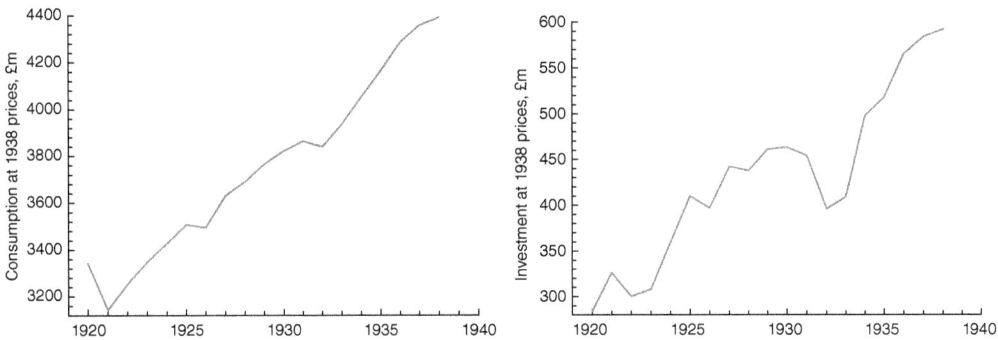

Figure 7.2. Consumption and investment

Feinstein (1972), Table 5.

Feinstein (1972), Table 5.

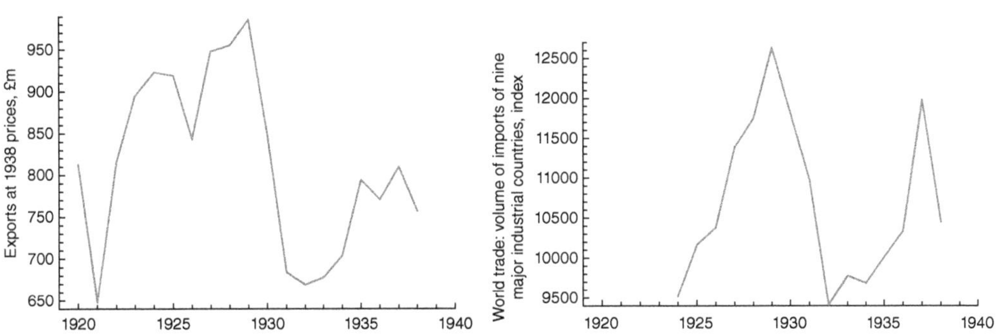

Figure 7.3. UK exports and a measure of world trade

Feinstein (1972), Table 5.

Andrews (1987), Table SA 4.

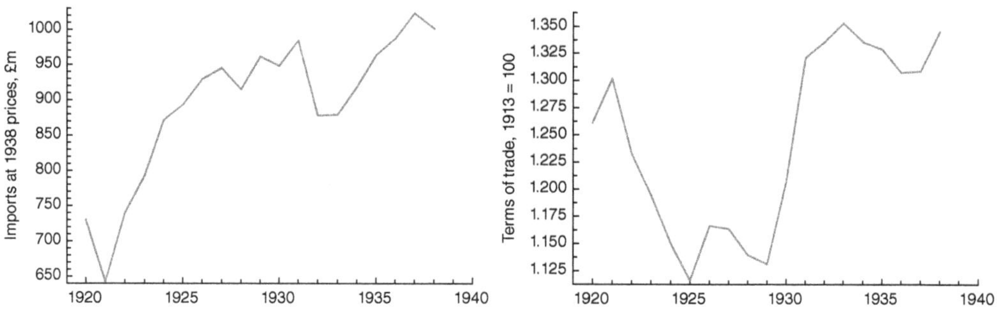

Figure 7.4. UK imports and the terms of trade

Feinstein (1972), Table 5.

Feinstein (1972), Table 64.

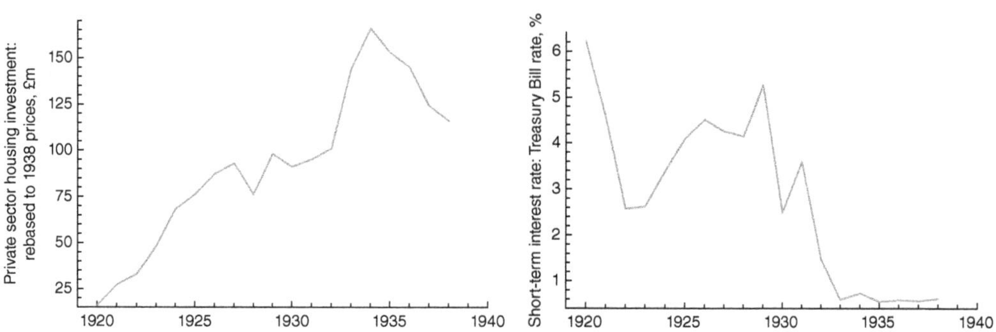

Figure 7.5. Investment in private sector housing and short-term rate of interest (TBR)

Feinstein (1972), Table 3.34.

London and Cambridge Economic Service (1971).

equation for housing investment. By contrast the revival of private sector investment, excluding housing, shown in Figure 7.6 came later in the recovery from about 1934 and it was highly responsive to gross domestic product. Hence the equation for this component of demand shows investment depending upon changes in output.

Figure 7.7 shows government expenditure on goods and services. It indicates that public spending on goods and services showed a good recovery from 1933, which became stronger after 1935 with rapidly growing expenditure on defence. Figure 7.8 shows the close relationship between civil employment and gross domestic product, which is a feature of the employment equation.

We next look at the relationship between the real product wage, that is the money wage divided by the price of output, and unemployment, which is shown in Figure 7.8. It will be seen that there was a rise in the real wage in the recession and real wages continued on a gradual upward course in the recovery.

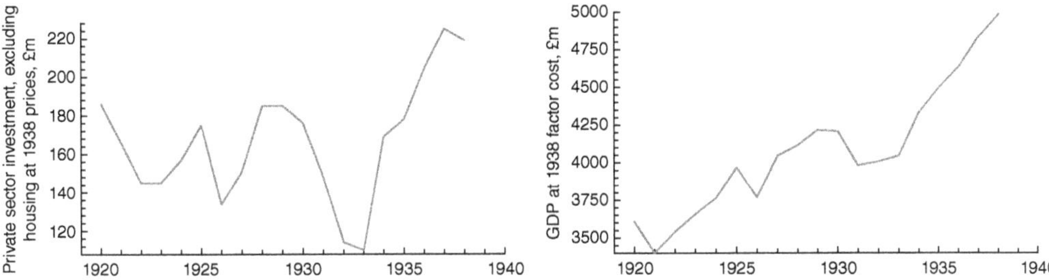

Figure 7.6. Private sector investment, excluding housing, and GDP

Gross fixed investment at 1938 prices in Feinstein (1972), Table 5, less housing investment and other public investment in Feinstein (1965), Table 3.34, rebased to 1938 prices.

Feinstein (1972), Table 5.

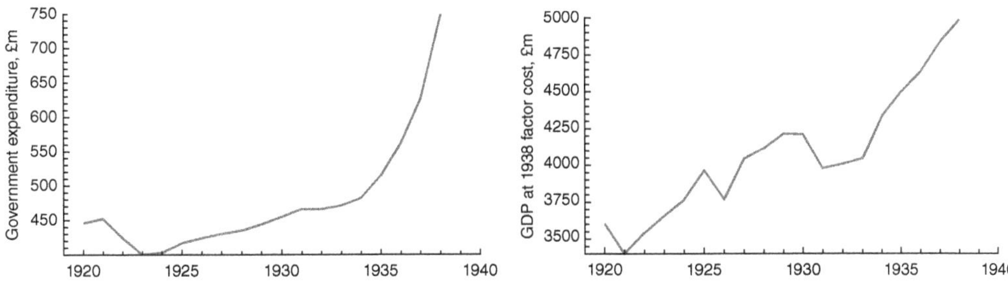

Figure 7.7. Government expenditure on goods and services and GDP

Feinstein (1972), Table 5.

Current expenditure on goods and services at 1938 prices, Feinstein (1972), Table 5, plus public sector investment, Feinstein (1965) Table 3.34, rebased to 1938 prices.

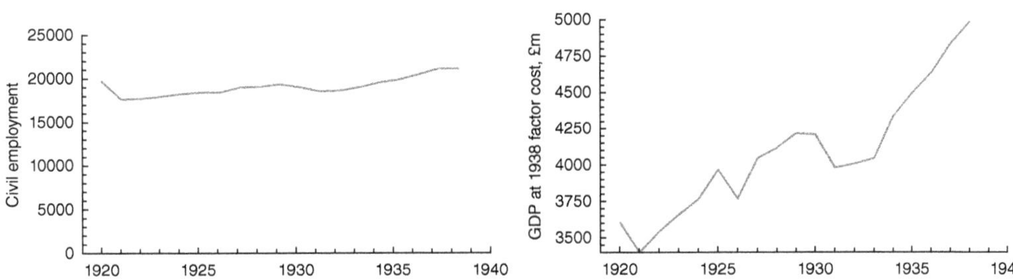

Figure 7.8. Civil employment and GDP

Feinstein (1972), Table 57.

Feinstein (1972), Table 5.

The impact of real wages on employment was not found to be high in the employment equation. The course of the real wage charted here is different from that shown by Eichengreen and Jeanne (2000). In their Fig 1.3 the real wage rises steeply in the depression and declines as the economy recovers from 1932. This difference may be explained by their use of the unsatisfactory Bowley monthly index of wage rates combined with the use of a cost of living index as a deflator, when what is needed is a measure of the price of output. The other main wage series available to us is the quarterly index of wage rates compiled by the Board of Trade, which gives a similar picture to Figure 7.8. The Board of Trade index of wages rates deflated by the price of output is shown in Dimsdale et al. (1989: 272).

Our model indicates that the Great Depression was transmitted to the British economy through a decline in exports. This reduced gross domestic product and checked investment. The world slump also caused a fall in import prices, reflecting largely the decline in the price of food and raw materials. The fall in the cost of living combined with stickiness in money wages resulted in a rise in the real consumption wage. As the demand for labour was found to be relatively inelastic with respect to the real wage, higher real wages did not have a large effect in reducing employment. The rising real wages of those in employment enabled real personal income to rise in the downturn and also consumer spending, which was highly dependent upon it. Thus both personal disposable income and consumers' expenditure rose in the depression years (Figure 7.9).

In the recovery there was some growth of exports due to a gradual revival in world trade and also the depreciation of sterling following suspension of the gold standard. While the recovery in world trade was limited, activity was higher than the depressed levels of 1931–2. There was strong growth in private housebuilding in 1932 and later on in private industrial investment. The rise in housebuilding was largely attributable to the fall in interest rates after the suspension of the gold standard, while the recovery in gross domestic product from 1933 induced higher industrial investment. Rising government spending on goods and services was a feature of the recovery from its early stages and this was reinforced by the rapid growth of expenditure on rearmament from 1935.

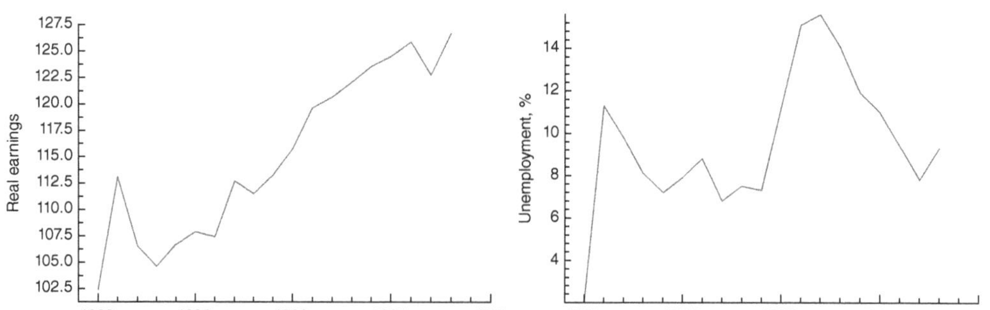

Figure 7.9. Real earnings and unemployment

Wages and salaries deflated by the total final expenditure deflator, Feinstein (1972), Tables 10 and 5. Feinstein (1972), Table 57.

7.4 SIMULATION RESULTS

We carry out a series of simulations of the model. The first group of simulations relates to the effects of the suspension of the gold standard and the worldwide depression on the British economy. The second group looks at the forces making for recovery in the later 1930s. The results of the simulations are expressed as percentage of base run values. These are defined as the output generated by the model when the exogenous variables take their actual values. We do not discuss long-run effects, since we concentrate on the effects achieved in the period up to 1938.

7.4.1 The Effects of the Great Depression on the British Economy

First we look at the effect of holding the exchange rate at the 1929 level of $4.86/£1 and the Treasury bill rate at the average 1931 level of 3.6 per cent. Simulation 1 compares the result of holding sterling and the Treasury bill rate at the pre-devaluation parity with the base run in which sterling is devalued and the Treasury bill rate follows its actual course.

We find that holding the exchange rate at the 1929 level would have reduced exports by 20 per cent in 1932–4 and gross domestic product by 5 to 6 per cent. The combination of a higher interest rate and lower gross domestic product would also have reduced fixed investment, investment in private sector housing falling by 25 per cent and in non-housing investment by about 20 per cent. The decline in consumer spending is 5 per cent, while employment falls by 3 per cent. It is a feature of the model that the change in employment is less than that of gross domestic product.

In Simulation 2, world trade is held at the 1929 level, implying a considerably higher level of activity than that experienced in the early 1930s. It results in exports being 40 per cent higher than the depressed level of 1932–3 and gross domestic product is 11 to 12 per cent higher than in the base run. As a result of the higher level of activity both consumers' expenditure and employment rise by 5 per cent. Non-housing investment benefits from the higher level of gross domestic product, but the effect on investment in private sector housing is smaller.

It may be concluded that the fall in world trade in the early 1930s had a major effect on British exports, gross domestic product, and employment. As exports were 32 per cent of gross domestic product in 1929, it is not surprising that their decline had a major impact on gross domestic product. The effect of the fall in world trade, which is included in the base run, reduced consumers' expenditure by 5 per cent. In fact there was a rise in consumers' expenditure in 1929–32, despite the decline in world trade and exports, which needs to be explained. We shall consider this issue after reporting the results of the next simulation.

Simulation 3 examines the effect of holding the Treasury bill rate at the average 1929 level so that there is no benefit from the cheap money policies of the 1930s. The higher interest rate has a negative impact on private house-building, which is reduced by 30 per cent in 1933–4 compared with the base run, but the effects on non-housing investment, consumption, and gross domestic product are considerably smaller. While private sector housebuilding is sensitive to the interest rate, it is a relatively small component of expenditure, which may explain its limited effect on movements in gross domestic product. Private sector housing investment was only 2 per cent of gross domestic product in 1929 and at its peak in 1934 it reached 4 per cent of gross domestic product (Feinstein, 1965, 1972). Our simulation results suggests that the effects on the level of activity of the boom in housebuilding in the 1930s was less than claimed by Worswick (1984) and see also the useful discussion in Howson (1975: 108–16).

Since the effects of a higher interest rate in our simulation appear to have been relatively modest, it would appear that the impact of the exchange rate was more powerful than that of the interest rate in Simulation 1, which includes both effects.

We return to Simulation 2 on the effect of world trade being held at the 1929 level, because it is of interest in explaining the behaviour of consumers' expenditure. We have seen that consumption is raised by 5 per cent in 1932–3 by the higher level of world trade relative to the base run. This result implies that the effect of the fall in world trade was to reduce consumption by 5 per cent. As consumption actually rose by 5 per cent from 1929–32, there is a difference of 10 per cent which needs to be explained. However both the base run and the simulation include the effects of the decline in import prices on consumption. In the Great Depression of 1929–31 import prices fell by 25 per cent and both consumer prices and the price of final output fell by 10 per cent. In the consumption function of the model a reduction of 10 per cent in the consumer price index raises both real personal income and consumption by 10 per cent. What happened in the Great Depression was that the reduction in consumption due to the decline in world trade was more than offset by the impact of the decline in import prices. Consumer prices declined which raised real disposable income and hence consumption. This reconciles the effects of the decline in exports in reducing employment with those of falling prices in raising consumer spending due to lower import prices.

The dynamic effect of falling prices is important in the consumption function of the model and also that of Hendry (1983). We have carried this work further in estimating a quarterly consumption function for the UK in the interwar period, comparing the results with US and German experience (Dimsdale, Horsewood, and Van Riel, 2006). We find that the consumption function for non-durables has similar price effects to the results reported for the aggregate consumption function in the annual model used in our simulations.

These results for consumption support the views of those economic historians, such as Richardson (1967), who have pointed to the rise in consumer spending in 1931–2 in moderating the impact of the Great Depression on the UK. We have tried to explain the processes which produced this outcome which has not been addressed by previous writers. In particular it is necessary to explain why the rise in real wages associated with the fall in consumer prices, combined with stickiness in money wages, did not have a major effect in reducing employment and hence the aggregate real income of employees. The employment function of our model shows that the demand for labour was relatively inelastic with respect to the real wage, so that a rise in the real product wage did not have large effects on employment. The real wage bill, that is employment times the real wage, rose as a result of the fall in prices, due to the higher real wages of those who were still employed. The real wage bill is the predominant constituent in real personal income. Hence real personal disposable income and consumption could rise at a time of rising real wages, despite the decline in employment. This enabled rising consumption to offset the effects of the large negative shock due to the decline in exports. As a result the impact of the Great Depression on the British economy was remarkably mild, compared with the experience of other leading economies, such as the US and Germany. Crafts and Fearon (2010: 287) give a useful comparison of Britain and the United States in the Great Depression.

7.4.2 Simulations of the Recovery

In the next group of simulations we look at factors contributing to economic recovery in the 1930s. Simulation 4 holds the level of world trade at its low point of 1932. This has a discouraging effect on exports, which are reduced by more than 25 per cent in 1937 compared with the base run. Non-housing investment falls by 20 per cent as it is highly responsive to movements in gross domestic product, which declines by more than 8 per cent in the wake of the reduction in exports. Employment is reduced by 3 per cent. The effects on private sector housing investment and on consumers' expenditure are smaller. The result of this simulation is to show that a failure of world trade to revive would have had serious consequences for the recovery of the UK in the later 1930s. Although world trade was lower in the late 1930s than in 1929, there was an important recovery compared with the depressed levels of 1932. Since exports were a major component of gross domestic product, even a comparatively modest recovery in export volumes made an important contribution to economic recovery in the later 1930s.

The effects of lower interest rates on the recovery have already been examined in Simulation 3. These are found to be strong for private sector housing, but the effects on consumption and gross domestic product are relatively modest. It should be noted that this refers only to the direct effects of lower interest rates on domestic demand. It does not take account of the effect of lower interest rates on activity via the weakening of the exchange rate. In our model the exchange rate is exogenous since the level of sterling is assumed to be set at the level desired by the policymakers rather than being determined as a freely floating exchange rate. This accords well with the account of the management of sterling after the suspension of the gold standard in Howson (1980).

Our last two simulations examine the effect of public expenditure on the recovery. In Simulation 5 defence expenditure is held at the 1935 level, which is considerably lower than the actual level of expenditure included in the base run. The results suggest that gross domestic product would have been reduced by about 2 per cent of gross domestic product in 1937–8, if expenditure had been held at the 1935 level. The dynamic effects on consumption may not have had time to work themselves out fully, so the long-run effects could be larger than allowed for in a simulation which does not go beyond 1938. The reduced level of defence spending has a discouraging effect on non-housing investment which is 8 per cent lower in 1937–8, but the effects on consumption are smaller. These results for defence expenditure can be compared with those found by Thomas (1983). The effects which we find here are smaller than those which he reports. Defence spending was 2.8 per cent of gross domestic product in 1935 and reached 6.4 per cent in 1938. Our model indicates that the impact of rising defence expenditure from a low base meant that it did not have a major effect on output and employment up to 1938.

Our last simulation holds public expenditure at its 1932 level. Expenditure in Simulation 6 includes current public expenditure on goods and services and public sector investment. The simulation shows public expenditure as having major effects on the economy. If expenditure had been held at the 1932 level, gross domestic product would have been reduced by 7 to 8 per cent in 1937–8 with marked effects on non-housing investment. Consumer spending would have been reduced and employment lowered. While the growth in the broader measure of public spending is less than that in defence spending, it is a considerably larger aggregate, which enables it to have a larger effect on gross domestic product.

Overall it would appear that the limited recovery of world trade made a major contribution to the revival of the later 1930s. It also seems that government spending, broadly defined, was important in the recovery. Effects are much smaller if the increases in public spending are confined to expenditure on defence from 1935. In addition we do not find major effects of lower interest rates via private sector housebuilding on gross domestic product. This is due to investment in private housebuilding being a relatively small component in national expenditure.

7.5 CONCLUSIONS

We have first discussed the events leading up to the decision to suspend the gold standard in 1931. We conclude that cooperation among central banks was crucial in the operation of the restored gold standard. By contrast movements in Bank rate were downgraded and were less important than before 1914. The main effort of the Bank was directed towards putting pressure on the Labour government to reduce the budget deficit. Cuts in the deficit were necessary for the Bank to be able to secure credits which would enable it to defend sterling. Failure to resolve this issue resulted in the fall of the Labour government and its replacement by a National Coalition, which was willing to make reductions in government expenditure. At this time the political situation became confused, as it was widely believed that Labour might win the rapidly approaching general election leading to confusion on the foreign exchange market. Our interpretation is based on an examination of the full account of the events leading up to the 1931 crisis in Sayers (1976).

We argue that the crisis in the exchange rate was due to the relatively weak position of sterling combined with confusion in the foreign exchange market about the state of fundamentals after the fall of the Labour government. For this part of our argument we rely upon the model of exchange rate crises proposed by Morris and Shin (1998).This emphasizes that it is not the weakness of fundamentals itself which precipitates a crisis. Such an event could occur at a time when the underlying state of a currency is improving, but the foreign exchange market is confused about prospects. In this case it was the general belief, which proved to be erroneous, that Labour would be re-elected in the impending election and the measures taken by the Coalition to reduce the budget deficit would be reversed. Hence the attack on sterling, which set off the crisis, occurred at a time when fundamentals were improving. In the event the fears of agents about the return of Labour to power proved to be groundless as the Coalition won the election comfortably.

The suspension of the gold standard and the depreciation of sterling meant that the British financial system was largely insulated from the international financial crisis. The impact of the ensuing Great Depression was felt through the decline in British exports associated with the contraction of world trade. By contrast Britain benefited from the marked improvement in the terms of trade due to the sharp fall in imports prices. These forces tended to offset each other and the outcome was that the contractionary pressures on gross domestic product were not severe.

We explore these issues using an econometric model in Dimsdale and Horsewood (1995), which is now fairly familiar to economic historians. It has been cited by Eichengreen and Jeanne (2000) and Middleton (2010). The model can explain the stability of consumers' expenditure despite shocks to the economy. It was this which enabled gross domestic product to be resilient in the face of a sharp decline in exports and a setback to non-housing investment. The key factor was the fall in import prices, which, combined with sticky money wages, raised real wages. As demand for labour was relatively inelastic, the real wage bill and real disposable income could rise. This boosted consumption which rose in 1929–32, so partly offsetting the effect of the decline in exports.

In the recovery, the reduction of interest rates made possible by the departure of sterling from the gold standard contributed to the revival of private sector housebuilding, but this effect does not appear to be very powerful. The economy benefited from the modest recovery in world trade after 1933. In addition public expenditure, broadly defined, made an important contribution which exceeded the effects of the surge in expenditure on rearmament from 1935.

We conclude that our model gives a plausible account of the factors contributing to both the downturn and the recovery. It brings out the key role played by consumer spending in moderating the effects of the recession of the early 1930s.

APPENDIX—INTERWAR SIMULATIONS

List of Variables:

CE Consumers' expenditure
HINV Private sector housing investment
NHINV Private non-housing investment
EXP Exports
CEMP Civil employment
TBR Treasury bill rate

For data sources see Dimsdale and Horsewood (1995: 380–1, 396).

Simulation 1. Exchange rate held at 1929 level and TBR at 3.59% (1931 level).

Years	CE	HINV	NHINV	EXP	GDP	CEMP
1930	−0.01	−0.05	−0.25	−0.25	−0.07	−0.02
1931	−0.17	−0.65	−3.55	−4.09	−1.03	−0.26
1932	−0.95	−5.70	−16.86	−16.80	−5.05	−1.40
1933	−2.03	−25.88	−23.92	−20.68	−6.87	−2.47
1934	−2.52	−26.35	−16.97	−13.12	−5.71	−3.18
1935	−2.47	−20.78	−2.87	−8.21	−3.37	−2.83
1936	−1.58	−15.62	−10.24	−2.59	−0.96	−1.46

Deviation % from base run

Simulation 2. World trade held at 1929 level

Years	CE	HINV	NHINV	EXP	GDP	CEMP
1930	0.68	2.93	15.84	14.82	4.40	1.09
1931	1.87	3.84	36.42	27.90	8.35	2.52
1932	3.63	7.23	48.13	40.17	11.78	4.61
1933	5.16	7.88	41.89	39.63	12.17	5.86
1934	5.18	6.13	7.64	14.16	6.12	4.87
1935	3.89	6.41	−17.15	2.76	1.40	2.66
1936	1.87	4.56	−25.61	−6.27	−1.68	0.00

Simulation 3. Effect of interest rates on activity

Years	CE	HINV	NHINV	GDP
1930	−0.17	−4.50	−3.68	−1.09
1931	−0.36	−30.04	−3.29	−0.704
1932	−0.09	−22.91	−4.09	−1.45
1933	−0.16	−34.57	−3.25	−1.11
1934	0.25	−38.90	−0.96	−0.87
1935	0.80	−32.17	1.74	−0.22
1936	1.32	−26.69	4.92	0.56

Holding TBR at 1929 level of 5.26%

Simulation 4. World trade and economic recovery

Years	CE	HINV	NHINV	EXP	GDP	CEMP
1933	−0.23	−0.98	−5.13	−6.50	1.53	−0.37
1934	−0.64	−1.31	−10.34	−9.29	−2.77	−0.85
1935	−1.25	−2.55	−13.57	−13.22	−4.07	−1.59
1936	−2.01	−3.71	−16.99	−18.90	−5.67	−2.38
1937	−2.88	−5.38	−21.60	−25.52	−7.78	−3.24
1938	−3.36	−5.23	−15.57	−20.22	−6.40	−3.37

World trade variables held at 1932 level

Simulation 5. Expenditure on defence and recovery

Years	CE	HINV	NHINV	EXP	GDP	CEMP
1936	−0.08	−0.35	−1.88	0.01	−0.55	−0.13
1937	−0.36	−1.02	−6.67	0.06	−1.87	−0.51
1938	−0.75	−1.42	−9.27	0.15	−2.55	−0.94

Defence spending held at 1935 level

Simulation 6. Government expenditure and recovery

Years	CE	HINV	NHINV	GDP	CEMP
1933	−0.02	−0.10	−0.55	−0.16	−0.04
1934	−0.11	−0.30	−1.99	−0.55	−0.15
1935	−0.35	−0.96	−5.70	−1.63	−0.49
1936	−0.81	−1.80	−11.02	−3.20	−1.05
1937	−1.54	−3.21	−16.79	−5.20	−1.91
1938	−2.78	−5.96	−25.86	−8.72	−3.38

Government spending on goods and services held at 1932 level

8

Holding Shareholders to Account

British Banking Stability and Contingent Capital

John Turner

8.1 INTRODUCTION

Until 2008, the British banking system was regarded as one of the most stable in the world. This chapter[1] will seek to explain why it enjoyed such enviable stability and why it is necessary to look back to 1825 to find a systemic banking crisis in Britain on a par with the one that engulfed the banks in 2008. It is suggested that a key reason for the relative stability of the system was the role played by contingent capital.

For a large part of the period between 1825 and 2008 constraints were placed on banks' risk-taking by the presence of contingent capital, that is capital above and beyond that which shareholders had invested in a bank, and which was callable in the event of bank failure. From the genesis of joint-stock banking in 1825 until the early 1880s, contingent capital took the form of unlimited shareholder liability, and from this point until its demise in 1958, contingent capital in British banking took the form of uncalled capital, that is, fixed amounts of capital per share which could be called in the event of bank failure. As contingent capital resulted in managers and shareholders bearing substantial downside risk, this discouraged them from risk shifting (i.e. opportunistically increasing asset risk) at depositors' expense. Ultimately, it was the presence of this contingent capital which guaranteed the stability of

[1] This research was conducted during my tenure as the Alfred D. Chandler Jr Fellow at the Harvard Business School. Thanks to HBS for their hospitality. Thanks also to Sarah Millard, Jenny Mountain, and Kath Begley of the Bank of England's Archives and Information Centre for helping me negotiate the Bank's records. Earlier versions of this chapter were presented to Oxford University's Monetary History Group and the Munich symposium organized by Instituts für Bankhistorische. Thanks to Nicholas Dimsdale, Avner Offer, and Luke Samy for their comments.

the banking system. The analysis in this essay of banking crises over the long run finds that although bank failures occurred in the era of contingent capital, there were no systemic banking crises.

Although contingent capital was commonplace in other banking systems, particularly in their formative years, there have been few studies of its stability-enhancing role. For example, double liability in the US national banking system was effective at protecting depositors, and contingent liability discouraged bank risk-taking in the early-twentieth-century US banking system (Esty, 1998; Macey and Miller, 1992; Grossman, 2001). Similarly, a study of the history of early joint-stock banking systems around the world found that the presence of unlimited liability was correlated with the stability of these banking systems (Hickson and Turner, 2004). This chapter augments these studies and argues that contingent liability played a vital role in the stability of the UK banking system for over a hundred years.

Section 8.2 of this chapter explains how contingent capital enhances banking stability. Section 8.3 traces the long history of contingent capital in British banking. Section 8.4 assesses the stability of the British banking system since 1825, and discusses the correlation between contingent capital and banking stability. Section 8.5 addresses criticisms of contingent capital, which if true would effectively mean that contingent capital was worthless, and played no role in enhancing British banking stability. The concluding section suggests that although contingent capital may be a solution which ensures the long-run stability of the banking system, it is probably not a solution with a lot of political support.

8.2 WHY DOES CONTINGENT CAPITAL RESULT IN STABLE BANKS?

Banks engage in credit intermediation by taking in funds from depositors and lending them to borrowers. As the vast majority of deposits are usually lent out, the largest asset of a commercial bank is its loan portfolio. Loan portfolios are extremely fungible assets for at least two reasons. Firstly, borrowers value discreetness, implying that information about loans cannot be released into the public domain. Secondly, by releasing private information about loans into the public domain, banks can only earn partial returns on their investment in information gathering. Although, from a theoretical perspective, the high fungibility of the loan portfolio suggests that banks should be predominately funded by shareholder equity, the fundamental nature of banks (i.e. credit intermediation) means that they are highly leveraged institutions. This creates all sorts of incentives for bank managers to risk shift (i.e. shift the loan portfolio surreptitiously into riskier assets than promised *ex ante*), which can potentially threaten the stability of the banking system. This raises a couple of related questions. What prevents bank managers from risk shifting? What incentives do managers of commercial banks have to run their banks in a prudent manner, consistent with the stability of the wider system?

Depositors could restrain managers by monitoring banks and removing funds if they suspect that managers are risk shifting. The potential free-rider problem could potentially be overcome by relying on large depositors (England, 1988). Indeed, the sequential service rule of demand deposit contracts may actually incentivize large depositors to invest in monitoring, and thus ameliorate the free-rider problem (Calomiris and Kahn, 1991). Depositor discipline of this sort, however, runs into at least two difficulties.

Firstly, a combination of explicit deposit insurance, *ex post* bailouts and implicit too-big-to-fail policies weakens the incentives of depositors to engage in monitoring (Minsky, 2008: 282). Although it is traditionally believed that constructive ambiguity reduces the moral hazard associated with such implicit government guarantees, there is a time inconsistency problem associated with any such *ex ante* attempts by the authorities to commit themselves to not bail out banks that get into difficultly.

Secondly, and more fundamentally, as already discussed above, information concerning a bank's loan portfolio is private, and cannot be disclosed to depositors without damaging a bank's invaluable reputation for discreetness and reducing its return on its private-information gathering. In other words, the very nature of banking means that risk shifting cannot be observed by depositors, and no amount of depositor monitoring will uncover the quality and value of a bank's loan portfolio. In addition, even if depositors could monitor, they could not prevent a bank risk shifting in the last period. Admittedly, there may be uncertainty as to when the last period may occur, but when the discount rate is sufficiently high, it will be in the interest of bank managers to risk shift (Hickson and Turner, 2004: 908).

A further potential constraint on risk shifting by bank managers is that shareholders stand to lose the capital they have invested should managers engage in risk-taking which ultimately causes the bank to fail. Thus the incentive structure of residual claimants ultimately determines whether managers risk shift using depositors' funds. In order to ameliorate risk shifting, banks would need to hold large amounts of capital in the form of idle funds, which would incur a large opportunity cost. An agency cost could also arise from this need to raise large amounts of capital as the bank may have many small atomized shareholders and a separation of ownership and control.

As for the same reasons outlined above in relation to depositors, shareholders in a diffusely owned bank cannot get information on borrowers. In addition, shareholders cannot prevent a bank's management risk shifting in the last period at their expense. Knowing this, shareholders will only invest in a bank if they are sufficiently compensated by high returns. However, the cost of equity capital in these circumstances might actually be prohibitive. Consequently, managers' interests need to be somehow aligned with those of shareholders.

One way to reduce the above opportunity and agency costs, and at the same time potentially further reduce incentives to risk shift, is for shareholders to have some form of contingent capital, for example, unlimited liability, double liability, or uncalled capital. Contingent capital constrains bank shareholders from risk shifting as they bear considerable downside risk in the event of bank collapse (Esty, 1998). However, for such a scheme to work, bank managers need to be shareholders so that they personally bear the downside of their risk-taking, and so that their incentives are aligned with those of shareholders. Indeed, shareholders (and depositors) may have a preference for managers to be wealthy and have substantial stakes in the banks which they manage.

Banking systems where shareholders have contingent capital will be more stable in the presence of exogenous shocks than those without for several reasons. Firstly, banks with shareholder liability will have been less likely to have engaged in risk shifting so that exogenous shocks are less likely to reduce the value of their loan portfolios. Secondly, depositors are less likely to run banks with large amounts of contingent capital as they know that deposits are partially or even fully covered by contingent capital.

8.3 CONTINGENT CAPITAL IN BRITISH BANKING

Prior to 1826, only the five state-chartered banks (Bank of England, Bank of Ireland, Bank of Scotland, Royal Bank of Scotland, British Linen Company) were permitted to form as joint-stock companies with limited shareholder liability. Every other bank was constrained to the partnership organizational form and, apart from in Scotland, note-issuing banks were restricted to a maximum of six partners. Each partner in these banks had joint and several unlimited liability for the debts of their bank.

After the severe financial crisis of 1825, British banks were permitted to establish as joint-stock companies, but shareholder liability was jointly and severally unlimited.[2] This meant that each bank shareholder was liable down to their last 'acre and sixpence' for the debts of their bank. In the event of bankruptcy, calls would be made to shareholders on a *pro rata* basis based on the number of shares they held. If some shareholders were unable to pay the full value of their call (because they had been personally bankrupted by it), then a *pro rata* call would have been made on the remaining solvent

[2] Irish Banking Copartnership Regulation Act (6 Geo. IV, *c*.42); Banking Copartnership Act (7 Geo. IV, *c*.46).

shareholders, and so on until the debtors were paid or all shareholders were bankrupted. As can be seen from Table 8.1, a quarter of a century after banking incorporation law was liberalized, there were 141 banks in the UK, with over 35,000 shareholders who were unlimitedly liable for the debts of their bank.

Banks were initially excluded from the provisions of the Joint Stock Companies Act (1856),[3] which granted businesses the freedom to adopt limited liability, due to concerns over depositor safety (Alborn, 1998: 129). However, following legislation in 1857 and 1858, banks were permitted to limit their liability. As can be seen from Table 8.1, by 1869, 41 English banks as well as one Irish bank were operating as limited liability banks. The vast majority of these banks were newly created companies rather than established banks limiting their liability. Indeed, the majority of the established banks did not limit their liability until the early 1880s as unlimited liability was 'thought by the shareholders more conducive to profit, and by the depositors, more likely to give safety' (Wilson, 1879: 69).

The limited liability banks which established after this liberalization had very high levels of uncalled capital. Uncalled capital is where banks (or any

Table 8.1. Shareholder liability regimes in British banking, 1849–1900

	1849	1869	1889	1900
England & Wales				
No. banks with unlimited liability	113	73	2	0
No. limited liability banks	1	42	103	72
No. limited liability banks with uncalled capital and/or reserve liability	—	40	102	71
Number of shareholders	22,031	40,583	95,701	125,859
Ireland				
Number unlimited liability joint-stock banks	10	7	0	0
Number limited liability joint-stock banks	1	2	9	9
No. limited liability banks with uncalled capital and/or reserve liability	—	1	8	8
Number of shareholders	3,083	8,487	20,226	23,974
Scotland				
Number unlimited liability joint-stock banks	18	9	0	0
Number limited liability joint-stock banks	3	3	10	10
No. limited liability banks with uncalled capital and/or reserve liability	—	—	8	8
Number of shareholders	11,157	10,865	19,192	23,435

Sources: *Banking Almanac and Yearbook*, 1850, 1870, 1890, 1900; *Investor's Monthly Manual*, Dec. 1870; Acheson et al., 2010: 250.

Notes: The five state-chartered banks are included as limited liability banks. Shareholder numbers were not available for several small banks.

[3] 19 & 20 Vict. *c*.47.

company) issued shares at a nominal value of say £50, but only called up a proportion of this amount (e.g. £10), with the remainder (£40) being called in the event of bank failure or by directors at any time. In effect, a shareholder's liability in the event of failure was a fixed amount which depended on the number of shares they held. As the newly created limited banks were typically small, the vast majority of British banking up until the early 1880s was conducted by unlimited liability banks.

As can be seen from Table 8.1, all except one of the newly created limited liability banks had uncalled capital in 1869. The median and mean uncalled capital per share for limited banks in 1875 was £18.75 and £32.36 respectively, with the average proportion of uncalled capital being 2.74 times paid-up capital.[4] The levels of uncalled capital were so high that for the median limited bank, 50.6 per cent of deposits were covered by uncalled capital, with a further 30.5 per cent of deposits covered by paid-up capital and reserves (Acheson and Turner, 2011b: 210). Consequently, these banks were viewed by contemporaries as being as safe as unlimited banks (Dun, 1876: 28).

The demise of unlimited liability was precipitated by the collapse of the City of Glasgow Bank in October 1878. At the time of its failure, it was one of the largest banks in Scotland and had one of the largest branch networks of any British bank. The bank's shareholders had unlimited liability, and the subsequent calls they faced resulted in the personal bankruptcy of 86 per cent of the bank's 1,819 shareholders. The fallout from this disaster was such that Parliament passed legislation in 1879 to encourage the unlimited banks to limit their liability (Crick and Wadsworth, 1936: 33). The central idea behind this legislation was the creation of 'reserve liability', which was exactly the same as uncalled capital except it could only be called in the contingency of bankruptcy and was not therefore callable at directors' discretion. According to one of its advocates, reserve liability existed purely for the protection of bank depositors (Rae, 1885: 258).

Most banks subsequently limited their liability and, as can be seen from Table 8.1, unlimited liability had all but disappeared from British banking by 1889. Notably, in 1889, every single limited liability bank apart from four of the state-chartered banks had uncalled capital, or reserve liability, or quite frequently both. After the wholesale limitation of liability, the extra liability carried by bank shareholders in the form of uncalled capital and reserve liability was substantial as for every £1 a shareholder had invested in a bank, they were liable for another £3.10 on average.[5]

As can be seen from Table 8.2, in 1900 every limited bank (apart from three of the state-chartered banks) had some form of contingent liability, and the average ratio of callable capital to deposits was 33.9 per cent. However, by

[4] Author's calculations based on data from *Investor's Monthly Manual* (Dec. 1875).

[5] Figure calculated from data contained in *Banking Almanac and Yearbook*, 1885.

Table 8.2 Contingent liability in British banks, 1900–1958

	Callable capital/deposits (%)			Number of banks	Number of banks with callable capital
	Mean	Median	Mean of top five banks		
1900	33.9	28.6	20.6	90	87
1910	29.3	24.4	19.2	57	54
1921	10.3	10.5	8.7	25	22
1931	11.3	11.9	8.5	22	19
1940	9.4	10.1	7.1	16	13
1950	3.7	4.2	2.5	16	13
1958	0.0	0.0	0.0	17	0

Sources: Based on data from *Banking Almanac* (1900 and 1910), *Bankers' Almanac and Yearbook* (1921 and 1931), and *Stock Exchange Official Yearbook* (1940, 1950); Memo on Bank Capital (Sept. 1958) in Bank of England Archives, C40/102.

Notes: The Bank of England is excluded from the above figures. Southern Irish banks are excluded from 1921 onwards.

1921, this ratio had fallen substantially, mainly due to the monetary (and hence deposit) expansion during the First World War. Bank amalgamations also contributed slightly to this decrease as banks sometimes decreased their reserve liability and uncalled capital as part of the merger process, which ultimately came at the expense of depositor safety.[6] By 1940, the position was much as it was in 1921, apart from the top five banks having a slightly lower callable capital to deposit ratio. However, the monetary expansion during the Second World War without a similar expansion in bank capital resulted in the callable capital to deposits ratio falling to a lowly 2.5 per cent.

Barclays was the first bank to remove its callable capital when it extinguished its unpaid capital in 1921 by reorganizing its capital and capitalizing some shareholder reserves. However, other major banks only removed their callable capital between 1956 and 1958 in a move coordinated by the Bank of England.[7] As can be seen from Table 8.2, by 1958, callable capital had been removed from British banking.

It was argued in the section above that contingent capital only constrains managers from risk shifting if they themselves are shareholders and thus subject to potential calls on their personal wealth. In the case of UK banks, directors were required by banks' deeds of settlement or articles of association to hold a minimum number of shares in the bank before they could assume office. Although share qualifications may have been small in relation to the overall share issue of the bank, they would have constituted a sizeable proportion of a director's personal wealth, particularly in the nineteenth

[6] See the *Report of the Treasury Committee on Bank Amalgamations*, 5–6.

[7] See Bank of England Archives C40/102, confidential internal memo, 30 April 1958.

and early twentieth centuries. Banks with unlimited liability were typically controlled by those who had most to lose in the event of bankruptcy, that is, the wealthiest (Hickson and Turner, 2003). However, once liability was limited and calls on shareholders were *pro rata*, the wealthiest shareholders no longer had as much incentive to be involved in bank governance, but yet bank governance was still restricted to the wealthy due to share ownership qualifications (Acheson and Turner, 2006: 342–3). Even by 1940, directors of four of the 'big five' banks faced an average potential call on their personal wealth of £3,762, assuming they held the minimum number of shares necessary to qualify as a director. In reality, many directors held much more than the minimum share qualification.

8.4 BANKING STABILITY, 1800–2008

The question now arises as to whether the presence of contingent capital for bank shareholders made the banking system more stable. In order to do this, we need to analyse the stability of the banking system over the past two centuries. As banking stability is difficult to quantify over the long run, economists usually adopt a narrative approach to determine whether a banking system has experienced a crisis (Grossman, 2010: 58–9; Reinhart and Rogoff, 2009). How does one define a banking crisis? Reinhart and Rogoff consider the failure of one large or several small commercial or merchant/investment banks as a crisis. Consequently, they identify banking crises as having occurred in the UK in the following years: 1810, 1815–17, 1825–6, 1836–9, 1847, 1857, 1866, 1878, 1890, 1914, 1974, 1984, 1991, 1995, and 2007–8.

Including investment/merchant banks in the definition of banking crises is probably not helpful, particularly in an historical context, as they are not directly linked to the money supply (via deposits) and are not directly involved in credit intermediation. In addition, bank failures may indicate that a shock has hit the money markets, and may therefore be a useful way of identifying pressure in the money markets, but by themselves they do not necessarily mean that the banking system is unstable. Indeed, periodic bank failures may actually encourage banking stability. Banks can fail because depositors run them suspecting that they are vulnerable, and this fear of runs and subsequent failure can effectively act as a device which encourages banks to be prudent in the first place (Calomiris and Kahn, 1991). For example, in the case of the UK banking system, it has been suggested that banks in the nineteenth century became more conservative as a result of observing banks around them failing (Collins, 1990: 84–5; Baker and Collins, 1999).

As we are more interested in whether or not there was a systemic failure of the banking system, we examine the bank failure rate and the extant literature to ascertain whether each of the crises identified by Reinhart and Rogoff were banking system failures. As a rough rule of thumb, if the failure rate (in terms of number or capital) is more than 10 per cent (which is a very low threshold), we will classify that episode as a banking crisis.

8.4.1 Pre-1826 Stability

Prior to 1826, the banking system experienced several shocks and the failure rate was 1.6, 7.0, and 18.4 per cent in 1810, 1815–17, and 1825–6 respectively; these are the three periods identified as banking crises in this era by Reinhart and Rogoff.[8] The high failure rate in 1815–17 was triggered by post-war austerity due in part to the Bank of England preparing for the eventual resumption of specie convertibility (Clapham, 1966: ii: 58–62). The trigger for the financial crisis of 1825–6 was an asset price reversal in the commodity and equity market. The high failure rate (18.4 per cent) during this crisis does not adequately reflect the stresses on the country banking system at the time. It is believed that nearly every English bank approached the Bank of England for help. As a consequence of the crisis, there was a rapid fall in the money supply accompanied by a credit crunch (Pressnell, 1956: 491).

As banks' owners in the pre-1826 system had unlimited liability, the presence of one major and one minor systemic crisis in the space of a decade would appear to undermine the thesis that contingent capital contributes to the stability of the banking system. However, banks in this period were constrained to the partnership organizational form, and in the case of England and Ireland, note-issuing banks could have no more than six partners. Aside from limiting a bank's ability to diversify its assets and liabilities, the six-partner restriction reduces a bank's equity cushion, thus undermining its ability to absorb losses as a result of monetary or real shocks. More importantly, however, as partners have unlimited liability, the more partners there are, the greater the ability of the bank to cover losses in the event of bankruptcy. Indeed, note-holders and depositors would prefer to see the ownership of the bank dispersed amongst many partners, as there is less risk that many owners would lose their entire wealth as compared to a small number of owners (Hickson and Turner, 2005: 197).

The high failure rate for 1825–6 was largely due to the collapse of the English banking system as the Scottish banking system was largely stable during this episode. The historiography of British banking has attributed the relative stability of the Scottish banking system to the absence of the six-partner rule (Kerr, 1884: 69–70; Cameron, 1967: 97–8; Munn, 1981: 236;

[8] The pre-1826 failure rate data are based on figures from Munn, 1981: 222–4; Pressnell, 1956: 11, 538; Gilbart, 1837: 110.

White, 1995: 47–8). However, the six-partner rule was not a binding constraint, as English country banks would have been small anyway due to the inherent hold-up problems faced by partnerships formed under the common law (Acheson et al., 2011). Scottish partnership law, on the other hand, enabled businesses to have facets of legal personality, which subsequently facilitated the formation of large partnerships as contracting and governance decisions could only be made by a managerial hierarchy. As a result, Scottish partnership banks had multiple partners, with the result that their notes and deposits were backed by the wealth of many heterogeneous owners. Notably, the changes to English banking incorporation law in 1826 deliberately emulated these features of the Scottish system by permitting the establishment of banks with multiple owners and unlimited liability.

The instability of the banking system prior to 1826 was largely confined to England, and appears to have been due to the constraints placed upon English banks. What this demonstrates, however, is that on its own contingent liability is not enough to prevent banking instability. Banks also need to have the joint-stock organizational form, which enables them to have a large and diffuse shareholder body. Such a body makes it much easier for banks with contingent liability to weather periodic exogenous shocks.

8.4.2 Stability in the contingent capital era, 1826–1958

During the era where joint-stock banks had some form of contingent liability, there were seven banking crises according to Reinhart and Rogoff, with five of these occurring whenever unlimited liability was the dominant form of contingent capital. However, as we will see below, none of these can be defined as systemic crises.

The first crisis identified by Reinhart and Rogoff in this era occurred in 1836–9. During 1834–6, many banks and railways were floated on the equity market. The collapse of railway stock prices in late 1836 and early 1837 resulted in pressures in the capital and money markets. In November 1836, the Agricultural and Commercial Bank of Ireland, which had been established in 1834, collapsed. Subsequently, several other banks failed in 1837, with the most prominent being the Northern and Central Bank of England. Despite these two prominent collapses, the failure rate in 1836–7 was only 3.7 per cent, and the two notable bank failures were newly established banks, which had expanded rapidly and had made overly risky loans and investments (Collins, 1990: 84).[9] If anything, the failures in 1836–7 made the banking system more stable by removing weaker (and riskier) institutions.

[9] The failure rate is based on data from Thomas (1934) and the *Bankers' Almanac and Yearbook* (1931: 279–330).

It is important to note at this point that unlimited liability (or any other form of contingent capital) did not necessarily prevent banks from failing. What it does mean, however, is that losses during crises will be borne by shareholders not depositors, and hence the incentive for depositors to run banks during periods of financial stress are substantially reduced. In addition, the presence of unlimited liability will mean that risk shifting will not have occurred *ex ante*, with the result that banks are better able to withstand shocks.

The second crisis identified by Reinhart and Rogoff is the commercial crisis of 1847, which was precipitated by a fall in wheat prices and disruption in the money and capital markets arising from calls on railway shareholders, who had witnessed the value of their investment fall substantially over a period of 18 months. Although the commercial crisis resulted in the bankruptcy of many small merchants and commercial enterprises (Evans, 1849), only 1.0 per cent of banks failed.[10] There were no large or notable bank failures, which, allied to the low bank failure rate, would suggest that there was not a systemic banking crisis during the 1847 commercial crisis.

The third crisis identified by Reinhart and Rogoff during this era was in 1857—this episode has been identified as the first global financial crisis (Kindleberger, 2000: 129). Although the bank failure rate in 1857–8 was only 3.3 per cent, there was one notable and substantial bank failure—the Western Bank of Scotland, which had the largest branch network (101 branches) of any Scottish bank. The Western Bank was also one of the largest in the UK at time, constituting 4.9 per cent of the British banking system's paid-up capital in 1855. The other significant failure in 1857 was the Northumberland and Durham District Banking Company, which was one of the larger English provincial banks at the time; it had 2.1 per cent of the British banking system's paid-up capital at the time of its failure.[11] Thus, in terms of capital, 1857 falls just short of the 10 per cent definition of a banking crisis. What is notable, however, is that despite the size of these two banks, their failure did not result in a widespread banking panic and the collapse of other banks.

Following the collapse of the Western Bank, its 1,280 shareholders paid calls totalling £1,089,577 (or £36 per share) in order to repay depositors (Checkland, 1975: 468). For this reason, depositors did not lose a penny as result of this failure, and other Glasgow banks accepted the Western's notes, thus allaying fears of further failures. Similarly, the *c*.433 shareholders of the Northumberland and Durham District initially faced calls totalling £2,233,826 (or £35 per share); although some of this was subsequently recovered (Orbell and Turton, 2001: 418–19).

[10] The failure rate is based on data from Thomas (1934: 656–62); *Bankers' Almanac and Yearbook* (1931: 279–330).

[11] Data from *Banking Almanac and Yearbook*. This figure excludes the Bank of England.

These two banks were also similar in that they had expanded aggressively in the years prior to their collapse. In the case of the Western Bank, it was well known to contemporary bankers that it was a risk-loving bank, having experienced liquidity difficulties in 1834, 1837, and 1847. In the run-up to 1857, it was running on very low reserves, had made substantial investments in overseas trade, and its loan portfolio was concentrated amongst a small group of businesses (Checkland, 1975: 467). Indeed, one could argue that the failures removed two overly risky banks from the banking system, thus making it more stable. Furthermore, the failure of these two banks would have proved a salutary reminder to shareholders and managers of the dangers of rapid expansion and overly risky lending.

The fourth crisis identified by Reinhart and Rogoff was the 1866 financial crisis, which was precipitated by the collapse of Overend and Gurney, a discount house connected to the banking system via the money market. The failure rate in 1866–7 was only 4.2 per cent, but apart from the Birmingham Banking Company, four of the other five UK commercial banks which failed were small, newly established, and had limited liability.[12] The Birmingham Banking Company had been around for nearly three decades, and similar to previous failures, its shareholders had to make good the deficit between the bank's assets and liabilities (Holmes and Green, 1986: 46). Despite its size, this bank only constituted 0.70 per cent of the British banking system's paid-up capital, and the total paid-up capital of the banks which failed was 4.1 per cent.[13] Overall, there were not enough failures of large banks for us to classify this as a crisis. Notably, from the perspective of this chapter, limited liability played a central role in the crisis—Overend and Gurney had limited their liability in 1865, the majority of banks which failed during the crisis had limited liability, and the stresses on the capital markets were mainly due to the failure of new limited liability companies which had formed following the 1862 Companies Act.

The fifth crisis identified in this era was in 1878, which is when the City of Glasgow Bank failed. At the time of its failure in October 1878, it was one of the country's largest deposit-takers, having the third largest branch network in the UK. The failure rate in 1878/9 was 4.2 per cent, but apart from the City of Glasgow Bank, the banks which failed were very small. Although the City of Glasgow Bank was one of the largest banks in the country, it only constituted 2.0 per cent of the British banking system in terms of paid-up capital, and the total paid-up capital of all the banks which failed in 1878–9 was only 3.9 per cent.[14] Although the failure rate was low, the British banking system

[12] The failure rate is based on data from *Bankers' Almanac and Yearbook* (1931: 279–330), Thomas (1934: 656–62) and various issues of the *Banking Almanac*.

[13] Data from *Banking Almanac and Yearbook*. This calculation excludes the Bank of England.

[14] Data from *Banking Almanac and Yearbook*. This calculation excludes the Bank of England.

faced severe liquidity pressures in late 1878, but the system was robust enough to weather these pressures (Collins, 1989). Ultimately, however, the stability of the banking system is measured not by its freedom from liquidity pressures, but by its ability to remain solvent in the face of these pressures.

Depositors of the City of Glasgow Bank lost nothing as shareholders met the deficit between the bank's assets and liabilities out of their personal wealth. Indeed, depositors did not even have to wait for the bankruptcy process to begin to get their money back as other Scottish banks immediately accepted City of Glasgow Bank notes, and they also allowed its depositors (except those who were stockholders of the City of Glasgow Bank) to transfer their deposits. This was only possible because the City of Glasgow Bank's stockholders had unlimited liability.

After the demise of unlimited liability in the early 1880s, banks had various types and amounts of uncalled capital up until the 1950s. During this period of time, there are only two crises identified by Reinhart and Rogoff—1890 and 1914. 1890 has been identified as a banking crisis by Reinhart and Rogoff due to the privately organized bailout of Barings Bank, a merchant bank which was in financial difficulties as a result of the collapse in value of South American securities. As no commercial banks failed during this episode, it cannot be classified as a systemic crisis. However, it could be argued that the Bank of England's co-ordination of the guarantee fund, to which the major joint-stock banks contributed large funds, averted a financial panic. The main reason joint-stock banks were happy to contribute to the guarantee fund was that Barings' acceptances were so widely held that it would cause major problems in the market for bank acceptances as well as the wider money markets (Clapham, 1966: ii: 333). It was therefore in the self-interest of banks to prevent this happening by contributing to the Barings' guarantee fund. Although banks were criticized for doing this, no guarantor lost a single penny as Barings was nursed back to full financial health in the aftermath of its collapse (Clapham, 1966: ii: 337). Indeed, during this episode, there was no threat to the solvency of any joint-stock bank.

The collapse of European capital markets and a foreign exchange crisis in the summer of 1914 resulted in severe liquidity pressures for the UK banking system, which were exacerbated by some banks' aggressive liquidity hoarding. Rather than the usual practice of suspending gold convertibility, a severe liquidity crisis was avoided by extending the usual August Bank Holiday by four days and by an issue of Treasury notes (Sayers, 1976: 74–6). Only the National Penny Bank, a small savings bank which had been in difficulties since 1911, failed in 1914. Although one could argue that a banking crisis was avoided by the actions of the Treasury, there were no question marks over the stability of UK banks.

Unlike many other economies, the UK did not experience a banking crisis during the Great Depression of the 1930s (Grossman, 1994; Jonker and van

Zenden, 1995). Although the presence of contingent capital may have had something to do with this, other factors may also have had a bearing on the system's stability after 1920. First, banks may have become intrinsically more stable due to the large national banks which emerged from the pre-1920 amalgamation process (Sykes, 1926: 162; Sayers, 1976: 11). These large banks were better able to absorb shocks due to their size and better diversification (Capie, 1995: 399; Holmes and Green, 1986: 119). Second, after 1920, British banks appear to have had a tacit agreement with the government whereby they were allowed to operate a cartel in return for holding large amounts of government debt (Griffiths, 1973: 8; Cottrell, 2003: 64). For example, in 1933, the long-term government debt held by UK banks was equal to 31 per cent of total bank deposits (Sheppard, 1971: 126–7). Ultimately, this would have limited the ability of banks to engage in risk shifting.

8.4.3 Banking Stability, 1958–2008

Over the half century since the disappearance of contingent capital, there were five banking crises according to Reinhart and Rogoff—1974, 1984, 1991, 1995, and 2007–8. However, as we will see below, only the final one of these can be defined as a systemic crisis.

In 1974, UK commercial banks, under the guidance of the Bank of England, provided about £1,300 million of liquidity support to secondary banks, institutions which raised funds on the wholesale money markets to make property and consumer finance loans (Reid, 1982: 192). This liquidity support, which was known as the 'lifeboat' operation, prevented the difficulties faced by the secondary banks from becoming a full-blown financial crisis (Reid, 1982: 200). Although several secondary banks failed, there were no question marks against any commercial bank.

Johnson Matthey Bankers got into difficulties in 1984 and was taken over by the Bank of England after a failed attempt at coordinating a private sector rescue. In 1991, the Bank of Credit and Commerce International (BCCI), a large international bank with offices in London, failed. These banks were not large relative to the clearing banks, and it is even questionable as to whether one could consider them as commercial banks. Therefore, it is erroneous to classify these isolated failures as banking crises. Similarly, we cannot consider the Barings failure in 1995, which was due to losses accumulated by a trader, as a banking crisis as it was an investment bank.

Before the 2007–8 bank bailouts, there were nine major institutions which dominated British commercial banking. In 2008, the Northern Rock and Bradford and Bingley were nationalized. In the midst of the crisis, Lloyds-TSB merged with HBOS as part of the government's strategy to save the latter and stave off a contagion-induced panic. However, within a matter of weeks,

Lloyds-TSB and the Royal Bank of Scotland were the recipients of huge taxpayer-funded capital injections, with the result that the UK taxpayer owned the large majority of the equity in these banks. In terms of total assets, 51.8 per cent of the British banking system required a government bailout either in the form of complete nationalization or large capital injections, and this is not even considering the unprecedented assistance offered to banks by the Bank of England.[15] Consequently, the 2007–8 crisis easily meets our definition of a systemic banking crisis, and clearly is the worst banking crisis in the UK's history.

8.4.4 Summary

During the era when UK banking was dominated by joint-stock banks with contingent capital (1826–1958), the UK banking system did not experience a systemic banking crisis. Although there were episodic stresses on the system which resulted in some banks failing and calls on shareholders, the overall system was robust in the face of these shocks, and may even have been strengthened by the failure of high-risk banks. Admittedly, in the last three or four decades of the contingent-capital era, the amount of contingent capital was relatively low, and banking stability may have been attributable to the tacit agreement between banks and the government, whereby banks held large quantities of government bonds.

After the removal of contingent capital, the UK banking system was relatively stable for fifty years until the banking crisis of 2008. This raises the following question: if contingent capital was so important in ensuring banking stability, why did it take fifty years for the banking system to collapse? The answer, which has been hinted at above, is that there were government constraints and regulations on bank risk shifting, which in effect were substitutes for contingent capital. The 2008 crisis occurred after a lengthy period of deregulation, where many of these constraints had been removed or gradually eroded.

8.5 CRITIQUES OF CONTINGENT CAPITAL IN BANKING

The main thesis of this chapter is that contingent capital resulted in a stable banking system as it prevented risk shifting because shareholders and

[15] This is based on total assets in 2006, which were obtained from bank balance sheets.

managers had all or some of their personal wealth at stake should their bank fail. However, throughout its existence, contingent capital in banking was criticized in two related ways which greatly undermines its efficacy in ameliorating risk shifting. First, it was claimed that bank shareholders were low-wealth individuals, and that over time, as bank failures occurred, wealthy individuals were less inclined to invest in bank shares. Second, it was believed that bank shares were dumped at the onset of a crisis by shareholders attempting to avoid calls.

The claim that shareholders of banks with contingent capital were low-wealth had several major proponents in the nineteenth century (Turner, 2009a). For example, William Clay MP, in a major parliamentary speech in 1836, argued that 'unlimited liability has a tendency to deter persons of fortune, intelligence, and respectability, from becoming partners or managers of joint-stock banks', (Clay, 1837: 117). Although he did grant at the time that wealthy persons owned bank shares, he suggested that the dynamic was that bank failures would result in wealthy individuals selling their bank shares (Clay, 1837: 66). Similarly, Walter Bagehot, writing in 1856, stated that 'we enact that every person joining a bank shall be liable for every sixpence contained in it, to his last acre and shilling. The consequence is that persons who join banks have very commonly but few acres and shillings' (Bagehot, 1856: 312). This particular criticism of unlimited liability in banking reached its zenith in the aftermath of the City of Glasgow collapse, with *The Economist* suggesting that its failure revealed that most bank shareholders were low-wealth investors (*The Economist,* 1879: 'City of Glasgow Bank': 1480). In addition, it was widely believed by contemporaries that, following the bankruptcy of the vast majority of City of Glasgow shareholders, remaining wealthy shareholders in unlimited liability banks would rapidly sell off their ownership stake (*The Bankers' Magazine*, 40 (1880); Levi, 1880: 56; Rae, 1885: 257).

Bank shares were tradable, and as with all companies with such shares, it would have been quite easy for shares with contingent capital to end up in the hands of low-wealth individuals. To solve such problems, economists typically suggest that each incumbent owner could verify applicant owners and regularly monitor existing co-owners (Jensen and Meckling, 1976: 331; Carr and Mathewson, 1988: 769; Winton, 1993: 490; Woodward, 1985: 605). In UK banks, however, verification of applicant owners was the role of the firm's directors; they effectively controlled entry into the shareholding body and ensured that shareholder aggregate wealth was not diluted (Acheson et al., 2010: 255). Bank directors had incentives to exclude low-wealth individuals because (a) they were shareholders themselves, (b) they were typically amongst the wealthiest owners, and (c) liability was joint and several, which meant that if some shareholders could not pay calls, directors typically faced further calls on their wealth (Hickson and Turner, 2003: 952). When the banks limited their liability in the early 1880s, directors still had a vetting role (Rae,

1885: 233). The incentives to vet circumspectly may have reduced somewhat after banks limited their liability as the admission of low-wealth individuals imposed less of an externality once liability was no longer unlimited (Acheson et al., 2010: 255). In addition, the administrative costs of director vetting may have increased due to increasing shareholder numbers, which was primarily a result of amalgamations. The average number of shareholders in the top five UK banks was 10,104 in 1900.[16] However, evidence submitted to the US's National Monetary Commission categorically stated that bank directors vetted candidate shareholders very carefully even in the first decade of the twentieth century (Withers and Palgrave, 1910: 93).

By the late 1920s, when the average number of shareholders in the top five banks was closer to 60,000, one observer suggested that most bank shareholders were individuals of modest means (Sykes, 1928: 141). However, this was not a problem in the 1920s as the levels of uncalled capital were so low relative to bank stock prices that banks could easily admit investors with modest sums of wealth. In addition, even if this was the case, bank directors were required to invest significant amounts capital in banks in order to qualify as a director, which meant that they had incentives to ensure that shareholders had adequate wealth and, more importantly, they also had incentives to ensure that managers did not risk shift.

The director vetting of shares was a privately arranged scheme designed to prevent shares ending up in the hands of low-wealth individuals. Such a scheme, however, may not have prevented opportunistic share dumping by directors and other wealthy owners during times of financial distress in order to escape potential calls. Indeed, *in extremis*, banks shares could have had a negative value to wealthy shareholders, with the result that it was optimal for them to assign their shares to impecunious straw-men. If this happened, contingent capital would have been a toothless tiger, and ultimately would not have prevented managers engaging in risk shifting. Consequently, the joint-stock bank acts of the mid 1820s imposed a post-sale-extended liability on shareholders of unlimited liability joint-stock banks, which meant that individuals were liable for the bank's debts for up to three years after they had ceased being a shareholder.[17] Shareholders of limited liability banks with uncalled or reserve liability also faced a post-sale-extended liability requirement as the 1862 Companies Act made shareholders liable for unpaid capital

[16] Figure based on data obtained from 1900 *Banking Almanac*.

[17] Irish Banking Copartnerships Act, 1825 (6 Geo. IV, *c*.42) and the English Banking Copartnerships Act, 1826 (7 Geo. IV, *c*.46). In Scotland, former owners of unlimited liability joint-stock shares were liable for debts incurred during their time as a shareholder (Bell, 1858: 224). Established English, Irish, and Scottish banks which registered as unlimited liability companies under the Companies Act of 1862 (25 & 26 Vict. *c*.89) were able to reduce their post-sale-extended-liability requirement to one year.

for up to one year after they had sold their share (Plumptre, 1882: 507). The post-sale-extended liability requirement effectively prevented the director-vetting system breaking down in the last period (Acheson et al., 2010: 258).

How effective were these mechanisms outlined above at preventing the wealth dilution of bank stockholding constituencies? The available evidence suggests that these mechanisms were successful. First, several studies which have examined the wealth and socio-occupational characteristics of bank shareholders in the nineteenth century and early twentieth centuries found that they were wealthy individuals and that they had more than sufficient wealth to pay any potential calls (Hickson and Turner, 2003; Acheson and Turner, 2006, 2008a, 2011a; Turner, 2009b). Second, a recent study of the City of Glasgow Bank found that its shareholders were wealthy individuals, with the average shareholder being asked to pay £12,000 (which is over £1m in today's money) (Acheson and Turner, 2008a: 243). In addition, evidence from the share-trading records of contemporary banks shows no evidence of bank shares being dumped after the City of Glasgow crisis, especially by wealthy individuals (Acheson and Turner, 2008a: 245–7). Furthermore, the fall in share prices of Scottish unlimited liability banks after the collapse of the City of Glasgow was not due to investors dumping their stock; rather it was due to City of Glasgow Bank shareholders having to sell their shares in other banks in order to meet calls (Acheson and Turner, 2008a: 249).

8.6 CONTINGENT CAPITAL REDUX

The stability in the UK banking system from 1825 onwards was associated with the presence of contingent capital in the form of unlimited liability and then uncalled capital. The basic argument is that contingent capital acted to discourage bank managers from risk shifting at depositors' expense. Given the great collapse of the banking system in 2008, the question naturally arises as to whether regulatory authorities need to reintroduce some variant of contingent capital into banking in order to protect depositors and taxpayers. Notably, there have been several proposals made which attempt to mimic aspects of contingent capital. For example, Flannery has suggested that banks issue contingent capital certificates, which are simply debt securities that convert into equity in the event that a bank's capital asset ratio falls below a trigger level (Flannery, 2009). Admati and Pfleiderer (2010) have suggested that the liability of bank equity be unlimited and that this equity be placed in an equity liability carrier, which also holds safe debt and is financed by investors bearing limited liability. From the perspective of the UK's experience with contingent capital, these proposals are only a second-best option as shareholders and managers are not personally liable in the event of default. Ultimately, it is this potential personal liability, particularly that borne by managers, which discourages risk shifting in the first instance.

Prior to the recent crisis, some scholars suggested that contingent capital in its historical form should be re-introduced into banking systems (Macey and Miller, 1992; Grossman, 2001). More recently, Conti-Brown has suggested that systematically important financial institutions should have *pro rata* unlimited liability (Conti-Brown, 2011). However, these policy proposals are largely ignored and viewed as interesting curiosities of financial history and therefore somewhat anachronistic. The economic arguments against contingent capital largely revolve around the issue of the cost of bank capital and fears that calling in capital may exacerbate a crisis. As contingent capital would reduce the marketability of bank shares due to the necessity of having a large administrative structure so as to ensure that bank shares are not sold to impecunious individuals, bank capital may become overly costly. These costs, however, may not be that great. For example, bank shares traded on the London and regional stock exchanges relatively freely in the nineteenth century even when most banks had unlimited liability (Acheson and Turner, 2008b). Indeed, changes in liability regimes in the nineteenth century had no impact on the liquidity of shares (Acheson et al., 2010: 263–4). However, the fact that modern banks have shareholders numbering in the hundreds of thousands may make the administrative costs prohibitively high in the modern context (Acheson et al., 2010: 270). Furthermore, with such large numbers of shareholders, calling in capital could exacerbate a crisis as many individuals would be attempting to liquidate their financial and real assets simultaneously. Consequently, any attempt to introduce contingent capital into banking would probably necessitate banks having fewer shareholders (Acheson et al., 2010: 270).

The main opposition to contingent capital would be banks and their shareholders, who would much rather have taxpayer-funded bailouts and deposit insurance than bear the downside of their own risk-taking decisions. Political opposition to such reforms would also be expected as powerful banks would lobby against such changes, and politicians in democracies may be concerned about proposals which would ultimately restrict ownership of bank shares to the wealthy or potentially impose huge costs upon middle-class bank shareholders.

9

Narrow Banking, Real Estate, and Financial Stability in the UK *c.*1870–2010

Avner Offer

9.1 INTRODUCTION

For more than a century after 1866, the stability of the banking system in Britain was never in question. This period of stability can now be seen as exceptional. During this period, Britain maintained a steady level of economic growth, provided a rising standard of living for the majority of its people, and made a transition from workshop of the world to consumer society. This banking system was different from the one we have today, and appears quite alien to economists trained in modern finance theory. In contrast, the banking system that came into being after the 1970s initially seemed to sustain continued prosperity but fell into crisis in 2007, and remains out of control. Economic growth came to a halt, much of the banking system has had to be bailed out, subsidized, or nationalized, and there is no agreement on where to go next. The banking system that existed in Britain up to the 1970s may provide some clues as to how financial stability might be restored.

The main attribute of this world we have lost was the functional specialization of different parts of the banking system. Each activity in the financial system was undertaken by a different set of institutions. This is in contrast with the encompassing 'universal banking' institutions which emerged after the 1970s and which came to dominate. The earlier system kept the risks of different areas of financial business in different compartments, insulated from each other. In particular, the special risks arising from the finance of housing and commercial real estate were contained within separate institutions with self-limiting constraints. The financial system operated with self-regulating prudential constraints on liquidity and credit, which kept its expansionist tendencies in check, and allowed liquidity to grow at the same pace as the rest of the economy, and no more. This is the world we have lost, and we might wish to consider how much of it we might want to recapture.

Money has three functions, and in late-Victorian Britain, each one of them was provided by a separate set of institutions. The most immediate use of money is as a medium of exchange. Institutionally, this was embodied in the payments system. On the High Street, the most imposing buildings belonged to the clearing banks, whose main function was to make and receive payments. 'Clearing' was a daily process in which agents of the banks got together to cancel out their mutual liabilities, and to pay over any remaining balances. Another set of institutions, mostly in the City of London, provided credit ('discounting') against short-term commercial paper.

The second function of money is as a store of value. A hierarchy of financial institutions collected savings, and transformed them into investments and loans. At retail street level, there was a class of saving banks; one level higher were insurance companies. In the City of London, investment banks specialized in underwriting bonds and equity issues, while the stock exchange (and other specialized markets) traded in financial and other assets. A special set of institutions, the building societies, accepted deposits, and lent them out on mortgage for house purchase. Insurance companies also lent on mortgage, but other institutions kept clear of the real estate markets.

Money also serves as a unit of account. The Bank Charter Act of 1844 made the Bank of England responsible for the value of the currency, the level of prices, and the integrity of the financial system. Despite being a private corporation, the Bank understood this function, and on the whole, discharged it well.

9.2 PAYMENTS AND SAVINGS

Economists are used to thinking of banks as performing 'maturity transformation', taking short-term deposits, and converting them into long-term loans. It comes as a surprise for them to realize that the core institutions of late-Victorian banking did not engage in this activity. Late-Victorian banks were a kind of urban utility. By the end of the nineteenth century, the routine everyday business of banking in England and Wales had concentrated in five large institutions based in London, with hundreds of branches each, scattered in every town (Sayers, 1967: Ch. 3; Collins, 1990: Ch. 3). Like gas and water utilities, their function was to provide liquidity for business wherever required. Legal tender in Britain, either gold coins or Bank of England notes, was limited in quantity by the Bank Charter Act of 1844, and most of the money supply was provided by the clearing banks, in the form of bank deposits and overdrafts. They used this form of liquidity and credit to gradually increase the money supply, more or less in line with economic growth, by operating a sort of 'real-bills doctrine', which accommodated advances to the level of legitimate business requirements (Higonnet, 1957; Goodhart, 1972: 209–10).[1] The judgements that bankers formed on legitimate business were disciplined by the personal risk they took, as bank officers, if advances were not serviced and repaid (Holgate, 1938: 743).

The main function of the 'clearing' banks was to facilitate business payments. They did not lend a great deal, and lent cautiously. Thus Walter Leaf, Chairman of the Westminster Bank said:

> The main credit system of the country, the gigantic amount carried by trade in the form of capital or capital debts, is independent of the banker altogether . . . The banker deals in 'short money' on both sides. He is essentially a broker whose business it is to link up money needing temporary investment with borrowers needing temporary loans. (Leaf, 1935: 93, 97)

Credit was advanced in the form of deposit overdrafts or as short advances for a few months, although it was often easy to roll over. In 1909, one expert estimated that nearly three-quarters of bank deposits were created by loans and advances (Withers, 1909: 63), while the scale of outstanding loans was typically no more than about half of deposits (Goodhart, 1972: 158). Deposits were means of payment: liabilities were discharged by debiting and crediting bank accounts. These accounts either paid no interest, or a low interest rate, and sometimes even incurred a charge. Depositors could obtain their money on demand. This exposure to the volatility of business payments made banks averse to risk. They controlled it by keeping a large proportion of liquid assets (such as government bonds and money on call), typically up to a third of their assets; capital ratios of 12 to 14 per cent in the late-Victorian period, and down to about half that level in the interwar years; and even their own reserves of gold. In 1913 the clearing banks were aiming to accumulate gold reserves comparable to those used by the Bank of England for monetary policy, which they wanted in order to insulate themselves from the effects of that very policy (Offer, 1983: 132–3; Goodhart: 1972, 223–6). Another source of discipline was 'skin in the game', the personal liability of bank shareholders.

From the 1870s and until the Second World War, the Bank of England succeeded in maintaining a stable level of prices. That made money attractive as a store of value. Two types of institutions took money from individuals and locked it away for safekeeping. Saving banks provided a 'store of value' for small savers. Trustee savings banks began early in the nineteenth century as not-for-profit mutual associations for saving. The primary consideration was the safety of deposits. The government entered this business with the Post Office savings bank in 1861, which gave a sovereign guarantee for the small accounts of low-earning households. The Post Office also provided a poor

[1] The 'real-bills' doctrine was applied by the Bank of England to regulate the money supply when convertibility to gold was suspended during the Napoleonic Wars (Viner, 1937: 148–9).

man's payment system, in the form of money orders and postal orders (for smaller sums) (Horne, 1947). The funds deposited in these institutions could only be invested in government bonds, and they rose so much that in the years before the First World War, the Post Office savings bank became the most readily available and reliable source for government borrowing (Offer, 1983: 134). By 1938, the total deposits in all savings banks was about £775 million, or about 3 per cent of a net personal wealth of £24,289 million (Sheppard, 1971: Table (A) 3.1; Solomou and Weale, 1997: Table 6, 311). Another form of lower-class savings was through self-help. Friendly societies (and 'industrial assurance', i.e. burial insurance companies) had £1,760 million worth of funds in 1938, about 7.2 per cent of net personal wealth (Sheppard, 1971: Table (A) 2.9).

For the middle classes, a popular form of saving was insurance policies sold by life offices. Most of these policies were for a fixed term of years, and constituted a form of saving. The life insurance element was attractive at a time when life expectation was volatile at all ages. Only a minority of these policies were converted into annuities, which provided coverage for the risk of living too long. Insurance companies strove to maintain financial claims over the long term, and to control professionally for known actuarial risks. There were scores of firms and the industry was quite competitive. There was a certain amount of concentration at the top, but it would still be interesting to investigate what kept these firms honest. This industry needs to be studied more closely. It is possible that competition kept the reserves relatively low, and so the attraction of steady premium flows was larger than various ways of absconding with the money. It was easier to operate a system of this kind with an expectation of stable prices. Also many of the firms were mutual societies, and their presence in the market would have restrained their joint-stock competitors (the Post Office also entered this business). These companies invested for the long-term in bonds, solid equities, and mortgages. They were managed conservatively, and one of their selling points was the sharing of opportunity and risk with the clients (the 'with-profits' policies). In a time of poor accounting standards, it is a remarkable that policyholders placed such confidence in the insurance companies, but they did. The scale of insurance company funds in 1938 was £1,023 million, a smaller proportion of total personal wealth than the funds held by friendly societies, which provided contingency insurance for manual workers and the lower middle class (Sheppard, 1971: Table (A) 2.6).

9.3 HOUSING

A truism worth restating is that the purpose of saving is to transfer financial claims from one point in time to another. This process is fraught with a variety of risks, and one of the methods of coping with them is to own real estate. Housing is tangible, and provides a flow of shelter regardless of its financial value. Historical experience over the twentieth century also shows that housing held its value remarkably well, typically rising in value as fast or faster than gross domestic product, about seven or eight times more than the retail price index, two to three times more than labour earnings (Offer, 2014: 214–16). Victorian bankers were advised not to take real estate into their portfolios and that they heeded this advice is an important reason for a century of banking stability (Rae, 1885: 94–8, 106–7, 113–16; this was the leading banking handbook of the period). Real estate is poor collateral: its value is uncertain and it is difficult to sell. It is also exposed to taxation. Banks foreclosing on mortgages in recent times typically take a large loss on market value.

In Victorian England, housing was typically owned not for shelter, but for profit. It was provided by small capitalists on the 'buy to let' system. Houses were erected by speculative builders and were sold on to these landlords. House property was subject to large cyclical value swings. The greatest of these swings took place towards the end of the nineteenth century, when house values rose to a peak in the late 1890s at a time when overseas investment (the other main outlet for savings) was not attractive. In the following years, house values fell sharply, typically declining by more than a third over the Edwardian period, one of the largest house-price collapses recorded (Offer, 1981: Ch. 17). At that point the First World War broke out, and within a year, most of the housing in Britain was placed under a regime of rent control which was not fully lifted until the 1980s. Then as now, housing was a very large household asset class (about a fifth before 1914, less than a tenth between the wars, about a third in the last twenty years; Offer, 2014: Table 8.1; also Solomou and Weale, 1997). But these violent fluctuations in its value had little adverse effect on the financial system up to 1939. It actually came out stronger as a consequence. One reason was that rents held up much better than property values, so nominal revenue flows held up as well (Offer, 1981: Figure 17.9, 278). And these assets, on the whole, were not liabilities on anybody's books. When rental flows were capped by regulation, the losses were taken by the owners, and the demise of houses as an investment class cleared the way for owner-occupied housing, financed by mortgage lending. And owner-occupation opened up a new domain for finance.

Building societies had been lending to owner-occupiers since the beginning of the nineteenth century, but their activities were circumscribed by the dominance of the 'buy to let' rental sector. The introduction of rent control opened a new scope for owner-occupation, and building societies developed the institutional capacity to provide the finance. Their heyday was between the wars, when they financed the great bulk of new construction, and developed new methods to do so. The building societies were not-for-profit mutual societies. They took deposits (mostly from middle-class savers), and lent the money out on mortgage. Their mode of operation had built-in prudential constraints. The loans were funded entirely from time deposits, some of which were classified as 'shares' in the society, whose assets were junior to those of ordinary depositors. The incentive was that shareholders received a higher rate of interest, and might get priority for borrowing. Initially loan-to-value ratios were low, and borrowers had to advance large cash deposits, and to have a good saving record. Mortgages had always provided a rate of return more than twice as high as government bonds. What building societies discovered, was that the borrowers they selected could be relied upon, and that their time depositors were genuine savers, and thus more patient than the businessman depositors and shareholders of the clearing banks. Without needing to maintain stock market value, they could share the mortgage markup with their depositors, and offer them a competitive rate of interest, substantially above the return on government bonds. This attracted a flow of middle-class and even financial industry savings in the 1920s, and even more so after the downwards conversion of interest on government bonds in 1932. On the other hand, they were constrained in the amount that they could lend by the funds deposited in their accounts, together with any reserves they had built up. Unlike the clearing banks, building societies were not able to create money. Their funds were not ledger-book credits, but had been earned by households, and were genuinely withdrawn from consumption. Building society deposits were genuine liabilities, secured only on illiquid housing, and so lending had to be prudent (Cleary, 1965).

Not that it always was prudent: in the 1930s in particular building society managers developed innovative methods of lending high ratios of house value, coming close to 100 per cent. Success led to rapid growth, and credit evaluation became less personal. During the 1930s, building societies began to take on greater risk. The managers rose in status as their societies rose in size. They began to compete with each other for market share, and in the process, may have sailed a little close to the wind. Their innovative lending policies largely dispensed with borrowers' equity. Much lending was made directly to developers, who paid insurance to cover the risk of default. Fortunately, the societies were never tested by a substantial downturn, and came out of the Second World War in a stronger position to resume their activities, which continued in the same form up until the 1980s. They rarely, if ever, borrowed money on the financial markets, they built up substantial reserves, and their leverage was low. Their lending was rationed by the savings of their depositors. In consequence, in the interwar years, although demand for housing was buoyant and economic conditions (for the middle-class) were good, and although the lending response was ample, it did not overstep prudential limits, and house price levels did not substantially rise between the wars. Although a number of large societies emerged and the sector became more concentrated, the societies did not on the whole pose a systemic risk. Housing finance was insulated from the payments system. The value at risk was only depositors' and shareholders' funds, which were secured amply by the revenue flows that serviced the mortgages (Speight, 2000; Samy, 2010).

These financial innovations helped to build up Britain's large stock of owner occupied housing, much of it eventually transferred from the moribund rental sector. This achievement was remarkable in view of the attributes of housing markets. In Britain and the United States during the twentieth century, demand for housing was insatiable: it rose faster than income, if credit was available to feed it. To paraphrase Samuelson on stocks, 'if people buy because they think houses will rise, their act of buying sends up the price of houses... no one apparently loses what the winners gain' (Samuelson and Samuelson, 1980: 601). This is actually incorrect: once houses rise, the next cohort of people finds it more difficult to buy, and can only be accommodated if credit is expanded. Seen as an asset, for long periods houses appeared to deliver their proverbial safety. The reason, however, was that they have been poor assets economically, the one major commodity which has failed to benefit from economic growth: it did not become any cheaper, either in relative or in absolute terms.

Housing is the main source of financial volatility: as Leamer says, 'Housing *is* the Business Cycle' (Leamer, 2007). Real estate fever is often implicated in financial crashes (Herring and Wachter, 1999): looking back over the last forty years, there was a commercial property crisis in in the UK in 1973, a large Savings and Loans crisis in the United States in the 1980s. Real estate speculation brought down the Japanese boom of the 1980s, and the economy has never really recovered. Credit loosening in Scandinavian countries in the 1980s was quickly followed by a real estate lending boom and by financial crises and sharp contractions in the early 1990s (Jonung et al., 2009; Honkaphoja, 2009). Imprudent mortgage lending led to a massive crisis in 2007–8 which is still unfolding, especially in the United States, Spain, Ireland, and the UK. Germany, which has a large rental sector, and whose house prices did not escalate, largely escaped a direct financial crisis, and is only affected by the imprudent investment of German banks in overseas mortgages.

The mechanisms of these crises are driven by two factors. Shelter is a necessity, and housing is one of the most visible signals of social status, one that is difficult to make and difficult to fake. Demand for accommodation consequently appears to be quite rigid, and is thus not tightly constrained by income. If house prices rise, consumers will continue to compete as long as they can. This is demonstrated by the long duration of housing 'hot-spots' on the coasts of the United States, and for decades at a stretch in the UK. All the more so, if consumers are provided with credit. In that case, they are merely constrained by their ability to service debt, and can extend the working hours of their households (i.e. with income from two or more adults) in order to service these debts. The uneven increase in house prices across different regions in the USA suggests that it is credit supply which has driven the booms. We now need to consider what factors first constrained and then facilitated the supply of credit after Second World War.

9.4 BANKING *c.*1945–1970

The Second World War ended with a large government debt overhang, and most of the lending capacity of the banks was utilized in rolling over this debt. Commercial lending was restricted. At the same time, a demand for credit opened up. Full employment, rising incomes, and the end of rationing in the early 1950s built up demand for consumption. A housing boom was financed partly from building society sources, and partly by the government. New housing is usually accompanied by the purchase of consumer durables like furniture and carpets. At the same time, a pent-up demand had built up for household appliances, for washing machines, cookers, and refrigerators, and also for motor cars to facilitate commuting from the new outlying suburban locations, and to make use of public investment in highways and motorways. Banks responded by providing, for the first time, loans for consumption purposes, and a system of credit scoring for consumer borrowers. The first credit card came in 1966. The production and sale of consumer goods also needed to be financed and accommodated, generating demand for factories, retail premises and for office space in town centres. Credit for these purposes required longer maturities than the existing banking system was used to provide. Commercial property required large new sources of mortgage lending. The existing clearing bank system, constrained as it was with lending controls, was not able to respond adequately to these demands, which were met in large part by hire-purchase credit companies and by secondary banks.

The issue was investigated in the Radcliffe committee on the working of the monetary system, which sat between 1957 and 1959. The Bank of England, and the Treasury, who between them managed the monetary system, faced four tasks that were not easily squared. One was to roll over and begin to discharge the large overhang of government debt. A second was to maintain price stability, primarily at this stage in order to maintain the exchange rate. A third was to maintain full employment and the momentum of growth, and a fourth was to accommodate the new demands for credit. The committee dismissed the concept of 'money', and instead focused on the larger issue of liquidity, which was determined by the supply of credit overall. This earned it some scorn from contemporary and subsequent commentators of a monetarist bent (Capie, 2010: 134–7), but in my humble view it was right. It identified no magic bullet, and instead recommended a pragmatic mix of administrative, regulatory, fiscal, and monetary controls, involving a good deal of regulatory judgement, to try to keep the lid on credit expansion. This turned out to be messy to manage and not very precise. But the decade that followed only looked bad at the time: in retrospect those were years of prosperity and growth, albeit with upwards inflation creep. By the end of the sixties, however, the regulators had tired of regulating, and the policy mood had changed.

The Radcliffe Committee took evidence painstakingly for two years. It wanted to find out how banking worked, and to improve it by the application of reason and judgement. A decade later, policymakers had lost their patience. The British economy, bound to a fixed exchange rate, struggled from one apparent crisis to another. From Chicago blew the winds of market efficiency and monetarism, and the drafts penetrated the Bank (Davies, 2012: 5–6). The central bankers pushed aside the lessons of practice and judgement, and reached for the convictions of faith. On Christmas Eve 1970, the chief economist of the Bank of England, John Fforde, wrote in an internal memo to senior colleagues:

> He who argues for fundamental change must to some degree, be preaching a faith. If one does not believe that competition is capable of stimulating efficiency and innovation, then presumably one ought not to object to a permanent system of ceiling controls on banks. But if competition has any virtue, we ought not to have a system that stifles. (Fforde, 1970: 6)

This line of reasoning justified a root and branch reform, known as 'Competition and Credit Control', applied in September 1971 (Bank of England, 1971). It replaced controls on borrowing with competition for credit by means of interest rates. More important for our story is the intention of breaking down functional barriers between the clearing bank cartel and other finance companies in order to create a uniform credit market and allow market forces free rein. That is a good idea, if one believes that the unfettered operation of market forces is benign. At the height of Victorian laissez-faire, the Victorians did not hold this belief. And despite the dominance of efficient market doctrines during the last three decades, there is no analytical proof that markets necessarily have such benign outcomes, while the empirical evidence is very mixed.

Shortly afterwards, the Bank of England gave a strong indication that those who took liberties with market freedoms would not be punished. Competition and Credit Control (CCC) was consistent with Edward Heath's dash for growth. But instead of an industrial investment boom, what followed was a consumer boom, with rising property values and imports. Inflation rose and was followed by widespread industrial unrest. Following the oil shock of 1973, the secondary banks which had largely financed the boom faced the prospect of failure, and were rescued by the Bank of England. Those who took excessive risk were bailed out (Reid, 1982).

In this respect as well, CCC was a genuine turning point. It started a withdrawal from prudence, and an increase in lending which continued unabated for more than three decades, until 2008. The underlying faith in competition and markets was the new policy metaphysics. The unleashing of credit also shook up the City of London. The stock markets revived, overseas banks began to arrive in large numbers, and a large Euromarket in dollars developed in London for corporate financing.

9.5 CREDIT LIBERALIZATION, 1979–2008

The Thatcher government which came into office in 1979 shared the intuitive faith in market efficiency. It followed on CCC with a sequence of moves to deregulate finance. There is no need to go through these shifts in detail. In outline, capital controls were abolished in 1979, deposit insurance was introduced in the same year, ceilings on lending were lifted in 1980, and the 'Big Bang' reform of City of London institutions in 1986 changed the culture of finance, by admitting Wall Street investment firms with their risk-taking bonus culture; eventually they absorbed or crowded out British investment banks. In the course of the 1980s, the separate compartments by function of British finance were finally dismantled.

Housing finance, which was still prudently rationed by the building societies, was also opened up from 1980 onwards. The residue of rent control was abolished, and council houses were offered for sale to their tenants, with councils forbidden to use the money to build new houses. This extended the market for housing finance, although housebuilding actually stagnated. Banks were allowed to enter mortgage lending in 1980, and from 1986 onwards, the building societies began to convert themselves from mutual societies into traded public shareholder companies. Their managers took the opportunity to help themselves to the accumulated reserves built up over several generations. The chief executives increased their pay about threefold (Shiwakoti et al., 2004). The shareholders were given between £135 each (Abbey National) and up to £2,000 (Halifax). Overall, about £36 billion in shares and cash were distributed by 1997. With the exception (among the giants) of the Nationwide, all the large societies (notably the Abbey National and the Halifax) took this route, although some sixty societies remained mutual. The prudence that had built the privatized societies into greatness now deserted them, and none of them managed to survive as an independent private entity. Banks and privatized building societies competed avidly to lend, and drove up house prices rapidly. The rise of house equity made homeowners feel wealthier, and discouraged them from saving.

The challenge for finance from the 1970s onwards was quite different from what it was in the early post-war years. The 1970s were also a transition period into a new type of economy. Labour productivity rose more slowly, and business profits also declined. Exporters were increasingly challenged, and the domestic manufacturing and coal mining sectors went into decline. The cyclical shock of high oil prices was mitigated by the development of North Sea oil fields, whose royalties also helped to reduce the fiscal burden on government. But the consequent strong pound (pushed up by oil and the high-interest rates of anti-inflation policy) was another burden for manufacturing, which lost ground to competitors in Europe and in East Asia. Instead of British export earnings, City banks now managed the earnings of exporters *into* Britain. International capital mobility and floating exchange rates made it easier for large international balances to find their way into London.

Bankers faced a new challenge: how to recycle the large amount of liquidity placed in their hands. Financial deregulation gave them a free hand to lend it out. The problem was to find profitable outlets. Initially, the balances arose from the large surpluses of oil exporting countries. From the 1980s onwards, as domestic and international inequality surged, large domestic funds had to be recycled as well. It is difficult to be more precise. A reform of the presentation of the National Accounts in 1997 means that flow of funds accounts before 1987 are no longer available online, so it is difficult to monitor where the money came from and where it went.

The structural change in finance is dramatic: in the course of somewhat more than three decades, bank lending has risen from less than half of gross domestic product, a level at which it had rested since the 1880s, to ten times as much, that is, more than five times gross domestic product. Liquidity ratios, which had been firmly regulated, declined from about 30 per cent (on the broadest definition) down to almost nothing by the end of the century. Capital/asset ratios, which were more than ten per cent before the First World War, fell down to less than 5 per cent. Banking business, previously a sedate activity delivering between 5 and 7 per cent return on capital, acquired the attributes of highly profitable, and by implication, highly risky business, returning between 20 and 30 per cent, an order of magnitude higher than the typical 2 to 3 per cent of long-term economic growth a year (Haldane and Alessandri, 2009).

These changes transmitted themselves to the structure of the economy. Let us reduce the economy to four sectors: (a) manufacturing and mining, (b) government, health and education, (c) construction, utilities, and trade, and (d) finance and business services. Taking the gross value added to gross domestic product of each sector, then between 1970 and 2005, sectors (b) and (c) each remained approximately constant. Manufacturing and mining declined from around 37 per cent to 16 per cent. At the same time finance and business services replaced it almost precisely, rising from less than 20 per cent to

36 per cent. Movements in employment were similar in magnitude, with manufacturing and mining declining sharply, and finance and business services taking their place. Financial intermediation on its own rose to some 14 per cent of GDP value added (Offer, 2012: Figure 4, 33).

For the financial system, making a profit in this service economy became a problem. This is where housing became so important. Housing is a long-lived commodity, and new construction only adds a tiny fraction in any given year. Supply cannot expand rapidly, but price was responsive to the supply of credit. With public housing declining and stigmatized, with private rental property inferior in quantity and quality, people in work competed for housing by bidding up prices. In doing so, they were supported by the deregulated financial system and by low interest rates. Up to the 1980s, mortgages, despite the large aggregate quantities, were a lacklustre asset almost entirely issued by non-traded mutual societies. The deregulation of mortgage lending, and the privatization of the building societies, opened up what seemed to be a secure and open-ended supply of assets with a good financial yield. Effectively it allowed financial institutions to capture a rising share of the labour income of the country. For borrowers the deal was mitigated by the prospect of capital gains, as house prices increased much faster than incomes. Financial institutions leveraged their small capital with deposits from overseas, and from selling off the loans and lending the proceeds again, thus creating as much new credit as they dared, with leverage ratios rising up to levels of between 40 and 50 (Vickers Commission, 2011: Figure 5.4, 128). On the borrowing side, mortgage-borrowing debt rose about fourfold in relation to income between 1975 and 2005, while unsecured debt rose about the same (Fernandez-Corugedo and Muellbauer, 2006: Chart 3, 43). By the end of the period, outstanding UK debt amounted to about three times gross domestic product, and about 80 per cent of that was secured on housing and commercial real estate (Vickers Commission, 2011: Figure 3.4, 51; Treasury Select Committee, 2009–10, Lord Turner's evidence, 2 March 2010, Ev83).

The decline of productive investment opportunities also caused finance to turn its attention to the public services, to utilities, transport, infrastructure, education, and health, which are mostly financed by the government. It is beyond the scope of this essay to deal with privatization in its various forms. Suffice it to say here that the privatizations of utilities and other infrastructure provision in education and health and defence constituted a successful move by finance to convert tax revenues that support these activities into profit streams (Offer, 2012: 30–4). Financial enterprise was not about identifying new productive opportunities, but about capturing a share of the labour income flow, the most reliable and stable revenue source available. It was this revenue source which underpinned the huge profits, salaries, and bonuses earned in the financial sector.

9.6 A PROPERTY WINDFALL ECONOMY

The unshackling of credit in the UK in the 1970s eventually created what might be called a property windfall economy. It continued for more than thirty years, and for a long time had more winners than losers. For that reason, it enjoyed broad popular support. When costs increase, that is a sign of reduced efficiency, but in the property windfall economy, rising property values were taken by the media, in line with popular perceptions, to be a sign of health. Indeed, even four or five years after the crisis, much effort is being expended in restarting the property boom.

Among the winners may be listed, first, the borrowers. If they had to take out larger loans, and if their monthly outlays tended to rise (which they did; Offer, 2008: Figure 4, 551, and unpublished data from CML Research, provided by John Muellbauer), they acquired an appreciating asset. This asset could then be used to rise another step up the housing ladder, to bleed off some equity to finance consumption, to act as a nest egg in a world of unstable values and relentless inflation, and to bequeath to their children. Many of the baby-boom generation, who came of age in the 1960s and 1970s, did well out of the property windfall economy, and were hardly inclined to question it.

For the lenders, the property boom provided an expanding market for their activities. In rolling over increasing quantities of liquidity that accumulated within the system in consequence of global trade imbalances and the rise of domestic inequality, the open-ended housing market provided what seemed to be reliable and safe returns. The lending profits were creamed off by a small elite of lending companies and by their executives, who took a lion's share of the profits, with the rest going to shareholders, some of them pension funds, whose managers also paid themselves well. These large payouts to managers exacerbated the inequality that had helped to cause them in the first place.

The 'Great Moderation' of expanding housing, low consumer inflation, and asset price inflation, gave credibility to market efficiency doctrines. They appeared to vindicate the regimes of Thatcher, Reagan, Clinton, Blair, and Brown, and their de-regulatory reforms. So much so, that the political left largely embraced these doctrines as well, and indeed went further in implementing them, pushing financial institution de-regulation beyond the boundaries still respected by their conservative predecessors. The Great Moderation also vindicated the exponents of market efficiency within economics.

Voters increased their standards of living, mostly due to cheaper manufactures of rising quality, imported from the Far East. In the 1980s and 1990s, the low cost of liquid energy and gas heating also stimulated motorization, and gas central heating. The transactions economy, with its large profits and large incomes, helped to maintain employment, and provided a strong flow of taxation. In gratitude, governments gave financiers substantial tax breaks, in the form of lower taxation on capital gains and on non-domiciled residents. From the 1990s onwards, governments also drew on the City to finance infrastructure investment through public-private arrangements (PFI) at mark-ups greatly in excess of the cost of public borrowing. In the process, both ministers and civil servants benefited personally through a 'revolving door' system, in which ministers moved on to lucrative directorships, and civil servants moved in and out of the private companies they contracted with (Transparency International, 2011; Kremer, 2012). On a fairly crude measure of an annual sample of instances of corruption reported in *Private Eye*, reported corruption rose about tenfold between the 1970s and the 2000s, with private-public deals generating the largest number of instances (author's work in progress with Danyal Arnold).

Who lost? When Old Labour morphed into New Labour, it moved into the centre ground of J.K. Galbraith's 'Economy of Contentment', in which the weak minorities were sacrificed for the benefit of comfortable majorities. As houseowners became increasingly wealthy, newcomers into the housing market were increasingly shut out. After 2001, house prices rose three times more than incomes in ten years (National Housing Federation, 2012). In the more affluent parts of the country, it became impossible for ordinary workers in average types of jobs, even professional jobs, and even working couples, to move from rental into purchase (Offer, 2006: 284–5; Batchelor, 2007). The surpluses accumulated by houseowners and lenders (and speculatively, by some borrowers) were then channelled into providing rented accommodation, much of it of lower quality, for those who could not afford to buy. By 2011, renting families were spending almost half their pay for housing (Rawlinson, 2011). In order to be able to buy many had to put in much longer hours of work, requiring mothers to earn rather than look after children, and to spend what was left over on childcare. The effects on family structure and functioning have yet to be studied.

9.7 CLIMAX

In 2007–8 the music stopped. Debt could be rolled over no longer. As in Japan and Scandinavia earlier, the housing and commercial property finance boom collapsed. In order to maintain the flow of real estate lending, prudential standards in the USA and in Britain had been lowered, and by 2006, the high levels of property values and debt could no longer be supported out of the incomes of increasingly marginal borrowers. Once default began, it began to spiral downwards, and eventually shook the foundations of the whole financial system, which fell into a crisis that is far from ended (Duca et al., 2010).

A good deal of the debate about the crisis has taken the form of a technical discussion about the structure of financial institutions. In the UK, Competition and Credit Control of 1971 began the dismantling of functional specialization in British finance, and the unclasping of the credit 'corset' in 1980s and mortgage lending by the banks, and the Big Bang in the City of 1986 opened the way for universal 'one-stop' global banks, which combined payments, lending, investment, mortgages, and 'investment banking', that is, speculative financial activity for corporate clients, wealthy individuals, and on their own account.

The UK did not have any Glass-Steagall legislation to go back to, of the kind that had separated retail and investment banking in the United States. After the collapse of much of the UK banking system, and its bailout by government at taxpayer expense, many voices advocated the erection of such barriers. The Vickers Commission, which reported in 2011, recommended a porous separation, further diminished by uncertainty and the postponement of its implementation until 2019.

Is that likely to restore stability to the banking system, let alone that kind of stability it had enjoyed for more than ten decades after 1866? What are the fundamental requirements? It seems to me that the core function of the banking system, that public policy needs to safeguard, is the payment systems. In the summer of 2012, the electronic payments system of several banks failed for short periods. That provided a reminder of the importance of this function. Reliable and secure payment is what the great Victorian and inter-war clearing banks provided.

The second issue is what to do with real estate. If the banking industry is to be broken up by function, then housing loans are not a suitable activity for narrow banks. Real estate provides the collateral backstop for the bloated banking system. The attributes of real estate as an asset make it unsuitable as security for the institutions that manage the payments system. The maturities are long, the assets are costly to liquidate, their value can fluctuate enormously, and they are exposed to taxation. The strictures of George Rae, in *The Country Banker* (1885), still hold. The Victorians knew why they kept away. There are several housing finance models available. Housing has been (and to some extent remains) in the public sector. That, in effect, was the nature of public housing. In the United States, no bastion of socialism, housing finance was kept under federal control by means of the FHA, and then of 'Fannie' and 'Freddie', until they were privatized in 1969, and they continued under semi-official tutelage afterwards, though not a very prudential one. Another option is the mutual/ethical model, like the North American savings and loans societies, which had been regulated strictly until the 1980s, or the British building societies, which had built-in constraints on their expansion. The largest mutual institutions in the UK, the Nationwide Building Society, and the Co-operative Bank, survived the crisis unscathed, although the

Nationwide did indulge in some wholesale borrowing, and the Co-op has recently come to grief due to an imprudent merger with the Britannia Building Society.

In the Vickers Commission report (2011), there is no consideration of keeping housing and commercial property finance beyond the reach of the ring-fenced banks. After the financial crisis in Sweden in the early 1990s, the Swedish government had sufficient independence and moral capital to deal quite brutally with the banks. No such detachment appeared to be possible for British governments. The Vickers Commission itself, despite being described as 'Independent' in its title, had two bankers among its five members. Its 'ring-fenced' banks would still be able to provide housing finance. Implicit in this decision (and the decision to place its functional boundaries *within* institutions, and not between them) was an acceptance that financial crises would continue; that the property windfall economy, or some variant of it, would be allowed to operate, at half-cock if necessary; that the immediate cost of preventing crises in the future was greater than their discounted future cost. The City honeypot was too dangerous to tamper with. The economy had changed so much since the 1970s that unwinding finance was too large a task to attempt.

Which leaves the problem still on the table. Finance is a heavy cost on the economy. If I believed in efficient markets, I would say a 'deadweight cost', a large rent levied for the benefit of those who administer the surpluses of Britain's suppliers, and the assets of its rich. Financial stability, it appears to me, is not just a matter of institutional design. It is not only a question of where boundaries will run, and which type of institution will be allowed to generate which type of credit. A return to stability requires a return to that credit rationing that gave so much pain to the bankers of the 1960s. It requires taking the windfall away. It requires pushing credit back into the bottles from which it had escaped. Is that possible? That is not just a banking question, but a social and political one. Its resolution, or the failure to do so, will determine the future course of the British economy and society. The stakes are that high.

10

Do Financial Crises Lead to Policy Change?

Youssef Cassis

10.1 INTRODUCTION

Have financial crises led to significant changes in policy? The question has been repeatedly asked in the wake of the financial crisis of 2007–8, as the world's informed opinion became intensely aware of the failure and dramatic consequences of a quarter of a century of ever-increasing financial deregulation. Good regulation, it is commonly assumed, should prevent the outbreak of financial crises, and financial crises have tended to spark off a strong demand for a change in the regulatory environment. Yet crises have kept recurring. This is not surprising. Policy changes are not a straightforward process. In particular, economic, political, ideological, or technical divergence, if not outright conflict—between bankers, customers, politicians, and regulators themselves—can easily blur the picture and compromise the outcome. And measures taken in the wake of one crisis can prove woefully inadequate to contain the following one—a classic case of fighting the previous war. Striking the right balance between insufficient or excessive control, self- or state regulation, national or international compliance has historically proved a huge challenge.

This chapter[1] considers the question from a long-term historical perspective, by looking at the effects that global financial crises have had on financial regulation at both domestic and international levels.[2] Its main argument is

[1] This chapter is based on my recent book *Crises and Opportunities: The Shaping of Modern Finance*, 2011.

[2] Eight global financial crises have broken out during this period: the Baring Crisis of 1890; the American Panic of 1907; the financial crisis of July–August 1914; the banking crises of the Great Depression of the 1930s; the financial instability of the early 1970s and the ensuing bank failures; the international debt crisis 1982: the Japanese banking crisis of 1997–8; and the financial debacle of 2007–8. The number might appear limited, given the hundreds of financial

that these effects have, on the whole, proved limited, including after the Great Depression of the 1930s, and that there have been significant differences between the United States and Europe. Section 10.2 of this chapter deals with the perception and understanding of past financial crises, on which the degree of intensity of the need for change ultimately depends; section 10.3 with the way the opportunities for improving the existing regulatory framework were actually seized. Section 10.4 reflects on the financial debacle of 2007–8 and its effects on policymaking in the light of these past historical experiences.

10.2 UNDERSTANDING PAST CRISES

The 'never again' feeling is a good indicator of the perception of a financial crisis—of its severity, its causes, the risks of a relapse, and how to prevent it. Perhaps surprisingly, the 'never again' feeling, while present in all crises, has only occasionally been very strong in the eight financial crises that hit the major economies in the last 120 years. The financial crises of the Great Depression mark a watershed, both because of the strength of the feeling and the fact that financial crises would never be perceived in the same way again.

The Baring crisis of 1890 shook the City but did not traumatize it, or not for long. The news that Barings had fallen was of course astounding, but it was revealed once the crisis had actually been solved and the panic was short-lived. More significantly, the Baring Crisis did not lead to much soul-searching in the City or Westminster about the national or international financial system. The severity of the crisis in Britain was primarily due to Barings' immense reputation and role in the markets. Its problems were attributed to individual mistakes rather than structural deficiencies. The other giant, Rothschilds, was above suspicion, doubts about the creditworthiness of other leading houses were soon dissipated, and the joint-stock banks were rapidly gaining power within the banking community. The other correlated cause of the crisis was of course Argentina: the Argentine foreign debt was renegotiated with a group of London bankers known as the Rothschild Committee.[3] Foreign issues did

crises recorded in recent quantitative analyses (see for example C. Reinhart and K. Rogoff, *This Time Is Different. Eight Hundred Years of Financial Folly*, Princeton, 2009). However, the vast majority of financial crises have taken place in emerging economies and have presented a different reality, at economic, social, political, as well as global levels, from those occurring in advanced economies.

[3] The Argentine Funding Arrangement was in practice a moratorium that relieved the Buenos Aires authorities of having to make full payments on their debt during a period of three years in exchange for new bonds printed by the Argentine state; Marichal, 1989: 159–70.

decline in the years following the crisis but, unlike what would happen nearly a century later, there was no debate about the risks associated with sovereign loans and more generally emerging markets. The City of London had a long experience of capital exports, the first Latin American debt crisis had taken place in the 1820s, and in 1875 a Select Committee on Loans to Foreign States had inquired on the conditions in which such loans were issued, centring on the role of Stock Exchange—without, however, making binding recommendations (House of Commons, 1875). A country's risk was evaluated on the basis of its budget, more precisely through the ratio of the cost of servicing its debt to its income from taxes. And the reputation of the issuing house offered guarantees to investors (Flandreau and Flores, 2009). The main concern raised by the Baring crisis was about Britain's gold reserves: were they really insufficient or was it acceptable to count on London's ability to attract gold if need be? There was also the matter of safeguarding these reserves: should the gold reserves accumulated by the clearing banks be deposited at the Bank of England? Or should each bank keep its own gold bars and coins and publish their total amount on its balance sheet? At the heart of the matter lay the contradiction between the Bank of England's responsibility as a central bank and its commercial activities as a private bank. No solution was found before 1914 (Sayers, 1976: 28–65).

Unlike the Baring crisis, the American panic of 1907 was not radically different from the recurrent banking crises that had marked American banking history in the nineteenth century, even though it mainly involved a new type of financial institution, the trust companies (Calomiris, 2000: 3–4).[4] The crisis was widely perceived as exceptionally severe—'the industrial paralysis and prostration was the very worst ever experienced in the country's history', according to the *Commercial and Financial Chronicle* (Livingston, 1986: 172)[5]—and was primarily attributed to deficiencies in the American banking system, in particular the absence of a central bank. The fact that banking crises in the United States were more frequent and more severe than in Western Europe or in its northern neighbour Canada did not escape contemporaries. On 30 May 1908, Congress passed the Aldrich-Vreeland Act which, in addition to enacting a scheme allowing banks to issue emergency notes, created the National Monetary Commission, whose mission was to 'inquire into and report to Congress . . . what changes are necessary or desirable in the monetary system of the United States or in the laws relating to banking and currency'. The Commission, chaired by Nelson Aldrich, a Republican Senator close to Wall Street banking circles, embarked on a formidable international inquiry, commissioning reports, written by leading national experts, and

[4] Crises erupted in 1819, 1837, 1839, 1857, 1861, 1873, 1884, 1890, 1893, and 1896.

[5] Though the number of failed banks in 1907 was smaller than in 1893 (73 as against 503), their total liabilities were over 20% higher (Wicker, 2000: 5, 87).

conducting interviews on the banking and currency systems of all major economies.[6] Another concern, of a more political nature, underlay the perception of the 1907 crisis: the concentration of power in the hands of Wall Street's financial elite. J. P. Morgan might have single-handedly saved the financial system, but the country's fate could not be left in the hands of one man. The Pujo Committee was appointed in 1912 to investigate the 'concentration of money and credit' and the fears aroused by the possible existence of a 'money trust' helped overcome the resistance to creation of the Federal Reserve System in 1913—the major regulatory outcome of the panic of 1907.

The financial crisis of July–August 1914 was of course different. The crisis was caused by the approach and then the outbreak of hostilities and subsequent financial disturbances were overwhelmed by the magnitude of the demands of a total war. And yet the war acted as a revelation, first of the fragility of the financial system, both nationally and internationally. As one of Baring Brothers' partners wrote in a letter: 'It is mortifying in the extreme to find how instantaneously the credit edifice which we have built for generations could tumble to pieces in a night' (Ziegler, 1988: 320). The war also revealed the new role of the state in financial affairs—saviour, customer, but also supervisor. To a remark made by Edward Holden, chairman of the London City and Midland Bank, one of the world's largest banks, that the state should take the responsibility if it had forced the banks to lend a lot of money wrongfully, David Lloyd George, the Chancellor of the Exchequer, answered: 'It takes the responsibility and the control' (Kynaston, 1999: 7). The relationship between the state and financial world would never be the same again. However, this was not yet clearly perceived in the aftermath of the war, nor that the world economic situation was very different from what it had been four or five years earlier. On the contrary, both financial and political leaders were determined to return to the pre-war order, longingly remembered as the belle époque. Nowhere was this clearer than in monetary matters, with the restoration of the gold standard in the early 1920s, which proved to be the most important contributory factor to the severity of the Great Depression (Eichengreen, 1992).

Unlike other crises, the Great Depression has been analysed time and again by economists and historians. As Ben Bernanke put it: 'To understand the Great Depression is the Holy Grail of macroeconomics' (Bernanke, 2000: 5). This particular status of the Great Depression as one of the defining moments in the world's history somewhat blurs the distinction between the perception of contemporaries and that of ensuing generations. The financial regulations inherited from the Great Depression go beyond the immediate measures taken

[6] Experts included Hartley Whiters and Inglis Palgrave for England, Alfred Neymarck for France, and Jakob Riesser for Germany, amongst others. See National Monetary Commission, 1910.

as a response to the banking crises, whatever their significance, and include the war and even the post-war years. The same goes with the analyses and interpretations of the crisis. Not only has the Great Depression become the reference against which subsequent crises have been judged, it has also altered the way subsequent crises have been dealt with—not least thanks to a far better understanding of economic and financial crises, from Keynes onwards.

Discussing how the banking crises of the 1930s were perceived by contemporaries would go far beyond the scope of this chapter. A few remarks can be made in connection with our general purpose. The first is the sense of the sheer enormity of the depression—the worldwide dimension of the crisis, the human misery of mass unemployment, the apparent collapse of capitalism, and also the rise of political extremism and growing international instability. The banking crises were only part of a much broader phenomenon, however intricate their links with the state of the economy. A second point to bear in mind is that, whatever the global character of the slump, it was felt very unevenly across countries, and analyses greatly differed as to the causes, nature, and impact of the financial crises. Britain was more concerned with the fate of the pound than its fairly stable banking system. In France, politico-financial scandals tended to overshadow a lingering though never really acute banking crisis. Opinions were divided in Germany, between those who attributed the crisis to the banks themselves—excessive foreign liabilities, insufficient equity, and ultimately the pernicious effects of universal banking—and those who saw the problem in the international politico-economic context—German foreign policy on reparations (Balderston, 1994). In the United States, the banking system remained, as in 1907, the main culprit, despite the creation, in the interval, of the Federal Reserve, which was supposed to have stabilized it. More than elsewhere, the blame was put on the speculative excesses of the 1920s and the financial crisis, and more generally the depression, linked to the Wall Street crash of October 1929 (Fraser, 2005: 367–418). Reactions to the crisis, in particular the necessity to do something, were thus motivated by a combination of economic and political considerations and, despite national differences, had their roots in a common zeitgeist—a sense that solutions should be found in state intervention rather than market mechanisms.

Like the financial crises of the 1930s, though in a far less dramatic way, those of the early 1970s were part of a broader economic crisis. Despite a number of bank failures (Bankhaus Herstatt in Germany, Franklin National Bank in the US, fringe banks in the UK), which required the intervention of the monetary authorities, it was the general economic climate—oil shock, 'stagflation', rising unemployment—and the crisis affecting other industries, not least iron and steel, which mostly exercised the minds of decision-makers. More generally, there was a pervasive feeling that an era was coming to an end—a change best expressed, in the field of economics, by the mounting neoclassical challenge to Keynesianism—to which the end of the regime of fixed exchange rates strongly contributed. As far as banking was concerned, the awareness of potential risks lying ahead was particularly strong. The crises marked the end of a long period of stability—these were the first banking failures of any significance since the Great Depression! While banking difficulties were seen as part of the adverse economic climate, in particular inflation and higher interest rates, this new instability was primarily attributed to the internationalization of financial activities and the higher risks they entailed—risks deriving from the growth of the foreign exchange market and the Eurocurrency interbank market. The frailty of the international banking system became apparent, raising the question of an international lender of last resort (Kindleberger, 1978; Spero, 1979; Reid, 1982).

The Mexican default in August 1982 came hard on the heels of the banking crises of the early 1970s and though different in many respects, the near panic was also linked to the development of the Euromarkets and, more generally, to an increasingly unstable international financial system. What became known as the International Debt Crisis was, on the one hand a violent though short-lived shock—there might have been less noticeable bank failures than in 1974, but the feeling that the international financial system could collapse was more vivid. On the other hand, it was a protracted affair, as what was also called the Latin American—and also the Third World—debt crisis lasted throughout the 1980s and beyond. This crisis triggered off much debate and analysis—politico-strategic, academic, and journalistic. Three interrelated problems came to the fore: the lending policy of the commercial banks; the level of indebtedness of Third World countries; and the global character of the crisis. Banks were judged severely—for lending at all costs and taking excessive risks. Attention, in particular, was drawn to their exposure to a single borrower, considered too high; and to their capital ratios, considered too low (Bird, 1989). In Europe and, especially in the United States, there were demands for stricter capital requirements and banking supervision, which increased after further banks' failures—Continental Illinois in the United States and Banco Ambrosiano in Italy. On the other hand, as with the Baring Crisis nearly a hundred years earlier, the problems at the periphery caused far more concern than those in the core industrial countries. Banks might have overlent, but for most analysts, the unsustainable debt level reached in countries such as Mexico, Brazil, or Argentina, was due to the poor conduct of their economy, in particular their lack of fiscal and monetary discipline. For some, however, the consequences of such mismanagement were compounded by adverse global economic conditions, in particular oil price increases and higher interest rates (Devlin, 1989). In any case, the 'structural adjustment' programmes of the International Monetary Fund and the World Bank were seen as the right solution here—despite being subjected, in several quarters, to strong criticism. More than ever before, the International Debt Crisis of 1982 was perceived as a global financial crisis, calling not only for an international response, but also for international cooperation in order to prevent the outbreak of another crisis.

The Japanese banking crisis of 1997–8 broke out several years into the slump, as the public was becoming progressively aware of the degradation of the economic climate—through rising unemployment, reductions in employee benefits, overtime hours, wage reductions, inability to sustain mortgage payments. The big banks had indeed fuelled the stock market and property booms during the 1980s. However, the causes of the banking crisis were not seen as lying exclusively with the deterioration of the Japanese economy. The Japanese banks appeared to be suffering from structural problems—in particular with regards to bad loans—and in need of radical reforms going beyond the type of regulatory measures usually taken in the wake of financial crises, such as tightening supervision and imposing higher capital requirements. In fact, the country's entire financial regulatory framework, especially the informal and personal relationships between the Ministry of Finance and the banks, was judged by Japanese and foreign observers alike as ill-suited to the demands of a severe crisis, hence the slow response of the authorities to the banks' problems (Amyx, 2004). Similar views were held about the Japanese economy as a whole. Public opinion has tended to eschew business cycle explanations of the economic crisis, implying targeted macroeconomic measures, in favour of structural explanations, implying a fundamental reform of the system (Takeshita and Ida, 2003).

10.3 CRISES AND REGULATORY REFORM

The level of regulation following a financial crisis has, to a large extent, been determined by the intensity of the 'never again' feeling, and the damage caused by unregulated innovation. From this perspective, the Great Depression apparently stands apart: it was the worst economic downturn in modern history and never before, or since, have such a battery of regulatory measures been adopted in order to tame financial activity. While there is some truth in this vision of events, the history of financial crises presents a more subtle picture. In the first place, financial crises have not automatically led to more regulation; on the contrary, this has been the exception rather than the rule. Secondly, state intervention and regulation, which marked the nearly half-century extending from the 1930s to the late 1970s, were the upshot of historical circumstances reaching beyond the Great Depression. Third, significant differences can be observed between the United States and Europe. And fourth, deregulation has also followed financial crises.

The Baring crisis of 1890 is the clearest case of no regulatory measures being taken in the aftermath of a financial shock. The Bank of England's preventive action was a model of intervention, which has been followed many times, not least during the secondary banking crisis in 1973, the international debt crisis in 1982 and the Long Term Capital Management collapse in 1998, but things ended there—because of the absence of panic, no real fear about the recurrence of such event, and the strength of Britain's laissez-faire tradition. Conversely, the panic of 1907 led to one of the most important pieces of legislation in American banking, the creation of the Federal Reserve System. The panic was real, the likelihood of its happening again strong, and the crisis widely attributed to the inadequacies of the American banking system. However, if there was a broad agreement behind the necessity of a central bank, there was much disagreement about the type of institution to be established—centralized or decentralized, under financial or political control? Antagonism against Wall Street remained vivid amongst Midwest country bankers and the solution could only be a compromise.

The Federal System aimed, above all, at solving the problem of the inelasticity of the money supply and the absence of a lender of last resort. It did so by setting up a decentralized structure, dividing the country into twelve districts, each provided with a Federal Reserve Bank located in the district's main city. Membership of the Federal Reserve was compulsory for the national banks though not for the state banks and trust companies. The Federal Reserve banks had the power of rediscounting bills, serving as a clearing house for member banks and monitoring banks. The entire system was overseen by the Federal Reserve Board, a body with eight members based in Washington and responsible for defining overall policy in agreement with the twelve Federal Reserve banks. How successful were the reforms that followed the panic of 1907? The creation of a central bank was undoubtedly a leap forward. However, all the opportunities for change were not and, for historical and political reasons, could not be seized. The creation of the Federal Reserve did not really alter the structure of American banking. On the one hand, it did not solve all the problems it intended to, in particular the pyramidal system of correspondent banking, whereby money centre banks held the reserves of provincial banks and this was seen as a destabilizing factor in times of crisis; and the separation between national banks and state banks, as many amongst the latter did not become members of the Federal Reserve. On the other hand, for many contemporaries and later observers, the main problem of the American banking system was the prohibition of branch banking—a question which was politically too sensitive to be addressed (White, 1983; see also Calomiris, 2000). The pre-1914 legislation did not prevent the outbreak of nineteenth-century-type banking panics in the early 1930s.

The 'never again' factor was especially strong during the First World War. This was indeed 'the war to end all wars'. The feeling, however, did not really extend to banking crises, whatever the acuity of those affecting some smaller European countries in the early 1920s. Legislative measures related to the banking sector, while being concerned with financial and monetary stability, were not primarily designed to prevent a return of the panic of August 1914. In the event, neither diplomacy nor finance was able to prevent the outbreak of another crisis and another war—the Treaty of Versailles and the restoration of the gold standard loom large in this context.

The Great Depression, on the other hand, was 'the crisis to end all crises'. In many countries, regulatory measures were taken to that effect, and in none more than in the United States. A series of radical reforms to the American financial market were introduced within the framework of the New Deal (White, 2000: 764–9). Two laws were passed in 1933, one on the capital market (the Securities Act) and the other on banks (the Banking Act, better known under the name of its two promoters as the Glass-Steagall Act). The first contained various provisions aimed at improving the quality of information about the securities offered and traded on the stock exchange. The second decreed the complete separation of commercial banking activities (taking deposits and making loans) from investment banking activities (issuing, distributing, and trading securities), including if these activities were shared between parent companies and subsidiaries or through either the cross-holding of shares or overlapping directorships. In practice, the commercial banks parted from their subsidiaries involved in securities transactions, whereas the vast majority of private banks opted for investment banking. The major exception was J. P. Morgan & Co, Wall Street's most famous bank, which chose to become a commercial bank, a decision that led several partners to resign and to found an investment bank, Morgan, Stanley & Co. (Chernow, 1990). The Glass-Steagall Act also introduced federal deposit insurance, compulsory for banks that were members of the Federal Reserve System, but optional and conditional for the others. The insured institutions paid a premium based on a percentage of their total assets, as a contribution to a guarantee fund intended to pay the depositors of a bankrupt bank. Six months after voting on the law, 14,000 banks had already decided to insure their clients, for a maximum sum of 5,000 dollars per deposit. Another federal regulation—Regulation Q—set a maximum interest rate that the banks could pay on savings deposits. Other laws completed this New Deal legislation, in particular the Securities Exchange Act of 1934, which created the Securities and Exchange Commission (SEC); the Investment Companies Act of 1940, which codified the rules governing investment companies; and the Banking Act of 1935, which reformed the Federal Reserve System, centralizing the conduct of monetary policy with the seven members of the Board of Governors in Washington.

Financial regulation did not go so far in the major European economies, including Germany, where universal banking managed to survive. Even so, owing to the particularly close links between banking and industry, its abolition was debated in a tense mood marked by populist anti-capitalism, rampant anti-Semitism, and politicians' paranoid fear of banking power. The banking law of December 1934, enacted under the Nazis, attributed the crisis to individual failings rather than to any shortcoming of the system; and it made do with strengthening bank supervision and introducing some restrictions on long-term deposits and on banks' representation on the supervisory boards of other companies. But even though universal banking survived, the government considerably strengthened its hold over financial institutions whose role in the economy grew weaker as a result of state subsidies granted to companies, the expansion of the savings banks, and the more or less automatic financing of growing public deficits through bank deposits (James, 1992: 277–9).[7] In France, things were left unchanged until 1941, when the Vichy government introduced a law, upheld and completed in 1944, which controlled and regulated banking activities that until then had been open to any newcomers. Henceforth, banks had to be registered according to their type of activity. The law made a clear distinction between an investment bank and a deposit bank. It also defined a number of specialized institutions, according to their operations or clientele, including finance companies and discount houses (Andrieu, 1990: 201–37). Britain, for its part, steered clear of the trend towards greater regulation of the banks, probably because there had not been any bank bankruptcies during the thirties, the financial system was more specialized than elsewhere, and the Bank of England effectively monitored it to ensure that it was working properly. Amongst other European countries, Italy and Belgium opted for abolishing universal banking, Switzerland for maintaining it. In Switzerland, the federal banking law of 1934, apart from setting some general rules and entrusting the supervision of the banking system to an independent commission, has above all been famous for its article 47 relating to banking secrecy—a measure which undoubtedly increased the competitive advantage of Swiss banks (Guex, 2000; Vogler, 2001).

With the exception of the United States, as well as Belgium and Italy, the measures of financial regulation taken in the wake of the Great Depression appear relatively mild and little intrusive. As far as most European countries were concerned, state intervention in banking affairs was as much a result of the depression as a consequence of the economic and political context of the thirties and, even more, the Second World War. Britain is a case in point. From an informal regulatory framework, mainly based on the personal suasion of the Bank of England's Governor, it emerged from the War with a nationalized central bank, though its governing structure at first remained virtually unchanged; and clearing banks still in the private sector but under the

[7] By 1938, savings banks had become the dominant element in the German banking system, with some 45% of total assets, compared with 15% for the commercial banks.

Treasury's and the Bank of England's strict control—as Keynes put it, in no need to be nationalized as in actual fact they already had been so. The London Stock Exchange was not only tightly regulated by the authorities, but its dealings were regarded with suspicion—options, considered highly speculative, were only reintroduced in May 1958 after an interruption of 19 years. In effect, the London Stock Exchange set itself up as the regulator of the securities market, with all the caution and conservatism that that implies (Michie, 1999: 326–422). In France, most of the financial sector came under state control after Liberation. The Banque de France was nationalized, together with the four big deposit banks[8] and all major insurance companies—though the *banques d'affaires* remained in private hands.[9] The state's grip ended up stifling the Parisian capital market, not only when it came to foreign issues, but also issues by French companies. The Paris Bourse became pretty sluggish. Having lost two-thirds of the nominal value of its securities through nationalizations, it went through a 'long depression' that lasted until the 1980s (Straus, 1992; Feiertag, 2005).

The 'lessons' from the Great Depression must, then, be put in their proper context. The regulations which characterized the third quarter of the twentieth century were the result of an exceptional historical period marked by two world wars, the redrawing of international boundaries, a devastating economic crisis, massive political upheavals and shifts in ideological outlooks—the 'Thirty Years War' of the twentieth century. This led to an ideological shift which, combined with a generational change, favoured state intervention and a more organized form of capitalism. Even in the United States, where the regulatory framework was essentially set up in the wake of the crisis, the Glass-Steagall Act appears to have been more ideological than pragmatic and was rooted in Americans' instinctive distrust of financial concentration and power, already denounced by the Pujo Commission of Enquiry at the beginning of the century (Smith and Sylla, 1993). In particular, the separation between commercial and investment banking did not really address the main cause of the banking crises: most of the small banks that failed between 1930 and 1933 were only commercial banks, and they failed because of the depression, their fragility, and the failure of the Federal Reserve to come to their aid. Conversely, the large New York and major city banks, which had securities affiliates, survived the crisis. And while there might have been conflicts of interests between commercial and investment banking, there is no evidence that the banks engaged in the two activities took more risks in the sort of securities they underwrote and marketed than specialized investment banks (White,

[8] Crédit lyonnais, Société générale, Comptoir national d'escompte de Paris, and Banque nationale pour le commerce et l'industrie.

[9] The leading French *banque d'affaire*, or investment bank, was the Banque de Paris et des Pays-Bas, also known as Paribas.

1986; Kroszner and Rajan, 1994). On the other hand, the introduction of deposit insurance, in other words a government commitment to make banks safer for depositors, could justify a measure limiting risk-taking.

The financial instability of the early 1970s did not give rise to wide-ranging regulatory reforms, but led to a closer supervision of a number of activities. In the United States, foreign exchange trading began to be monitored; the Federal Reserve imposed stricter capital and liquidity requirements to American banks expanding abroad; while foreign banks operating in the United States were brought under federal control, with the International Banking Act in 1978. In Germany, the federal authorities established limits to foreign exchange transactions by German banks and in 1976, the Lex Herstatt put limits on loans as a percentage of bank capital and increased the powers of the Federal Supervisory Office and the Bundesbank (Spero, 1979: 168–9). In Britain, where the crisis had been most acute, the Bank of England strengthened its supervisory organization and gave it a much more formal basis. This was complemented by the Banking Act of 1979, which put stricter conditions on the recognition of institutions as banks by the Bank of England. As Margaret Reid, a highly respected financial journalist, commented at the time: 'The Bank of England is indeed justified in insisting that the banking community should not again risk running into crisis through excessive mismatching and scarcity of liquidity' (Reid, 1982: 197). Everywhere, central banks extended their prerogative to prudential supervision (Spero, 1979: 153ss).

But it was the need for an international form of financial regulation which was most strongly felt, forty years after the Great Depression (on this topic, see in particular Alexander, Dhumale, and Eatwell, 2006; Davies and Green, 2008). A first step was the creation in December 1974 of the Standing Committee on Banking Regulation and Supervisory Practices—later known as the Basel Committee. It was formed by the central banks' governors of the Group of Ten, plus Switzerland and Luxemburg, with the BIS as its secretariat. The 'Basel Concordat' it issued the following year advocated sharing supervisory responsibility for banks' foreign activities between host and home country authorities. It took another crisis, the international debt crisis of 1982, for practical recommendations to emerge. Following the International Lending Supervision Act passed in the United States in 1983, the Basel Committee turned its attention to the issue of capital adequacy, with the aim of creating a level playing field for competition amongst international banks. The Basel Agreement—Basel I, more formally 'The International Convergence of Capital Measurements and Capital Standards'–was adopted in 1988 and implemented in 1992. It rested on three pillars–one measuring capital; a second weighting risk; and a third, with which Basel I is readily associated, setting a capital ratio of 8 per cent of risk-weighted assets.

In the meantime, while progress was being made towards some form of international regulation of the financial system, financial deregulation was the order of the day at national level from the late 1970s onwards, including in the wake of the shockwaves of 1974 and 1982. This was part of a much broader trend: the growing influence, first in the Anglo-Saxon countries, and then elsewhere in the world, of a neoliberal view of the economy and society, symbolically marked by the coming to power of Margaret Thatcher in the United Kingdom in 1979 and Ronald Reagan in the United States in 1981. Whatever the shifts in policies and attitudes, the fundamental dispensation—the smaller state and the strengthening of market mechanisms—was not really challenged until the crisis of 2007–8.

The movement started in the United States, with a liberalization of the financial markets. From 1 May 1975, the Securities and Exchange Commission abolished fixed commissions on the New York Stock Exchange, making competition there keener and leading to numerous small brokers disappearing and the largest ones, along with investment banks which henceforth had far greater equity capital at their disposal, being transformed into joint-stock companies. The City of London followed with 'Big Bang' on 27 October 1986, also a reform of the Stock Exchange abolishing fixed commissions and also the separation, unique to the London Stock Exchange, between the functions of brokers and jobbers.[10] Banks were also permitted to buy member firms, hitherto banned, bringing about the disappearance of almost all the leading brokerage houses, which were taken over by merchant banks, as well as the main commercial banks, both British and foreign. In Paris, the stockbrokers' monopoly was abolished in 1992. In Germany, the Bundesbank authorized certificate of deposits and floating-rate issues in 1984 and 1985, despite its distrust of financial innovation, and allowed foreign banks to act as lead banks for foreign issues in Deutschmarks.

Banking legislation was also relaxed in the United States. In 1980, Regulation Q was abolished by the Depository Institutions Deregulation and Monetary Control Act; in 1982, the Garn–St Germain Depository Institutions Act deregulated the savings and loans association—ushering in a crisis that devastated the industry; in 1994, with the Riegle-Neal Interstate Banking and Efficiency Act, banks were able to set up networks of branches throughout the country. Deregulation culminated in 1999 when the Glass-Steagall Act of 1933 was repealed by the Financial Modernisation Act. Commercial banking and investment banking could again be brought together on the grounds that new financial instruments justified greater concentration amongst the various intermediaries in the world of finance.

[10] Jobbers were securities traders, but they could not buy or sell them directly to the public, which did not have access to the Stock Exchange. For all its stock market transactions, the public was obliged to go through a broker who, in return for a commission, would negotiate with the jobber. A broker could speculate on his own account, but when working for a client, Stock Exchange rules did not allow him to sell a security for more than he had purchased it.

Deregulation was also the answer to the Japanese banking crisis, through a series of measures dubbed the 'Big Bang' and implemented between 1998 and 2001. They abolished, amongst others, barriers separating banking activities, securities transactions, and insurance; and liberalized foreign exchange transactions, bringing the national system into line with international standards. However, the powers of the bodies monitoring the financial system were strengthened while more autonomy was granted to the Bank of Japan.

At international level, in the face of criticisms, the evolution of the financial markets, and the financial crises of the 1990s, the Basel Committee undertook in 1998 to develop a 'Revised Framework on International Convergences of Capital Measurement and Capital Standards', known as Basel II, which was agreed in 2004, after six years of complex negotiations, still between the members of the G10, despite the growing number of countries adopting its standards.[11] While offering a more comprehensive approach to risk-weighting and capital ratios, Basel II was criticized for its excessive reliance on rating agencies and on the banks' internal risk models. The latter, in particular, was judged pro-cyclical and thus likely to make matters worse during a downturn, with all firms behaving in the same manner and facing increasing risks of illiquidity. The debacle of 2008 seems to have confirmed these doubts.

10.4 POLICYMAKING AFTER THE DEBACLE OF 2007–8

It is of course too early to draw a balance sheet of the perception of the financial debacle of 2007–8 and the policy changes carried out in its wake. However, the analysis of seven previous global financial crises and the events unfolding since September 2008 point to some possible directions.

Compared to previous experiences, the perception of the financial debacle of 2007–8 was at first that of a predominantly financial meltdown, more so than in the 1930s, the early 1970s, or the 1990s in Japan, when the banking crises were part of a broader economic downturn; the international debt crisis of the early 1980s was also primarily financial as far as advanced economies were concerned, but was closely linked with the deep economic problems of Latin American and other developing countries, as was the Baring Crisis in

[11] Basel II also rested on three pillars: the first, 'minimum capital requirements', offered a more comprehensive approach to risk-weighting; it also included capital to back operational risks and market risks in addition to credit risks on which Basel I was exclusively focused. The second pillar, 'supervisory review process', addressed the relationships between regulator and bank, with extended rights for the former. And the third pillar, 'market discipline', prescribed greater disclosure of capital and risk-taking positions to empower shareholders.

1890. The global character of the 2007–8 crisis was also underlined, with particular attention being drawn to the destabilizing effects of the growing world's economic imbalances since the turn of the twenty-first century; and the need for an internationally coordinated response to the crisis, including in terms of a global regulation of the financial system—a recurring theme since the 1970s. In terms of severity, comparisons were mainly done, though in a rather imprecise way, with the Great Depression of 1930s. As the effects of the financial crises started being felt on the real economy, attention turned to the nature of the recession, the risks of sliding into depression, the merits of fiscal stimuli, and exit strategies.

At the time of writing, the 'great recession' of the early twenty-first century was still unfolding and its perception was being shaped by new events, not least the austerity programmes adopted by most European countries in the face of growing budget deficits and, for some, the risks of a sovereign debt crisis. Four years after the fall of Lehman Brothers, three main observations could be made. First, no other crisis in history had ever been debated in such an extended way—by being for long and recurring periods on top of the political agenda; by sustained media coverage, despite the aridity of the topic; and by a flurry of publications, from highly academic analyses to popular books. It will be up to a new generation of historians to reflect on this phenomenon. Second, the 'never again' feeling had been very strong and almost unanimous, especially at the height of the financial collapse, with the spectre of 1929 reappearing more vividly than at any time since the end of the Second World War. However, and this is the third point, with time passing, the determination to push for radical change had been tempered by the inevitable return to business as usual—whatever the merits of the regulatory measures introduced in the aftermath of the crisis at both national and international levels (European Systemic Risk Board, Frank-Dodd Act, Vickers Report, Basel III).

The financial debacle of 2007–8 has probably not been severe enough to be followed by a fundamental overhaul of the financial system: a financial catastrophe has been avoided and however serious, the downturn has not been on the same scale as the Great Depression. This is in many ways warranted by the protracted Euro Crisis and the risks of an even more serious financial crisis still looming. Such a crisis would no doubt lead to a major change in the financial system, though it is unlikely to be a repeat of previous experiences—because of the complexity of financial operations, the economic weight of the financial sector, and the global character of financial activities, all far more pronounced that in any previous major crisis. But there are other factors possibly leading to policy changes. Financial crises should not be considered in isolation from other defining events. Two major turning points took place in the history of world capitalism in the twentieth century: one, during the depression and the Second World War, led to a marked level of state intervention; the other, during the 1970s, led, in far less dramatic circumstances, to a reversal of this trend. Financial crises were only one aspect of a wave of economic, political, socio-cultural, and geopolitical changes. There are signs of a turning point of similar proportions happening, not least with the rise of new economic powers and the neoliberal model reaching its limits.

Bibliography

Accominotti, O. (2012), 'London merchant banks, the central European panic, and the sterling crisis of 1931', *Journal of Economic History*, 72(1): 1–43.

Acheson, G. G., Hickson, C. R., and Turner, J. D. (2010), 'Does limited liability matter? Evidence from nineteenth-century British banking', *Review of Law and Economics*, 6: 247–73.

Acheson, G. G., Hickson, C. R., and Turner, J. D. (2011), 'Organizational flexibility and governance in a civil-law regime: Scottish partnership banks during the Industrial Revolution', *Business History*, 53: 505–29.

Acheson, G. G., and Turner, J. D. (2006), 'The impact of limited liability on ownership and control: Irish banking, 1877–1914', *Economic History Review*, 59: 320–46.

Acheson, G. G., and Turner, J. D. (2008a), 'The death blow to unlimited liability in Victorian Britain: The City of Glasgow failure', *Explorations in Economic History*, 45: 235–53.

Acheson, G. G., and Turner, J. D. (2008b), 'The secondary market for bank shares in nineteenth-century Britain', *Financial History Review*, 15: 123–52.

Acheson, G. G., and Turner, J. D. (2011a), 'Investor behaviour in a nascent capital market: Scottish bank shareholders in the nineteenth century', *Economic History Review*, 64: 188–213.

Acheson, G. G., and Turner, J. D. (2011b), 'Shareholder liability, risk aversion, and investment returns in nineteenth-century British banking', in D. R. Green, A. Owens, J. Maltby, and J. Rutterford (eds), *Men, Women, and Money: Perspectives on Gender, Wealth, and Investment 1850–1930*, Oxford: Oxford University Press: 207–77.

Admati, A. R., and Pfleiderer, P. (2010), 'Increased-liability equity: A proposal to improve capital regulation of large financial institutions', Stanford University Graduate School of Business Research Paper no. 2043.

Alborn, T. (1998), *Conceiving Companies: Joint-Stock Politics in Victorian England*, London: Routledge.

Aldcroft, D. H., and Fearon, P. (eds) (1972), *British Economic Fluctuations 1790–1939*, London: Macmillan.

Alderman, G. (1973), *The Railway Interest*, Leicester: Leicester University Press.

Alexander, K., Dhumale, R., and Eatwell, J. (2006), *Global Governance of Financial Systems: The International Regulation of Systemic Risk*, Oxford: Oxford University Press.

Ally, R. (1991), 'War and gold: The Bank of England, the London gold market and South Africa's gold, 1914–19', *Journal of Southern African Studies*, 17(2): 221–38.

Amyx, J. A. (2004), *Japan's Financial Crisis: Institutional Rigidity and Reluctant Change*, Princeton: Princeton University Press.

Andréadès, A. (1909), *History of the Bank of England*, London: P.S. King & Son.

Andrews, B. P. A. (1987), 'Exchange rate appreciation, competitiveness and export performance: the UK experience in the inter-war period', PhD thesis, University of Oxford.

Andrieu, C. (1990), *Les banques sous l'occupation: Paradoxes de l'histoire d'une profession*, Paris: Presses de la Fondation Nationale des Sciences.

Augar, P. (2000), *The Death of Gentlemanly Capitalism*, London: Penguin Books.

Bagehot, W. (1848), 'The currency problem', *Prospective Review*, 297–337, reprinted in N. S. J. Stevas (ed.), *The Collected Works of Walter Bagehot*, ix (1986), 15 vols. New York: Oxford University Press.

Bagehot, W. (1856), 'Unfettered banking', *Saturday Review*, 1 November 1856.

Bagehot, W. (1873), *Lombard Street: A Description of the Money Market*, London: King; New York: John Wiley and Sons, 1999 reprint.

Baker, M., and Collins, M. (1999), 'Financial crises and structural change in English commercial bank assets, 1860–1913', *Explorations in Economic History*, 36: 428–44.

Balderston, T. (1994), 'The banks and the Gold Standard in the German financial crisis of 1931', *Financial History Review*, 1(1): 43–68.

Balogh, T. (1947), *Studies in Financial Organization*, Cambridge: Cambridge University Press.

Bank of England (1961), 'Commercial Bills', *Bank of England Quarterly Bulletin*, 2 (4) (December): 26–31.

Bank of England (1971), Consultative document, 'Competition and credit control', 14 May 1971, reprinted in *Bank of England Quarterly Bulletin*, 11, (June 1971): 189–93.

Bank of England (1984), *The Development and Operation of Monetary Policy 1960–1983*, Oxford: Oxford University Press.

Banks, E. (1999), *Rise and Fall of the Merchant Banks*, London: Kogan Page.

Batchelor, R. A. (1986), 'The avoidance of catastrophe: Two nineteenth-century banking crises', in F. Capie and G. Wood (eds), *Financial Crisis and the World Banking System*. London: Macmillan, 41–76.

Batchelor, L. (2007), 'First-time buyers better off up North', *The Observer*, 9 September 2007. London.

Bean, C. R. (1981), 'An econometric model of manufacturing investment in the UK', *Economic Journal*, 91: 106–21.

Bell, G. (1858), *Commentaries on the Laws of Scotland*, 6th edition. Edinburgh: T. & T. Clark.

Bernanke, B. (1983), 'Nonmonetary effects of the financial crisis in the propagation of the Great Depression', *American Economic Review*, 73(3): 257–76.

Bernanke, B. (2000), *Essays on the Great Depression*, Princeton: Princeton University Press.

Bignon, V., Flandreau, M., and Ugolini, S. (2012), 'Bagehot for beginners: The making of lender-of-last-resort operations in the mid-nineteenth century', *Economic History Review*, 65(2): 580–608.

Bird, G. (1989), *Commercial Bank Lending and Third World Debt*, London: Macmillan.

Boot, H. M. (1984), *The Commercial Crisis of 1847*, Occasional Papers in Economic and Social History No. 11, Hull: Hull University Press.

Britton, A. (1986), *The Trade Cycle in Britain 1958–1982*, Cambridge: Cambridge University Press.

Broadberry, S. N., Campbell, B. M., Klein, A., Overton, M., and van Leeuwen, B. (2011), 'British economic growth, 1270–1870: An output-based approach', Department of Economic History, London School of Economics (18 December).

Broadberry, S. N., and van Leeuwen, B. (2010), 'British economic growth and the business cycle 1700–1870 annual estimates', Department of Economics, University of Warwick.

Bryer, R. A. (2003), 'Accounting for the "railway mania" of 1845—a great railway swindle?' *Accounting, Organisations and Society,* 16(5/6): 439–86.

Burk, K. (1989), *Morgan Grenfell 1838–1988,* Oxford: Oxford University Press.

Cairncross, A. K. (1953), *Home and Foreign Investment, 1870–1913: Studies in Capital Accumulation,* Cambridge: Cambridge University Press.

Calomiris, C. W. (2000), *U.S. Bank Deregulation in Historical Perspective,* Cambridge: Cambridge University Press.

Calomiris, C. W. (2011), 'Banking crises and the rules of the game', in G. Wood, T. C. Mills, and N. Crafts (eds), *Monetary and Banking History: Essays in Honour of Forrest Capie,* London: Routledge, 88–132.

Calomiris, C. W., and Kahn, C. M. (1991), 'The role of demandable debt in structuring optimal banking arrangements', *American Economic Review,* 81: 497–513.

Calvo, G. A. (1998), 'Capital flows and capital-market crises: the simple economics of sudden stops', *Journal of Applied Economics,* 1(1): 35–54.

Cameron, R. (1967), *Banking in the Early Stages of Industrialization: A Study in Comparative Economic History,* New York: Oxford University Press.

Capie, F. (1995), 'Commercial banking in Britain between the wars' in C. H. Feinstein (ed.) *Banking, Currency, and Finance in Europe between the Wars,* Oxford: Clarendon Press, 395–413.

Capie, F. (2002), 'The emergence of the Bank of England as a mature central bank', in D. Winch and P. K. O'Brien (eds) *The Political Economy of British Historical Experience 1688–1914,* Oxford: Oxford University Press, 295–315.

Capie, F. (2004), 'Money and economic development in eighteenth-century England', in L. Prados (ed.) *Exceptionalism and Industrialisation: Britain and its European Rivals, 1688–1815,* Cambridge: Cambridge University Press, 216–34.

Capie, F. (2010), *The Bank of England: 1950s to 1979,* Cambridge and New York: Cambridge University Press.

Capie, F., Goodhart, C. A. E., Fischer, S., and Schnadt, N. (1994), *The Future of Central Banking,* Cambridge: Cambridge University Press.

Capie, F., and Webber, A. (1985), *A Monetary History of the United Kingdom, 1870 to 1982,* London: Allen and Unwin.

Carr, J. L., and Mathewson, G. F. (1988), 'Unlimited liability as a barrier to entry', *Journal of Political Economy,* 96: 766–84.

Cassis, Y. (2011), *Crises and Opportunities: The Shaping of Modern Finance,* Oxford: Oxford University Press.

Casson, M. (2009a), 'The efficiency of the Victorian British railway network: A counterfactual analysis', *Networks and Spatial Economics,* 9: 339–78.

Casson, M. (2009b), *The World's First Railway System: Enterprise, Competition, and Regulation on the Railway Network in Victorian Britain,* Oxford: Oxford University Press.

Chamberlain, Sir Austen. (1935), *Down the Years*, London: Cassell.

Chapman, S. (1984), *The Rise of Merchant Banking*, London: Allen and Unwin.

Chatziioannou, M-C., and Harlaftis, G. (2007), 'From the Levant to the City of London: Mercantile credit in the Greek international commercial networks of the 18th and 19th Centuries', in P. L. Cottrell, E. Lange, and U. Olsson (eds) *Centres and Peripheries in Banking: The Historical Development of Financial Markets*, Aldershot: Ashgate, 13–40.

Checkland, S. (1975), *Scottish Banking: A History, 1695–1973*, Glasgow: Collins.

Chernow, R. (1990), *The House of Morgan*, London.

Clapham, J. (1966), *The Bank of England: A History, ii: 1797–1914*, Cambridge: Cambridge University Press.

Clarke, S. V. O. (1967), *Central Bank Co-operation, 1924–1931*, New York: Federal Reserve Bank.

Clay, Sir Henry, (1957), *Lord Norman*, London: Macmillan.

Clay, W. (1837), Speech of William Clay, Esq., M. P., *Moving for the Appointment of a Committee to Inquire into the Operation of the Act Permitting the Establishment of Joint-stock Banks*, London: J. Ridgway.

Cleary, E. J. (1965), *The Building Society Movement*, London: Elek Books.

Cleveland-Stevens, E. C. (1883), *English Railways: Their Development and their Relation to the State*, London: Routledge.

Collins, M. (1988), 'English banks and business cycles, 1848–89' in P. L. Cottrell and D.E. Moggridge (eds) *Money and Power*, London: Macmillan.

Collins, M. (1989), 'The banking crisis of 1878', *Economic History Review*, 42: 504–27.

Collins, M. (1990), *Money and Banking in the UK: A History*, London: Routledge.

Conti-Brown, P. (2011), 'Unlimited shareholder liability for systematically important financial institutions', Stanford University: Rock Center for Corporate Governance Working Paper.

Cottrell, P. L. (1988), 'Credit, morals and sunspots: The financial boom of the 1860s and trade cycle theory', in P. L. Cottrell and D. E. Moggridge (eds) *Money and Power*, London: Macmillan.

Cottrell, P. L. (2003), 'The financial system of the United Kingdom in the twentieth century', in L. De Rosa (ed.) *International Banking and Financial Systems: Evolution and Stability*, Aldershot: Ashgate.

Crafts, N. F. R., and Fearon, P. (2010), 'Lessons from the 1930s Great Depression', *Oxford Review of Economic Policy*, 26: 285–317.

Crick, W. F., and Wadsworth, J. E. (1936), *A Hundred Years of Joint Stock Banking*, London: Hodder and Stoughton.

Dale, R., Johnson, J. E. V., and Tang, L. (2005), 'Financial Markets can go mad: Evidence of irrational behaviour during the South Sea Bubble', *Economic History Review*, 58(2): 233–71.

Davies, A. (2012), 'The evolution of British monetarism: 1968–1979', Discussion Paper in Economic and Social History, no. 104, University of Oxford.

Davies, H., and Green, D. (2008), *Global Financial Regulation: The Essential Guide*, Cambridge: Polity Press.

Deane, P. (1968), 'New estimates of gross national product for the United Kingdom, 1830–1870', *Review of Income and Wealth Series*, 14: 95–112.

Deane, P. (1979), *The First Industrial Revolution.* 2nd edition, Cambridge: Cambridge University Press.
Devlin, R. (1989), *Debt and Crisis in Latin America: The Supply Side of the Story*, Princeton: Princeton University Press.
Dimsdale, N. H. (1981), 'British monetary policy and the exchange rate, 1920–1938', *Oxford Economic Papers*, 33: 306–49.
Dimsdale, N. H. (1990), 'Money, interest and cycles in Britain since 1830', *Greek Economic Review Supplement*, Autumn, 12: 153–96.
Dimsdale, N. H., and Horsewood, N. (1995), 'Fiscal policy and employment in interwar Britain: Some evidence from a new model', *Oxford Economic Papers*, 47: 369–96.
Dimsdale, N. H., Horsewood, N., and van Riel, A. (2006), 'Unemployment in interwar Germany: An analysis of the Labor Market, 1927–1936', *Journal of Economic History*, 66, 3: 778–808.
Dimsdale, N. H., Nickell, S. J., and Horsewood, N. (1989), 'Real wages and unemployment in Britain during the 1930s', *Economic Journal*, 99: 271–92.
Dornbusch, R., and Frenkel, J. A. (1984), 'The Gold Standard and the Bank of England in the Crisis of 1847', in M. D. Bordo and A. J. Schwartz (eds) *A Retrospective on the Classical Gold Standard, 1821–1931*, Chicago: University of Chicago Press.
Drees, B., and Pazarbasioglu, C. (1998), *The Nordic Banking Crises: Pitfalls in Financial Liberalization?* Washington DC: International Monetary Fund.
Duca, J. V., Muellbauer, J., and Murphy, A. (2010), 'Housing markets and the financial crisis of 2007–2009: Lessons for the future', *Journal of Financial Stability*, 6(4): 203–17.
Dun, J. (1876), 'The banking institutions, bullion reserves, and non-legal-tender note circulation of the United Kingdom statistically investigated', *Journal of the Statistical Society*, 39: 1–189.
Eichengreen, B. (1992), *Golden Fetters: The Gold Standard and the Great Depression 1919–1939*, Oxford: Oxford University Press.
Eichengreen, B., and Jeanne, O. (2000), 'Currency crisis and unemployment: Sterling in 1931', in P. Krugman (ed.) *Currency Crises*, Chicago: National Bureau of Economic Research.
Eichengreen, B., and Temin, P. (2000), 'The Gold Standard and the Great Depression', *Contemporary European History*, 9(2): 183–207.
England, C. (1988), 'Agency costs and unregulated banks: Could depositors protect themselves?' *Cato Journal*, 7: 771–97.
Esty, B. C. (1998), 'The impact of contingent liability on commercial bank risk taking', *Journal of Financial Economics*, 47: 189–218.
Evans, D. M. (1849), *The Commercial Crisis, 1847–1848*, London: Letts, Son and Steer; 1970 facsimile reprint of 2nd edition, Devon: David & Charles.
Feavearyear, A. E. (1963), *The Pound Sterling: A History of English Money*, 2nd edition revised by E. V. Morgan, Oxford: Oxford University Press.
Feiertag, O. (2005), 'The international opening-up of the Paris Bourse: Overdraft-economy curbs and market dynamics', in E. Bussière and Y. Cassis (eds) *London and Paris as International Financial Centres in the Twentieth Century*, Oxford: Oxford University Press, 229–46.

Feinstein, C. H. (1965), *Domestic Capital Formation in the United Kingdom, 1920–1938*, Cambridge: Cambridge University Press.

Feinstein, C. H. (1972), *National Income, Expenditure and Output of the United Kingdom: 1855–1965*, Cambridge: Cambridge University Press.

Fernandez-Corugedo, E., and Muellbauer, J. (2006), 'Consumer credit conditions in the United Kingdom', Discussion Paper, London: Centre for Banking Studies, Bank of England, and Nuffield College, Oxford.

Fetter, F. W. (1965), *Development of British Monetary Orthodoxy 1797–1875*, Cambridge, Massachusetts: Harvard University Press.

Fforde, J. (1970), 'Banking system (and credit control)'. Typescript memorandum, 24 December 1970, Bank of England.

Financial Services Authority (2009), *The Turner Review: A Regulatory Response to the Global Banking Crisis,* (March).

Flandreau, M., and Flores, J. (2009), 'Bonds and brands: Foundations of sovereign debt markets, 1820–1830', *Journal of Economic History*, 69(3): 646–84.

Flandreau, M., and Ugolini, S. (2013), 'Where it all began: Lending of last resort at the Bank of England during the Overend-Gurney panic of 1866', in M. D. Bordo and W. Roberds (eds) *The Origins, History, and Future of the Federal Reserve: A Return to Jekyll Island*, Cambridge: Cambridge University Press, 113–61.

Flannery, M. J. (2009), 'Stabilizing large financial institutions with contingent capital certificates', SSRN working paper available online at: <http://ssrn.com/abstract= 1485689>.

Francis, J. (1851), *A History of the English Railway*, London: Longman, Brown, Green & Longmans.

Fraser, S. (2005), *Wall Street: A Cultural History*, London: Faber and Faber.

Garber, P. M. (2001), *Famous First Bubbles: The Fundamentals of Early Manias*, Cambridge, Massachusetts: MIT Press.

Gayer, A. D., Rostow, W. W., and Schwartz, A. J. (1953), *The Growth and Fluctuation of the British Economy, 1790–1850*, Oxford: Oxford University Press.

Gelpern, A. (2009), 'Financial crisis containment', *Connecticut Law Review*, 41(5): 493–548.

Giannini, C. (1999), *'Enemy of None but a Common Friend of All?' An International Perspective on the Lender-of-Last-Resort Function*, Princeton: Princeton University.

Gilbart, J. W. (1837), *The History and Principles of Banking*, 3rd edition. London: Longmans.

Gillett Brothers (1964), *The Bill on London*, London: Chapman Hall.

Goodhart, C. A. E. (1972), *The Business of Banking, 1891–1914*. London: Weidenfeld & Nicolson.

Goodhart, C. A. E. (1989), 'The conduct of monetary policy', *Economic Journal*, 99: 293–346.

Gorton, G. B. (2008), 'The panic of 2007', *FRB Kansas City*, Jackson Hole Conference (25 August).

Gorton, G. B. (2009), 'Information, liquidity, and the (ongoing) panic of 2007', *American Economic Review*, Papers & Proceedings, 99, 2.

Gorton, G. B., and Metrick, A. (2010), 'Securitised banking and the run on repo', Yale ICF Working Paper, 09–14 (9 November 2010).

Griffiths, B. (1973), 'The development of restrictive practices in the UK monetary system', *Manchester School*, 41: 3–18.

Grossman, R. S. (1994), 'The shoe that didn't drop: Explaining banking stability during the Great Depression', *Journal of Economic History*, 54(3): 654–82.

Grossman, R. S. (2001), 'Double liability and bank risk-taking', *Journal of Money, Credit and Banking*, 33: 143–59.

Grossman, R. S. (2010), *Unsettled Account: The Evolution of Banking in the Industrialized World since 1800*, Princeton: Princeton University Press.

Guex, S. (2000), 'The origins of the Swiss banking secrecy law and its repercussions for Swiss federal policy', *Business History Review*, 74: 237–66.

Haldane, A. G., and Alessandri, P. (2009), 'Banking on the State', originally presented at Federal Reserve Bank of Chicago (25 September). Available online at <http://www.bankofengland.co.uk/archive/Documents/historicpubs/speeches/2009/speech409.pdf> accessed 11 April 2014.

Hawtrey, R. G. (1919), *Currency and Credit*, London: Longmans.

Hendry, D. F. (1983), 'Econometric modelling: The consumption function in retrospect', *Scottish Journal of Political Economy*, 39: 193–220.

Herring, R. J., and Wachter, S. (1999), 'Real estate booms and banking busts: An international perspective', Financial Institutions Centre, 99-27, The Wharton School, University of Pennsylvania.

Hickson, C. R., and Turner, J. D. (2003), 'Trading in the shares of unlimited liability banks in nineteenth-century Ireland: The Bagehot hypothesis', *Journal of Economic History*, 63: 931–58.

Hickson, C. R., and Turner, J. D. (2004), 'Free banking and the stability of early joint stock banking', *Cambridge Journal of Economics*, 28: 903–19.

Hickson, C. R., and Turner, J. D. (2005), 'The genesis of corporate governance: Nineteenth-century Irish joint-stock banks', *Business History*, 47: 174–89.

Higonnet, R. P. (1957), 'Bank deposits in the United Kingdom, 1870–1914', *Quarterly Journal of Economics*, 71(3): 329–67.

Hills, S., Thomas, R., and Dimsdale, N. (2010), 'The UK recession in context—what do three centuries of data tell us?' *Bank of England Quarterly Bulletin*, 50 (4): 277–91.

Holgate, H. C. F. (1938), 'Loans, overdrafts and deposits', *Bankers' Magazine*, (November): 739–43.

Holmes, A. R., and Green, E. (1986), *Midland: 150 Years of Banking Business*, London: BT Batsford Ltd.

Honkaphoja, S. (2009), 'The 1990's Financial Crises in Nordic Countries', Discussion paper 5/2009, Bank of Finland, Helsinki.

Honohan, P., and Laeven, L. (eds) (2005), *Systemic Financial Crises: Containment and Resolution*, Cambridge: Cambridge University Press.

Horne, H. O. (1947), *A History of Savings Banks*, London and New York: Oxford University Press.

House of Commons (1875), *Report from the Select Committee on Loans to Foreign States: Together with the Proceedings of the Committee*, Minutes of Evidence, Appendix, and Index.

Howson, S. K. (1975), *Domestic Monetary Management in Britain, 1919–1938*, Cambridge: Cambridge University Press.

Howson, S. K. (1980), *Sterling's Managed Float: The Operation of the Exchange Equalisation Account, 1932–39*, Princeton: Princeton University Press.

Hughes, J. R. T. (1960), *Fluctuations in Trade, Industry and Finance: A Study of British Economic Development, 1850–1860*, Oxford: Oxford University Press.

Jackson, P. (1996), 'Deposit protection and bank failures in the United Kingdom', *Bank of England Financial Stability Review*, Autumn.

James, H. (1992), 'Banks and bankers in the German interwar depression', in Y. Cassis (ed.), *Finance and Financiers in European History, 1880–1960*, Cambridge: Cambridge University Press, 263–81.

Janeway, W. H. (1995–6), 'The 1931 sterling crisis and the independence of the Bank of England', *Journal of Post Keynesian Economics*, 18: 311–25.

Jensen, M. C., and Meckling, W. (1976), 'Theory of the firm: Managerial behaviour, agency costs and capital structure', *Journal of Financial Economics*, 3: 305–60.

Jones, T. (1951), *Lloyd George*, London: Oxford University Press.

Jonker, J., and van Zenden, J. L. (1995), 'Methods in the madness? Banking crises between the Wars: An international comparison', in C.H. Feinstein (ed.), *Banking, Currency, and Finance in Europe between the Wars*, Oxford: Clarendon Press.

Jonung, L., Kiander, J., et al. (2009), *The Great Financial Crisis in Finland and Sweden: The Nordic Experience of Financial Liberalization*, Cheltenham: Edward Elgar.

Juglar, C. (1889), *Des crises commerciales et de leur retour périodique en France, en Angleterre et aux États-Unis*, 2nd edition. Paris: Guillaumin.

Kaul, C. (2004–10), 'Montagu, Edwin Samuel (1879–1924)', *Oxford Dictionary of National Biography*, Oxford: Oxford University Press.

Kerr, A. W. (1884), *History of Banking in Scotland*, London: Adam and Charles Black.

Keynes, J. M. (1914), 'War and the financial system, August 1914', *Economic Journal*, 24 (September).

Keynes, J. M. (1925), 'The economic consequences of Mr Churchill', *Collected Writings of J. M .Keynes*, ix: *Essays in Persuasion*, London: Macmillan, 1972.

Keynes, J. M. (1929), 'Can Lloyd George do it?' *Collected Writings of J. M .Keynes*, ix: *Essays in Persuasion*, London: Macmillan, 1972.

Kindleberger, C. P. (1978), *Manias, Panics and Crashes: A History of Financial Crises*, London: Macmillan.

Kindleberger, C. P. (2000), *Manias, Panics and Crashes: A History of Financial Crises*, 4th edition. New York: John Wiley and Sons.

Kindleberger, C. P., and Aliber, R. Z. (2011), *Manias, Panics, and Crashes: A History of Financial Crises*, Basingstoke: Palgrave Macmillan.

King, W. T. C. (1935), 'The extent of the London discount market in the middle of the nineteenth century', *Economica* (New Series), 2(7): 321–6.

King, W. T. C. (1936), *A History of the London Discount Market*, London: Cass.

Kirkaldy, A. W. (1921), *British Finance During and After the War, 1914–21*. London: Pitman.

Kostal, R. W. (1994), *Law and English Railway Capitalism*, Oxford: Oxford University Press.

Kremer, D. (2012), 'Market liberalism and the state: Corporate capture, corruption, and influence under the UK's Private Finance Initiative, *c.*1992–2012', MSc thesis, University of Oxford.
Kroszner, R. S., and Rajan, R. G. (1994), 'Is the Glass-Steagall Act justified? A study of the U.S. experience with universal banking before 1933', *American Economic Review*, 84(4): 810–32.
Krugman, P. (1979), 'A model of balance of payments crises', *Journal of Money Credit and Banking*, 11: 311–25.
Kynaston, D. (1999), *The City of London*, iii: *Illusions of Gold, 1914–1945*, London: Chatto and Windus.
Lawson, W. R. (1915), *British War Finance, 1914–15*, London: Constable.
Layard, P. R. G., Nickell, S. J., and Jackman, R. (1991), *Unemployment: Macroeconomic Performance and the Labour Market*, Oxford: Oxford University Press.
Leaf, W. (1935), *Banking*, London: Butterworth.
Leamer, E. E. (2007), 'Housing is the business cycle', Cambridge, Mass.: National Bureau of Economic Research Working Paper Series 13428.
Levi, L. (1880), 'The reconstruction of joint stock banks on the principle of limited liability', *Bankers' Magazine*, 40: 468–79.
Lewin, H. G. (1936), *The Railway Mania and its Aftermath, 1845–1852,* London: The Railway Gazette.
Livingston, J. (1986), *The Origins of the Federal Reserve System: Money, Class and Corporate Capitalism, 1890–1913*, Ithaca and London: Cornell University Press.
Lloyd George, D. (1938), *War Memoirs of David Lloyd George*, I, London: Odhams.
London and Cambridge Economic Service (1971), *The British Economy 1900–1970: Key Statistics*, London: Times Newspapers.
Macey, J. R., and Miller, G. P. (1992), 'Double liability of bank shareholders: History and implications', *Wake Forest Law Review*, 27: 31–62.
Macleod, H. D. (1891), *The Theory of Credit*, II: pt. 2, London: Longmans.
Macmillan Committee (1931), *Committee on Finance and Industry*, Cmd 3897, London: HMSO.
Mahate, A. A. (1994), 'Contagion effects of three late nineteenth-century British bank failures', *Business and Economic History*, 23(1): 102–15.
Marichal, C. (1989), *A Century of Debt Crises in Latin America: From Independence to the Great Depression, 1820–1930*, Princeton: Princeton University Press.
Matthews, K. G. P. (1986), 'Was sterling overvalued in 1925?' *Economic History Review*, 39: 572–87.
Matthews, R. C. O. (1954), *A Study in Trade Cycle History,* Cambridge: Cambridge University Press.
Matthews, R. C. O. (1972), 'The trade cycle in Britain 1790–1850', reprinted in D. H. Aldcroft and P. Fearon (eds) *British Economic Fluctuations, 1790–1939.* London: Macmillan.
Matthews, R. C. O., Feinstein, C. H., and Odling Smee, J. C. (1982), *British Economic Growth: 1856–1973*, Oxford: Oxford University Press.
Matthews, W. R. (1969), *Memories and Meanings*, London: Hodder & Stoughton.
May Committee (1931), Report of Committee on National Expenditure, Cmd 3920, London: HMSO.

McCartney, S., and Arnold, A. J. (2003), 'The railway mania of 1845–1847: Market irrationality or collusive swindle based on accounting distortions?' *Accounting, Auditing and Accountability Journal*, 16(5): 821–52.

Michie, R. C. (2007), 'The City of London as a global financial centre, 1880–1939: Finance, foreign exchange, and the First World War', in P.L. Cottrell, E. Lange, and U. Olsson (eds), *Centres and Peripheries in Banking*, Aldershot: Ashgate.

Michie, R. C. (1999), *The London Stock Exchange: A History*, Oxford: Oxford University Press.

Middleton, R. (2004–10), 'Sir George Paish (1867–1957)', *Oxford Dictionary of National Biography*, Oxford: Oxford University Press.

Middleton, R. (2010), 'British monetary and fiscal policy', *Oxford Review of Economic Policy*, 26: 414–41.

Minsky, H. P. (2008), *Stabilizing an Unstable Economy*, 2nd edition. New York: Macmillan.

Mitchell, B. R. (1964), 'The coming of the railway and United Kingdom economic growth', *Journal of Economic History*, 24(3): 315–36.

Mitchell, B. R. (1988), *British Historical Statistics*, Cambridge: Cambridge University Press.

Mitchell, B. R. (2003), *International Historical Statistics: Europe 1750–2000*, London: Palgrave Macmillan.

Moggridge, D. E. (1972), *British Monetary Policy 1924–1931: The Norman Conquest of $4.86*, Cambridge: Cambridge University Press.

Morgan, E. V. (1952), *Studies in British Financial Policy, 1914–25*, London: Macmillan.

Morris, S., and Shin, H. S. (1998), 'Unique equilibrium in a model of self-fulfilling currency attacks', *American Economic Review*, 88: 587–97.

Munn, C. W. (1981), *The Scottish Provincial Banking Companies, 1747–1864*, Edinburgh: John Donald.

National Housing Federation (2012), 'House prices rise three times as much as incomes over ten years', available online at: <http://www.housing.org.uk/media/news/house_prices_rise_three_times.aspx>, accessed 17 August 2012.

National Monetary Commission (1910), Interviews on the banking and currency systems of England, France, Germany, Switzerland, and Italy, under the direction of the Hon. Nelson W. Aldrich, chairman, Washington, National Monetary Commission, 61st Congress, 2nd session, Senate Doc. No. 405.

Neal, L. (1998), 'The financial crisis of 1825 and the restructuring of the British financial system', *Bank of St Louis Economic Review*, 80 (May/June): 53–76.

Nishimura, S. (1971), *The Decline of Inland Bills in the London Money Market, 1855–1913*, Cambridge: Cambridge University Press.

Norman, B., Shaw, R., and Speight, G. (2011), 'The history of interbank settlement arrangements: Exploring central banks' role in the payment system', Bank of England Working Paper 412.

O'Brien, D. P., and Creedy, J. (2010), *Darwin's Clever Neighbour: George Wade Norman and His Circle*, Cheltenham: Edward Elgar.

Offer, A. (1981), *Property and Politics, 1870–1914: Landownership, Law, Ideology and Urban Development in England*, Cambridge: Cambridge University Press.

Offer, A. (1983), 'Empire and social reform: British overseas investment and domestic politics, 1908–1914', *Historical Journal*, 26: 119–38.

Offer, A. (2006), *The Challenge of Affluence: Self-Control and Well-Being in the United States and Britain since 1950*, Oxford: Oxford University Press.

Offer, A. (2008), 'British manual workers: From producers to consumers, *c.*1950–2000', *Contemporary British History*, 22(4): 538–71.

Offer, A. (2012), 'The economy of obligation: Incomplete contracts and the cost of the welfare state', Discussion Paper in Economic and Social History, no. 103, University of Oxford.

Offer, A. (2014), 'Consumption and affluence', in R. Floud, J. Humphries, and P. Johnson (eds) *Cambridge Economic History of Modern Britain*, II: ch. 8, Cambridge: Cambridge University Press.

ONS (Office for National Statistics) (2013), *Quarterly National Accounts Time Series Dataset Q1 2013*, 16 July 2013 update, available: <http://www.ons.gov.uk/ons/rel/naa2/quarterly-national-accounts/q1-2013/tsd-quarterly-national-accounts–q1-2013.html> accessed 26 July 2013.

Ogden, T. (1991), 'An analysis of Bank of England discount and advances behaviour, 1870–1914', in J. Foreman-Peck (ed.) *New Perspectives on the Late Victorian Economy*, Cambridge: Cambridge University Press, 305–43.

Orbell, J., and Turton, A. (2001), *British Banking: A Guide to Historical Records*, Aldershot: Ashgate.

Pagan, A. R. (2003), 'Report on modelling and forecasting at the Bank of England', *Bank of England Quarterly Bulletin*, 43(1): 60–88.

Parliamentary Papers (1844, I). Bank of England Charter. A bill [as amended by the Committee] to Regulate the Issue of Bank Notes, and for giving to the Governor and Company of the Bank of England Certain Privileges for a Limited Period.

Parliamentary Papers (1844, IV). Railways. A bill to attach certain conditions to the construction of future railways, authorized or to be authorized by any act of the present or succeeding sessions of Parliament, and for other purposes in relation to railways.

Parliamentary Papers (1844, IV: 435). Railways. A bill (as amended by the Committee) to Attach Certain Conditions to the Construction of Future Railways, Authorized or to be Authorized by any Act of the Present or Succeeding Sessions of Parliament, and for other Purposes in Relation to Railways.

Parliamentary Papers (1844, XI: 5). Third report from the Select Committee on railways.

Parliamentary Papers (1844, XI: 6). Fifth report from the Select Committee on railways; together with the minutes of evidence, appendix and index.

Parliamentary Papers (1845, XXXIX). Railways. A return of the railway bills and projects, classified in their groups, which have been considered by the committees to whom they were referred; and whether such railway bills and projects were recommended or rejected by the said committees; the names of the members selected; and the number of days that the committee on each group has sat.

Parliamentary Papers (1846, I: 423). Corn importation. A bill to amend the laws relating to the importation of corn.

Parliamentary Papers (1847, I: 205). Corn, &c., importation. A bill to suspend, for a time to be limited, the duties on the importation of corn, maize, rice, grain, meal, flour, biscuit, and certain other similar articles.

Parliamentary Papers (1847–48, VIII, Pt. I). Reports from the Secret Committee on Commercial Distress; with an Index.

Parliamentary Papers (1847–48, VIII, Pt. II). Second report from the Secret Committee on Commercial Distress; with the minutes of evidence.

Parliamentary Papers (1847–48, VIII, Pt. III). Report from the Secret Committee of the House of Lords appointed to inquire into the causes of the distress which has for some time prevailed among the commercial classes, and how far it has been affected by the laws for regulating the issue of bank notes payable on demand. Together with the minutes of evidence, and an appendix.

Parliamentary Papers (1847–48, LXIII: 25). Railways. Return of the railway companies who have made application to the Commissioners of Railways under the 1st section of the act 11 Vict. c. 3, for an extension of the periods limited by their acts for the purchase of lands, or the completion of works, &c.

Parliamentary Papers (1850, XXXIII: 202–11). Bank of England, &c. Account of the Notes, Securities, Bullion, &c. of the Bank of England, as Published Weekly in the Gazette; and the Monthly Average Aggregate Amount of Promissory Notes, Payable to Bearer on Demand, in Circulation in the United Kingdom, from January 1846 to June 1849.

Parliamentary Papers (1852–53, LVII: 328–35). Bullion, &c. Account of the Notes, Securities, Bullion, &c. of the Bank of England, as Published Weekly in the Gazette; the Quarterly Averages of the Weekly Liabilities and Assets of the Bank of England; and the Monthly Average Aggregate Amount of Promissory notes, from January 1849 to June 1853.

Parliamentary Papers (1857, X). Report from the Select Committee on Bank Acts; together with the proceedings of the committee, minutes of evidence, appendix and index. Part I. Report and evidence.

Patterson, R. H. (1870), 'On our home monetary drains, and the crisis of 1866', *Journal of the Statistical Society of London*, 33(2): 216–42.

Peters, J. (1993), 'The British government and the City-Industry divide: The case of the 1914 financial crisis', *Twentieth Century British History*, 4(2): 142–7.

Plumptre, C. C. M. (1882), *Grant's Treatise on the Law Relating to Bankers and Banking Companies*, London: Butterworths.

Pressnell, L. (1956), *Country Banking in the Industrial Revolution*, Oxford: Clarendon Press.

Pressnell, L. S. (1968), 'Gold flows, banking reserves, and the Baring Crisis of 1890', in C. R. Whittlesey and J. S. G. Wilson (eds) *Essays in Money and Banking in Honour of R. S. Sayers*, Oxford: Oxford University Press.

Radcliffe Committee (1959), *Committee on the Working of the Monetary System*, Cmnd 827, London: HMSO.

Rae, G. (1885), *The Country Banker: His Clients, Cares and Work*, London: John Murray.

Railway Investment Guide (1845), *The Railway Investment Guide: How to Make Money in Railway Shares: A Series of Hints and Advice to Parties Speculating*, London: G. Mann.

Rawlinson, K. (2011), 'Families now spend half their income on rent', *The Independent*. 19 October 2011. London.

Redmond, J. (1980), 'An indicator of the effective exchange rate of the pound in the 1930s', *Economic History Review*, 33: 83–91.

Redmond, J. (1984), 'The sterling overvaluation in 1925: a multilateral approach', *Economic History Review*, 37: 520–32

Reid, M. (1982), *The Secondary Banking Crisis, 1973–75: Its Causes and Course*, London: Macmillan.

Reinhart, C. M., and Rogoff, K. S. (2009), *This Time Is Different: Eight Centuries of Financial Folly*, Princeton: Princeton University Press.

Richardson, H. W. (1967), *Economic Recovery in Britain 1932–39*, London: Weidenfeld and Nicolson.

Roberts, R. (1992), *Schroders: Merchants and Bankers*, Basingstoke and London: Macmillan.

Romer, C. D. (1990), 'The Great Crash and the Onset of the Great Depression', *Quarterly Journal of Economics*, 105(3): 597–624.

Samuelson, P. A., and Samuelson, W. (1980), *Economics*, New York: McGraw-Hill.

Samy, L. (2010), 'The building society promise: the accessibility, risk, and efficiency of building societies in England, *c.*1880–1939', DPhil thesis, University of Oxford.

Sayers, R. S. (1967), *Modern Banking*, Oxford: Clarendon Press.

Sayers, R. S. (1976), *The Bank of England 1891–1944*, 2 vols. Cambridge: Cambridge University Press.

Schwartz, A. J. (1986), 'Real and pseudo financial crises', in F. Capie and G. E. Wood (eds) *Financial Crises and the World Banking System*, London: Macmillan, 11–31.

Schwartz, A. J. (1987), 'Real and Pseudo-Financial Crises', in A. J. Schwartz (ed.) *Money in Historical Perspective*, Chicago: University of Chicago Press, 271–88.

Schwartz, A. J. (1995), 'Why financial stability depends on price stability', *Economic Affairs*, 15(4): 21–5.

Seyd, E. (1868), *Bullion and Foreign Exchanges, Theoretically and Practically Considered*, London: Effingham Wilson.

Sheppard, D. K. (1971), *The Growth and Role of U.K. Financial Institutions, 1880–1962*, London: Methuen.

Shiwakoti, R. K., Ashton, J. K., et al. (2004), 'Conversion, performance and executive compensation in UK building societies', *Corporate Governance*, 12(3): 361–70.

Skidelsky, R. (1983), *John Maynard Keynes*, i: *Hopes Betrayed 1883–1920*, London: Macmillan.

Smith, G. D., and Sylla, R. (1993), 'Wall Street and the U.S. capital markets in the twentieth century', *Financial Markets, Institutions, and Instruments*, Cambridge, Massachusetts.

Solomou, S., and Weale, M. (1997), 'Personal sector wealth in the United Kingdom, 1920–56', *Review of Income and Wealth*, 43(3): 297–318.

Sonne, H. C. (1915), *The City: Its Finance July 1914 to July 1915 and Future*, London: Effingham Wilson.

Speight, G. (2000), 'Building society behaviour and the mortgage-lending market in the interwar period: Risk-taking by mutual institutions and the interwar house-building boom', DPhil thesis, University of Oxford.

Spero, J. E. (1979), *The Failure of the Franklin National Bank: Challenge to the International Banking System*, New York: Columbia University Press.

Spring-Rice, D. (1923), 'The money market since the War', *Bankers' Magazine*, 115 (March).

Straus, A. (1992), 'Structures financières et performances des entreprises industrielles en France dans la seconde moitié du XXe siècle', *Entreprises et Histoire*, 2: 19–33.

Sykes, J. (1926), *The Amalgamation Movement in English Banking, 1825–1924*, London: P. S. King & Son.

Sykes, J. (1928), *The Present Position of English Joint Stock Banking*, London: Ernest Benn Ltd.

Sykes, E. (1915), 'Some effects of the war on the London money market', *Journal of the Institute of Bankers*, 36(2).

Takeshita, T., and Ida, M. (2003), 'An empirical study of economic reporting and public opinion', Seiki ronsô (Meiji University), 72(1): 1–42 (translated from Japanese by M. Bourqui).

Taylor, J. B. (1993), 'Discretion versus policy rules in practice', Carnegie-Rochester Conference Series on Public Policy, 39: 195–214.

Temin, P. (1974), 'The Anglo-American business cycle, 1820–1860', *Economic History Review*, 27: 201–21.

Thomas, M. (1983), 'Rearmament and recovery in the late 1930s', *Economic History Review*, 36: 552–79.

Thomas, S. E. (1934), *The Rise and Growth of Joint-Stock Banking*, London: Pitman.

Thornton, H. (1802), *An Enquiry into the Nature and Effects of the Paper Credit of Great Britain*, London: Hatchard, (London: Allen and Unwin, edition with introduction by F. A. Hayek, 1939; Fairfield, NJ: Augustus M. Kelley, 1978).

Transparency International UK (2011), *Cabs for Hire? Fixing the Revolving Door between Government and Business*, London: Transparency International UK.

Treasury, H. M. and Bank of England (1980), *Green Paper on Monetary Control*, Cmnd. 7858, London: HMSO.

Treasury Select Committee (2009–10), *Too Important to Fail—Too Important to Ignore*. House of Commons-261-II, London: The Stationery Office.

Truptil, R. J. (1936), *British Banks and the London Money Market*, London: Jonathan Cape.

Tucker, P. (2004), 'Managing the central bank's balance sheet: Where monetary policy meets financial stability', *Bank of England Quarterly Bulletin*, 44(3): 359–82.

Turner, J. D. (2009a), 'The last acre and sixpence: Views on bank liability regimes in nineteenth-century Britain', *Financial History Review*, 16: 111–28.

Turner, J. D. (2009b), 'Wider share ownership? Investors in English bank shares in the nineteenth century', *Economic History Review*, 62: 167–92.

Ugolini, S. (2010), 'The international monetary system 1844–1870: Arbitrage, efficiency, liquidity', Norges Bank Working Paper 2010/23.

Ugolini, S. (2012), 'Foreign exchange reserve management in the nineteenth century: The National Bank of Belgium in the 1850s', in A. Ögren and L. F. Øksendal (eds) *The Gold Standard Peripheries: Monetary Policy, Adjustment and Flexibility in a Global Setting*, Basingstoke: Palgrave Macmillan, 107–29.

Velde, F. R. (2007), 'John Law's System', *American Economic Review*, 97(2): 276–9.

Vickers Commission (2011), *Final Report of the Independent Commission on Banking*, London: The Stationery Office (12 September).

Viner, J. (1937), *Studies in the Theory of International Trade*, London: George Allen & Unwin.

Vogler, R. (2001), 'The genesis of Swiss banking secrecy: Political and economic environment', *Financial History Review*, 8(1): 73–84.

Waley, S. D. (1964), *Edwin Montagu*, London: Asia Publishing House.

Ward-Perkins, C. N. (1962), 'The commercial crisis of 1847', reprinted in E. M. Carus Wilson (ed.) *Essays in Economic History*, iii, London: Arnold.

Wells, H. G. (1916), *Mr Britling Sees It Through*, London: Cassell.

Wetenhall, J. (1843–50), *Course of the Exchange*, London.

White, E. N. (1983), *The Regulation and Reform of the American Banking System, 1900–1929*, Princeton: Princeton University Press.

White, E. N. (1986), 'Before the Glass-Steagall Act: An analysis of the investment banking activities of the national banks', *Explorations in Economic History*, 23: 33–54.

White, E. N. (2000), 'Banking and finance in the twentieth century', in S. L. Engerman and R. E. Gallman (eds) *The Cambridge Economic History of the United States*, iii: *The Twentieth Century*, Cambridge: Cambridge University Press.

White, L. H. (1995), *Free Banking in Britain: Theory, Experience and Debate 1800–1845*, 2nd edition, London: Institute of Economic Affairs.

Wicker, E. (2000), *Banking Panics of the Gilded Age*, Cambridge: Cambridge University Press.

Wilson, A. (1879), *Banking Reform: An Essay on the Prominent Dangers and the Remedies They Demand*, London: Longmans, Green and Co.

Winton, A. (1993), 'Limitation of liability and the ownership structure of the firm', *Journal of Finance*, 48: 487–512.

Wirth, M. (1890), *Geschichte der Handelskrisen*, 4th edition, Frankfurt am Main: Sauerländer.

Withers, H. (1909), *The Meaning of Money*, London: Smith and Elder.

Withers, H. (1910), 'The English banking system', in R. H. I. Palgrave, E. Sykes, and R. M. Holland, *The English Banking System* (Sixty-First Congress, Second Session, Senate Document No. 492: 3–148), Washington, DC: US Government Printing Office.

Withers, H. (1915), *War and Lombard Street*, London: Smith, Elder.

Withers, H., and Palgrave, R. H. I. (1910), *National Monetary Commission: The English Banking System*, Washington, DC: Government Printing Office.

Wood, E. (1939), *English Theories of Central Banking Control 1819–1858*, Cambridge, Massachusetts: Harvard University Press.

Woodward, S. (1985), 'Limited liability in the theory of the firm', *Journal of Institutional and Theoretical Economics*, 141: 601–11.

Wormell, J. (2000), *The Management of the National Debt of the United Kingdom, 1900–1932*, London: Routledge.

Worswick, G. D. N. (1984), 'The sources of recovery in the UK in the 1930s', *National Institute Economic Review*, 110: 85–93.

Xenos, S. T. (1869), *Depredations: Or, Overend, Gurney & Co., and the Greek and Oriental Steam Navigation Company*, London: The author.

Ziegler, P. (1988), *The Sixth Great Power: Barings, 1762–1929*. London: Collins.

Index

The manufacturer's authorised representative in the EU for product safety is Oxford University Press España S.A. of el Parque Empresarial San Fernando de Henares, Avenida de Castilla, 2 – 28830 Madrid (www.oup.es/en or product.safety@oup.com). OUP España S.A. also acts as importer into Spain of products made by the manufacturer.

www.ingramcontent.com/pod-product-compliance
Ingram Content Group UK Ltd.
Pitfield, Milton Keynes, MK11 3LW, UK
UKHW020926180926
475595UK00034B/152
* 9 7 8 0 1 9 9 6 8 8 6 6 1 *